DON'T BLAME
THE KIDS

DON'T BLAME THE KIDS

*The Trouble with
America's Public Schools*

GENE I. MAEROFF

McGRAW-HILL BOOK COMPANY

New York St. Louis San Francisco
London Montreal Paris Tokyo Toronto

Thomas H. Quinn, Michael Hennelly, and Karen
Seriguchi were editors of this book. Christine Aulicino
was the designer. Paul Malchow supervised the
production. It was set in Gael by Datapage, Inc.

Printed and bound by R. R. Donnelley and Sons, Inc.

Library of Congress Cataloging in Publication Data

Maeroff, Gene I.
  Don't blame the kids.

  Includes index.
  1. Public schools—United States.   I. Title.
LA217.M29   371'.01'0973   81–8320
                                          AACR2

ISBN 0-07-039465-2

1 2 3 4 5 6 7 8 9 DODO 9 0 8 7 6 5 4 3 2 1

TO MY PARENTS
and with special thanks
TO CANDICE

CONTENTS

Preface

I am indebted to the *New York Times* for the opportunity to have spent the last decade chronicling the issues and trends in American education. My work for the newspaper contributed to the reservoir of experience from which I have drawn in writing in this book. In particular, I benefitted from the support and encouragement of David Jones, the national editor for whom I worked most of the last 10 years. He and an able succession of assistant editors including John Herbers and Paul Delaney made certain that the *Times* was in a position to provide national coverage of education unequalled by any other daily newspaper in the country. In addition, I have had the advantage of a close professional relationship with Edward Fiske, my education writing colleague at the *Times* for at least half this period.

These 10 years of thinking about education from a base in New York, preceded by several years of similar work for the *Plain Dealer* in Cleveland, gave me time to formulate the observations and ideas in this book. There is no way I could thank personally all of the educators, students, and public officials whose good will helped along the way. Such seminal thinkers as Harold Howe II and Ernest Boyer, though they have committed precious few of their thoughts to books of their own, have provided a body of speeches, articles, and personal comments worthy of note by anyone hoping to learn about the schools.

Insight and inspiration have also come from a wide variety of other sources. The outpouring of books and journals devoted to education composes an ocean, the bed of which must be combed to ferret out the pearls. An indispensable treasure-trove for anyone interested in elementary and secondary education during the 1970s was contained within the pages of *Phi Delta Kappan,* a superb monthly magazine from which Stanley Elam retired as editor early this year.

There is no way of pinpointing when work on this book began. In a way, a reporter specializing in a field is continually accumulating background information that could find its way into a possible book. In my case, I began writing about education in the 1960s and there have been many conversations with individuals over the years that became part of the storehouse that eventually provided material for this book. Just a few of those people have been Kenneth Clark, Harold Enarson, Roger Farr, the Rev. Timothy Healy, Fred Hechinger, Terry Herndon, Clark Kerr, Robert Kibbee, Frank Macchiarola, Ewald Nyquist, Wilson Riles, and Albert Shanker.

In addition, there was the valuable experience gained in writing my last book, *The Guide to Suburban Public Schools,* with Leonard Buder as my co-author. The glimpses it provided into the operations of dozens of school systems were an important grounding for this book.

Though it may seem far afield at this juncture, I would also like to register my gratitude publicly to the late Carey McWilliams, who for many years edited *The Nation.* His confidence in me early in my career—during the late 1960s—gave me a vital boost. I value the chance I had to write for the magazine during that period.

Finally, I thank Thomas Quinn, my editor at McGraw-Hill, and his associate, Michael Hennelly. Working with Tom Quinn has been a pleasure and has added immeasurably to this endeavor.

Acknowledgments

ACKNOWLEDGMENTS for permission to use excerpts from copyrighted material include the following:

Robert Frost, "Stopping by Woods on a Snowy Evening," *The Poetry of Robert Frost,* Edward C. Latham, ed. (New York; Holt, Rinehart, & Winston). Reprinted by permission of the publisher.

Judith Guest, *Ordinary People* (New York: The Viking Press, 1976). Reprinted by permission of the publisher.

Marjorie Kirrie, "Teaching Writing in the World that Writing Built," *College Board Review,* Spring 1978. Reprinted with permission from *The College Board Review,* No. 107, Spring 1978 from an article by Marjorie Kirrie. Copyright © 1978 by College Entrance Examination Board, New York.

Neil Postman, *Teaching as a Conserving Activity* (New York: Delacorte Press, 1979). Reprinted by permission of the publisher.

Paul Simon, "Kodachrome."® © 1973 by Paul Simon. Used by permission. Kodachrome ® is a registered trademark for color film.

Thomas Wolfe, *Look Homeward, Angel* (New York: Charles Scribner's Sons, 1929). From Thomas Wolfe,

CHAPTER ONE

WHY *NOT* BLAME THE KIDS?

We have forty million reasons for failure,
but not a single excuse.

RUDYARD KIPLING,
The Lesson

"Students aren't what they used to be." As an education writer, I hear that sentiment more than any other from critics of public schools. These people complain about vandalism, truancy, and declining achievement, as well as lack of motivation and discipline among the current generation of students. They are certain that if young people would behave better and try harder the troubles of public schools would disappear like puffs of smoke into air. These critics are wrong and I am writing this book to tell them so.

The problems of schools are not as simple as they would have you believe, and their causes are so complex that, for example, even an elaborate study carried out by the College Entrance Examination Board could not pinpoint the reason why Scholastic Aptitude Test scores have been falling for almost two decades.[1] Those who like neat, easy answers were disappointed that the College Board speculated on factors ranging from the breakup of the traditional family, to the turbulence stirred up by the Vietnam War, to the kinds of courses students take in high school. The culprits between the covers of this book are the individuals, agencies, and institutions who are charged with making it possible for the schools to function in a manner that is productive for every child, but

1

who have instead contributed to the perilously low state of confidence in public education.

I will guide you through the unexplored corridors of America's public schools so that you can better understand the folly of blaming the students for the condition of education. It is akin to holding the Indians responsible for the ills of the reservation. Daniel Calhoun, a specialist in cultural history, tells us that in 18th and early 19th century America it was assumed when children did not learn that the fault lay with the quality of the instruction, not with the intelligence of the youngsters. "The unfortunate teacher whose pupils did not perform or move on had to answer for it," according to Calhoun. He maintains that "learning problems," defined as the inherent inability to master what is taught, were discovered partly in response to the difficulties encountered in the schools by defensive educators.[2]

Certainly youngsters must take some responsibility; I do not mean to imply they are faultless if they attack teachers or refuse to do homework or reach the seventh grade unable to distinguish a subject from a predicate. But the blame ought to be spread to where it belongs—to lawmakers who heap burden after burden upon the schools, to judges who interpret statutes as though schools had endless resources, to public officials who harass schools with regulatory minutiae, to teachers unfit to teach, to principals without leadership skills, to superintendents who ignore problems, to school board members who forget that they represent the public, to taxpayers who keep school systems on starvation diets, and to parents who evince more interest in the daily television listings than in the events of their children's schoolday.

It is not merely that schools have grown worse, but that the problems have expanded like steam billowing in a tea kettle. Children did not invent television and put a set in every house; nor did they manufacture the outpouring of drugs that are a blight upon so many of them. They were not the ones who changed social mores to accommodate an orgy of self-indulgence; nor did they dictate the public policy that altered the importance of a high school diploma. In another era, before the upheavals of the 1960s, when aspirations had not yet been raised and gratification could still be delayed, schools were able to treat students differently, and students, in turn, would respond to authority with deference. How can kids be blamed for no longer respecting their teachers when they are surrounded by adults who show disdain for the President of the United States and for the institutions of government? The rise of the Christian fundamentalist school with its enticing blend of old-time values is more than coincidence.

This, then, is a book that looks behind the ominous indicators of educational collapse to try to find out what has gone wrong and why. It may seem at times that I am indicting the educators, but—to the contrary—I believe that those who work in the schools have probably done more than others to keep the situation from deteriorating. It is just that teachers and principals are so directly involved that their failings will be the most obvious. And since they have freely chosen to place themselves on the front line they may be expected to bear the brunt of the fire.

Often, educators do better than their critics would suspect or statistics would show. Public School 155 in the Ocean Hill-Brownsville section of Brooklyn, for example, is a dilapidated, overcrowded, turn-of-the-century building in a neighborhood that became a symbol of urban strife during the late 1960s. Yet, it is now a peaceful, orderly place where teachers enjoy an esprit de corps and go about their daily duties under the leadership of a dedicated principal. A room in the school has been given over to the parents, and each day black and Puerto Rican mothers come to the school, sipping coffee with each other and with the teachers, sensing that this is a spot in which they and their children belong. There are other such elementary schools in New York City and elsewhere, schools whose purposefulness gives lie to the allegation that urban schools must necessarily be jungles.

What I have found especially disturbing in observing educational trends across the country is a growing tendency not only to hold the students totally responsible for their failures, but also to assess further penalties against them in the form of minimum competency tests required for diplomas. I will later devote a chapter to what is, in effect, a sop for a desperate and confused public.

Another chapter will deal with the continuing disaster of education in the inner city, where educational systems do less than they know how to do to help their students. Stuffed into overcrowded classrooms because their needs rank so low among urban fiscal priorities, inner-city youngsters do not get the individual attention that could very likely give them an essential boost in their learning. "If you have a question, she just gives you a little bit of time and you have to talk fast because she has to answer questions from a whole lot of other kids," Cory Simmons, a fifth-grader in a class of forty students at P.S. 163 on Manhattan's Upper West Side, said of his harried teacher.[3]

Because my writing for the *New York Times* has been about higher education as well as elementary and secondary education, I have had the opportunity to see how the educational jigsaw pieces fit together and to think about relations between what is taught in high school and what is taught in college. I am continually astonished by the indifference of higher education toward secondary education and in a chapter on this subject will offer some examples of what could happen to the benefit of students if education were viewed as a seamless puzzle and there were more cooperation between the various levels in assembling the parts.

How to pay for any improvement is an issue of paramount importance, especially at a time when the economic life of the country has become the dominant concern of government. I can no more solve in this book the persistent problems of school finance than you can prevent your living costs from rising. But I can give you a glimpse into this most arcane aspect of elementary and secondary education and discuss how fiscal difficulties have exacerbated the instructional troubles of the schools.

Finally, any book replete with criticism ought also to provide some notion of how to seek improvement. I will attempt to do this whenever possible, citing examples of efforts that are worthy of replication—the use of paraprofessionals to help strengthen reading instruction in rural Mississippi; an early exit test to allow bored teen-agers in California to leave high school with a credential, and a state-sponsored public high school for the mathematically gifted in North Carolina.

This book will end on a familial note, discussing in detail the role that parents can play and describing what is happening in the schools both to thwart and aid their efforts. I doubt that there is a single best form for parent participation, and their involvement will not be a panacea for the problems of education. But I do believe that the more that parents know about the possibilities for their involvement, the more likely their finding approaches that are suitable for them. If perhaps schools had done more to involve parents in meaningful ways, there might not now be the distrust that is making it so difficult to capture public support.

Public education is at a crossroads in the United States. Every citizen has a right to offer an opinion about the kind of elementary and secondary schools that ought to emerge from the ferment of this decade. There may be no issue—short of the question of preserving peace—that will have a greater impact on the shape of this nation at the end of the century. I hope that the following chapters will help you better understand what the schools face and why it will not be up to the students to determine the outcome.

CHAPTER TWO

THE
DUMPING GROUND

GIVING
SOCIETY'S BURDENS
TO THE SCHOOLS

How can I myself alone bear your
cumbrance,
and your burden, and your strife?

Deuteronomy

He was standing in front of the school, a forlorn figure in jeans, sneakers, and a thin windbreaker, shivering slightly in the crisp New England air. It was the autumn of his senior year, and he was wearing the class ring he had bought the previous spring, toward the end of his junior year. But the name of the school on the ring and the name on the building behind him were not the same. Here he was in this unfamiliar place, a part of Boston he did not know, waiting nervously to attend classes with students he had never seen. His last year in high school, the final rite which he had looked forward to sharing with friends, was in disarray. An order from a district court calling for the desegregation of the city's school system had made him one of thousands of students to be carted about the city in buses.

Such is the role that has been thrust upon the schools in the name of desegregation. The goal is a noble one. Too noble,

7

apparently, for the rest of society. For the schools are asked to do what the larger society will not do. People join churches and clubs according to skin color. They make friends and move into neighborhoods according to skin color. Ours is an exclusionary society; separatism by race is woven deep into its fabric. Yet schools are expected to bring the races together.

SCHOOLS AS SOCIAL REDEEMER

This is one of many extra burdens heaped on the schools. "When all else fails, turn to the schools," has become a habitual response to a social dilemma. Schools are supposed to absorb responsibilities that were traditionally vested in the home, in the church, in the hospitals, in the workplace, and in other institutions. They are expected to do what all the king's men and all the king's horses could not do, and have been assigned a leading role in the drama that calls for the redressing of society's ills. This idea has been the cornerstone for federal assistance to elementary and secondary education. Washington has given schools virtually nothing for general operating expenses. Almost all money from the federal government has been earmarked for specific programs to help those disadvantaged in circumstances and background. In other words, strings the size of mooring cables have been attached to the money.

Make no mistake. Schools have been viewed by Congress primarily as instruments of social change. It is perhaps flattering to public education that it was awarded so pivotal a role in the perfecting of society, but the responsibility is a burden nonetheless. Until the advent of the Reagan administration, the extent of the federal commitment to this approach was evident in the categories by which aid was allotted to local school districts. There has been money for the mentally and physically disabled, for those whose parents speak foreign tongues, for native Americans, and for the economically deprived. The largest single program funding has been for Title I of the Elementary and Secondary Education Act, which is allocated to the children of the poor. Title I pumped $29.6

billion into the nation's schools from its inception in 1965 through 1981. It provided $3 billion for remedial education for schoolchildren from impoverished families in the 1980–81 school year.

If Ronald Reagan gets his way, there will be an abrupt change of policy. The spending reductions that the President proposed during his first months in office would cut deeply into elementary and secondary education. He called for slashing twenty-five percent from the sums designated for the schools in the Carter budget. Furthermore, President Reagan broke with the traditional funding pattern and asked Congress to merge most of the school funds into block grants that would apparently give local educators more latitude in how to use the money, though they would get less of it. Thus, if Congress agrees, Ronald Reagan will abrogate the old relationship between Washington and the schools and, in the process, pull the fiscal rug out from under educators who for fifteen years were encouraged to sit on it and make themselves comfortable. Big-city school systems, which have become especially dependent on federal funds because of their large enrollments of disadvantaged pupils, face staggering losses if President Reagan pursues this revised policy throughout his time in the White House. Nonetheless, the public will undoubtedly expect the schools to continue to perform the social missions that have been assigned to them.

The notion that the schools should absorb responsibilities that the rest of society sheds or ignores is not new. It can be traced at least to 1917, when Congress passed the Smith-Hughes Act promoting vocational education in high schools.[1] Underlying the legislation was an emerging view of schools as a source of an unending labor supply for the factories and sweatshops of a burgeoning America. The three R's aside, it seemed appropriate that some young people—particularly those of a weaker academic bent—should be conditioned to accept their place in an industrial society that was coming to rely on the cultivation of a blue-collar class satisfied with its lot. The schools were to have a main part in that grand design.

In recent years, the belief that almost any task that involved children ought to be undertaken by schools has meant addressing even the nutritional needs of children. The schools now serve breakfasts. It is widely acknowledged that if pupils go to class hungry they cannot perform their best work. The answer to the problem is to feed them, and no one but the malevolent Mr. Bumble could possibly object to putting a decent meal into every youngster's belly at the start of the school day. But why are the schools always expected to intervene when others have abdicated responsibility?

In the life of every child, there are untold obstacles beyond the classroom walls inhibiting their potential for greater academic performance. Schools cannot take the lead in ameliorating all these conditions. Few of those being fed breakfast at school, for instance, are homeless waifs. It would seem reasonable to expect parents to feed their children at least a bowl of corn flakes at home in the morning.

What option is there, though, when parents do not fulfill their obligations and no one else steps into the breach? Only the schools remain, which is why the government—from federal, state, and city resources—paid a total of $14 million to provide 18 million breakfasts a year in the schools of New York City, where the almost one million pupils comprise the largest school system in the country. The state requires the New York City schools to serve a breakfast to each youngster who wants one. Until now, the poorest paid nothing and those who are not so poor were charged five cents. Yes, five cents. The obligation of the schools to serve breakfast came on top of a lunch program that made the New York City school system look more like a competitor of McDonald's than an educational enterprise. What will happen under President Reagan's budget is yet to be seen. The system's annual budget for lunches totaled more than $112 million, $1 million of which was strictly for warehouse space. Shipments arrived in rail car lots, and it took forty trucks to distribute the food. The milk order was so large, 700,000 half-pint containers a day, that forty dairies were under contract.[2]

The more that is foisted on the schools, the greater the inclination to add to the burden. When state and federal officials decided to promote inoculations against childhood diseases they decreed that children present proof of immunization at the schoolhouse door. Those without proper documentation were barred from kindergarten. Elaine Yaffe has pointed out that because of such a provision in Colorado, school secretaries and volunteers in one district spent 4,597 hours making sure that the immunization records of pupils were up to date.[3] Just what immunization in Colorado or any other state has to do with learning is not immediately apparent. Schools are obviously the most convenient place to carry out such a policy. Just once, though, it would have been refreshing to have seen the task given to some other agency with access to sites where children congregate.

The same mentality was behind a proposal to establish in the New York City schools medical clinics staffed on a part-time basis by physicians and nurses from local hospitals. The state board of regents recommended that Medicaid pay for the facilities and that the fees be charged to parents. As a first step, five pilot projects were to be set up in the early 1980s at schools in neighborhoods like the South Bronx and Brooklyn's Bedford-Stuyvesant section, the most economically depressed areas of New York, places desperately in need of better health care. The premise was logical: There is an indisputable link between good health and educational achievement, and many children from poor neighborhoods need medical services as much as they need schooling. A two-year study by the state board of regents showed that medical problems of students in New York City contributed to absences and disabilities affecting school performance.[4]

But where does the responsibility of the schools end and the obligation of other agencies begin? There is a growing sentiment in the country that schools should be incorporated into the health care delivery system. A move in that direction would begin with poverty-level youngsters whose families are eligible for Medicaid. One proposal that keeps reappearing in Congress would allow schools to be designated with clinics and hospitals as primary health providers, thereby making the schools eligible to administer Medicaid programs. Plans along this line have been developed under the name of the Child Health Assurance Program. It would be difficult for school systems to resist the incentives to participate. Among other inducements, there might be prepayments from the federal government, giving schools money even before they deliver the health services. Improved health care for children is a proposal not easily criticized, but someone at some point must be bold enough to define the limits beyond which social policy cannot be inflicted upon the schools.

Arthur Bestor recognized the danger of this approach several decades ago, when he wrote that "the idea that the school must undertake to meet every need that some other agency is failing to meet, regardless of the suitability of the schoolroom to the task, is a preposterous delusion that in the end can wreck the educational system."[5]

A congressman gets an idea for a pet project. A state legislature mandates a course of instruction. Local activists persuade a school board to add a program. Each time this happens, there is less money in the coffers and less time remaining in the school day for the real business of schooling— old-fashioned tasks like teaching children to read, write, and compute. Remember these quaint activities? Now there are programs about the evils of alcohol and drug abuse. There are programs about how to select a career and how to prepare for parenthood. There is even something called consumer education. And let us not forget ethnic heritage education and driver education. Just why driving instruction belongs in the curriculum, taking time and money from other subjects, is not clear. Could it be that the automobile insurance companies have done an efficient job of lobbying? Surely another agency, such as the state highway patrol, could handle driver education.

There is a tendency to confuse education with schooling. Many pursuits in life are educational, but not all belong within the province of the schools. Let the schools be free to concentrate on the teaching of literacy in all its forms, a job that no other agency is pursuing or is as well equipped to address. It is no accident that confidence in the schools has waned at the very time that so much is asked of them. It is as though they were being programmed for failure.

THE POLITICAL CROSS SCHOOLS BEAR

There is also the political cost of forcing the schools into controversial activities. Desegregation, its merits aside, has given the public one more excuse for not supporting schools. People who do not approve of what is happening in the schools are less likely to accept higher school taxes. It was more than coincidence in November 1977, when the voters of three of Ohio's biggest cities—Dayton, Columbus, and Cincinnati—all rejected ballot proposals to increase school taxes. All three cities were confronted by court-ordered desegregation orders. The outlook for approval of a much-needed school tax increase in Cleveland, also under court order, was so hopeless that the city did not even bother listing the item on the ballot. This does not mean that schools should be divorced from any connection with desegregation, but it is a reminder of the hazard that external concerns pose for the schools.

The Hazards of Sex and Prayer
No two issues better illustrate this point than sex education and prayer, both of which have engendered repeated controversies. The public is divided in the disputes and schools are compelled to reconcile the differences. Again, schools are asked to do what parents themselves will not do. Many parents, for instance, discover an unaccustomed shyness in themselves when they consider discussing sex with their children. Thus, the family leaves the subject untouched like some dangerous virus and efforts to bridge the generation gap are blocked by the embarrassment or self-doubts of the parents. The schools are shoved into the void. But deciding exactly what schools ought to teach about sex can throw an entire state into turmoil.

It happened in New Jersey in 1980 when the state board of education approved a plan to establish mandatory sex education in every public school from kindergarten through twelfth grade. In the lower grades, there was to be a year-by-year curriculum covering such topics as human reproduction, incest, sexual assault, venereal disease, dating, and social and emotional growth. In high school, the curriculum was to treat family planning, child rearing, and preparation for marriage and childbirth. Immediately, teachers' organizations and school boards rose in opposition, arguing that such a program was unworkable and invited trouble because it made no allowances for local differences over how to deal with the topics. The protests were so strong that the state senate called on the state board of education to reassess its plans. In the end, the board of education yielded to the pressure, remaining on record as favoring sex education, but rescinding the mandate and distributing a revised curriculum that could be used on an optional basis, beginning in 1983. Passions throughout the country are such that the controversy could have erupted almost anywhere.

The question of prayer in the schools splits the public in much the same way. Some families believe that making prayer a formal ritual in the schools is an intrusion upon religious freedom, as well as a violation of the constitutional stricture against the establishment of religion by the state. Others feel that prayer anywhere is inoffensive and that the divine presence can be properly invoked wherever people gather. The persistence of the dispute despite the U.S. Supreme Court ruling outlawing prayer in public schools shows the depth of feeling.[6] The schools, like the streets of Belfast, provide the battleground on which this religious war is fought. Massachusetts found this out in 1980, when devotional exercises were instituted in classrooms across the state in response to a directive by the legislature ordering teachers to permit students to pray aloud together voluntarily.[7] Pupils were permitted to leave the room during the prayer if they wished. The sanctity lasted five weeks. The Massachusetts Supreme Judicial Court, acting on a suit brought by the state's Civil Liberties Union, struck down the law as unconstitutional.[8] It was a victory for the alleged heathens and one more reminder of what can occur when the school is asked to play priest, rabbi, and minister, as well as mommy and daddy. Yet, some members of Congress persist in their sanctimonious quest for a national bill that would circumvent the decision of the U.S. Supreme Court and "put God back into the classroom." As if God needed their help.

There is no end to the chores that individuals and agencies would have the schools absorb. There are even those who would inject the debate over evolution back into the schools. A movement calling for the teaching of "scientific creationism" would require that theories purporting to prove the Biblical version of the origin of man be presented in science classes along with Darwinian theories. This particular proposal—already adopted in Arkansas—has not yet gathered enough support to pass in Congress, but the federal government has been gradually taking the lead in imposing other mandates. Washington's extensive involvement in public education is remarkable considering how recently it has unfolded. The debate over the propriety of a federal role in education was still raging strong in the mid-1960s, when Congress approved the Elementary and Secondary Education Act, the first in a series of giant steps that carried Uncle Sam through the schoolhouse door.

THE EDUCATION OF ALL HANDICAPPED CHILDREN

One of the latest of the federal directives is the Education of All Handicapped Children Act, Public Law 94–142, requiring schools to provide full educational opportunity for the disabled. The fact that Washington will pay for only about twelve percent of what it is demanding does not relieve schools of this burden. What this policy resembles is a regulation by the city council that you take your next-door-neighbor to dinner twice a week and pay for it out of your own pocket.

Since reimbursement for this extraordinary expense is minimal, the money has to come from somewhere within the school district budget. And indeed it does. Most school superintendents in the country can attest to how services for the nonhandicapped have had to be reduced to allow more to be done for the handicapped. The amount of thought given by Congress to the implications of this law does not do justice to an act with so humane an intent. Did Congress really mean to penalize other youngsters in order to help the handicapped? This is what has happened.

The need for attention to the plight of disabled school-aged children is indisputable. Until the passage of P.L. 94–142, the disabled and their families were supposed to be grateful for what little they got from the schools. Frequently, public schools simply refused to accept disabled students and parents had to make their own provisions for the education of their children. If admitted to school, disabled students were sometimes banished to dungeon-like classrooms in the basement. Out of sight, out of mind. The law delivered retribution with the vengeance of a Sweeney Todd.

The schools are obligated to accept children suffering the most extreme handicaps. Transportation must be provided by the school system even if it means incurring the expense of specially adapted vans to pick up disabled youngsters at their homes. Whatever is needed in the classroom in the way of individual attention and costly equipment must be supplied as well. The profoundly, multiply handicapped are not excluded by the law. This may make it necessary for a teacher to administer medicine or aspirate a child's throat so that he does not choke. Other times, the teacher may have to manipulate the youngster's limbs so that his muscles do not atrophy. It is like nothing a teacher ever learned in a college of education. Some of the children can barely hold up their heads or move parts of their bodies. Some wear diapers. Many of their needs are more medical than educational, but the schools must attend to them. A visit to some of these classrooms can leave an observer wondering if he has inadvertently come upon a hospital ward.

Educating the disabled is working out to be twice as expensive to the nation's schools as educating the nonhandicapped. Facilities must be equipped and specially trained teachers must be hired. Parents must be reimbursed for the cost of private schools if the public schools cannot meet the needs of the children. It is abundantly clear that the federal government means to wipe out the vestiges of discrimination against the disabled. Consequently, local school officials are anxious about any situation that may give the appearance of unfair treatment.

An example of how far this concern may be carried was seen in Pearl, Mississippi, a small rural community outside

Jackson, where figuring out how to serve one of the disabled students became an exercise of Solomonic proportions. The difficulty involved a child classified as educable mentally retarded, one of a group of youngsters attending classes in two one-story houses that the district had acquired across the road from the main school building. The living room and bedrooms of each house had been converted into classrooms for the retarded students, segregating them from the main school while keeping them close enough to use such facilities as the music room and the art studio. One of the teachers of the disabled found, however, in leading her youngsters across the road for music and art, that a girl in the class had a respiratory impediment that made her lose her breath after walking just a short distance. The strain seemed so great that the teacher finally decided that it would be best to leave the child behind with another class while her classmates went to the main building. And this is what was done until the girl's mother discovered that her daughter was not participating fully in her class's activities. The mother complained to school authorities that they were violating the federal law by not providing her daughter with all the educational services being given to her classmates.

The local school administrators were in a quandary. Finally, they decided to forbid the teacher to take any of the children across the road, supposedly assuring equal treatment for all of them. Then it occurred to someone that if the girl could be transported to the main building her classmates would not have to be denied the chance to attend music and art classes. The school district bought a wagon of the sort that children use for play and kept it outside the door of the converted house, assigning a junior high school student to pull the girl back and forth for music and art classes. This worked until the girl began gasping for breath just climbing in and out of the wagon. Art and music were again in jeopardy for the entire class, but at about this time the girl's mother decided to withdraw her from public school and enroll her in a private school that offered a more suitable setting for dealing with her multiple handicaps. The law requires the school district and the state to pay the tuition and transportation bills.

The burden imposed by the law is not only a financial one. Whenever possible, disabled children are to be assigned to classes with the nonhandicapped, a practice known as "mainstreaming." As the law phrases it, the "least restrictive environment" is required. The provision was adopted to prevent school systems from unnecessarily segregating the disabled. A youngster who can reasonably handle the work ought to have a chance to attend a regular class despite a physical, mental, or emotional disability. Formerly, students were sometimes shunted into separate classes for no more reason than their confinement in wheelchairs.

Unfortunately, some school districts are exploiting the mainstreaming provision and putting disabled students into regular classes when they ought to be in separate classes. This is a money-saving device that holds down costs because more pupils can be assigned to regular classes, which do not normally have problems of the sort that make it necessary to keep classes for the disabled smaller. Such abuses of the law by the schools hamper the education of both the handicapped and the nonhandicapped. The handicapped are denied the special help possible only in smaller classes and the nonhandicapped are robbed of instructional time because their teachers must give disproportionate attention to the needs of a few.

The law, defended in the name of equity, has escalated the trend of trying to make the schools all things to all people. Each clarification of the law by the federal government and the courts pushes the boundaries of responsibility a bit further. Parents of disabled children were given the right to demand that school systems serve their youngsters from the ages of 3 to 21. The idea is that the disabled need something beyond what is normally given to other children. This reasoning also underpinned verdicts in Pennsylvania, first by the Federal District Court, and then by the Third U.S. Circuit Court of Appeals, that the disabled are entitled to year-around classes because going to school during the summer reinforces their chance "to reach their maximum potential."[9]

School districts in Pennsylvania were told they could not arbitrarily limit the disabled to the 180-day school calendar. If this policy is endorsed throughout the country—similar suits have been filed in other states—it could cost the nation's school systems an extra $830 million a year, the National School Boards Association estimated.

Conflicts over P.L. 94–142 are inevitable because the act is vague on the question of how far the public's liability extends. In Illinois, for example, the federal government contended that the state and local school districts were not paying their full share of the cost of residential treatment centers to which some disabled students were sent when public schools were unable to meet their needs. In one situation a psychiatric institution charged the parents of a thirteen-year-old girl almost $30,000 a year, but state and local officials would reimburse the family only $14,700. The Governor's Purchase Care Review Board examines such cases in Illinois and sets a limit for the state's fiscal responsibility, allowing payment only for what it considers the educational portion of the expenses and not for the long-term treatment.

How much is enough? Local school districts have encountered similar problems even when they have tried to accommodate disabled students within the normal framework of the schools. Amy Rowley, deaf since birth, received the routine evaluation that the Hendrick Hudson School District, near Peekskill, New York, gave to disabled pupils. Amy was a motivated child, apparently able to keep up with other first-graders in a regular class if given the right kind of help, according to school officials. The individualized education plan developed for Amy by her school provided for her to sit near the front of the classroom. A lapel microphone was purchased for the teacher to wear and Amy was fitted with a wireless hearing aid. A receiver box was placed on her desk. A certified teacher of the deaf tutored Amy each day for thirty to forty minutes to supplement her regular instruction, and a speech therapist met with her twice a week for thirty to forty minutes a session. In addition, the district bought and installed in its office at a cost of about $1,200 a printer-telephone for communicating with Amy's parents, both of whom were deaf. The Rowleys were not satisfied. They said that Amy should have the benefit of a sign language interpreter to sit next to her in class because she would otherwise miss some of the instruction. The school district insisted that the interpreter was unnecessary.

"This wasn't a question of money," said Charles Eible, superintendent of the district, a middle-income system of 3,000 pupils encompassing the countrified suburbs to the south of Peekskill. "We reviewed all aspects of her progress and thought that a sign language interpreter might even be detrimental because she lip reads extremely well. The program provided for her was appropriate and effective and she was doing well."[10] A federal district court disagreed, ordering the school district to provide the interpreter. The school system took the case to the Second U.S. Circuit Court of Appeals and again Amy Rowley won. "She needs a sign language interpreter in her classroom to enable her to have the same educational opportunity as her classmates," the Appeals Court declared.[11]

Where will it end? What degree of financial responsibility will the nation's schools have to incur in their surrogate role of atoning for the public's collective built. A district court in Texas ruled in 1980 that the school district in Irving was obligated to provide catheterization for a five-year-old with a permanent bladder impairment, a procedure that school officials had argued was medical, not educational.[12] The question is not whether the disabled deserve fairer treatment, but how far the limited resources of the schools can be stretched for the few. The Education of All Handicapped Children Act is not the only such law with which the schools must cope. There is also Section 504 of the Rehabilitation Act of 1973, phased into effect during the late 1970s, which mandates that "no otherwise qualified handicapped individual . . . shall solely by reason of his handicap, be excluded from the participation in, be denied the benefits of, or be subjected to discrimination under any program or activity receiving financial assistance [from the federal government]."

The act is part of the growing list of reforms unassailable in their pursuit of justice but fraught with obligations for the nation's educational institutions. Section 504 means that the buildings and grounds of schools and colleges must be made accessible to the disabled. This has required installing ramps and elevators, removing curbs and constructing sidewalks, widening doorways, erecting signs in Braille, and putting up audible street-crossing signs. The deaf, the blind, and those in wheelchairs are supposed to be able to move around freely and without danger to themselves. Programs, as well as facilities, are affected by the law, as the disabled are apparently entitled to the interpreters, readers, tutors, and special equipment needed for them to enjoy full participation in all areas of the curriculum. The educational institution must bear the expense. There are no firm estimates of what the cost will be to elementary and secondary schools, but at colleges and universities the outlays are expected to total between $500 million and $2 billion, according to the National Association of College and University Business Officers. Higher education could barely afford such an expense in the best of times, let alone in the 1980s, when revenues will be slashed by dwindling enrollments.

In its brevity, Section 504 gives no hint of how far educational institutions must go to comply with its provisions. The federal government conceded that not every classroom in every building must be accessible, but the ambiguity has permitted arbitrary judgments of federal regulators, in effect, to become law. When Congress enacted the legislation, it consisted of only 46 words. It has already taken the U.S. Supreme Court, in the first case it considered on Section 504, thousands of words to begin interpreting it.[13] It is not a comfortable situation for educational institutions, supposedly bastions of enlightenment. They are not keen on adding to their mounting expenses, but they do not want to be portrayed as enemies of the disabled.

THE CHILDREN'S ARMY

Efforts to use schools as a wedge to pry open the door to equal opportunity for the disabled flow out of earlier attempts to employ schools as the nation's main device for implementing racial desegregation. In either event, the questions here concern not the goal, but the notion that schools must carry the load for the rest of society. The teen-ager shivering outside the high school to which he was bused in Boston symbolizes the problem. Desegregation exacts a terrible toll from the youngsters. They, not their parents, are the soldiers in the war on intolerance. The whole process of schooling gets tied into the effort, while other institutions are spared damage.

In many circumstances, students reassigned to distant schools find themselves spending as much as two to three hours a day in transit. The continuity in their schooling is broken and the benefit of being in a building where teachers can confer about the student's performance the previous year is lost. It can mean, as it did in Boston, being transferred from school to school as a desegregation plan is gradually refined. Court-ordered busing produced a 100 percent turnover in some Louisville, Kentucky, schools. Extracurricular activities are rendered subservient to transportation schedules. Parents often find it impossible to participate in the on-going life of a school that they cannot reach conveniently. After-school friendships are sacrificed to the great distances separating the students' homes. The social structure that is so helpful in creating a successful school is knocked apart.

There is nothing inherently iniquitous about a child having to ride a bus to school. Fifty-four percent of all public school pupils in the United States are transported to school, mostly because they live too far to walk, not because they are involved in desegregation plans. It is regrettable, though, to add long bus rides for those for whom it is unnecessary. The difficulty is that so long as housing segregation persists there seems to be no other way to desegregate schools.

More than the discomfort of sitting on a bus is in store for some of the youngsters whom society has anointed its Hessians. School desegregation itself can sometimes be life-threatening, as was seen in South Boston when that neighborhood rebelled against a desegregation plan imposed on the city by a federal district court. In South Boston, attitudes about race were frozen in glaciers of hate that could not have been thawed by the warmth of a thousand brotherhood dinners. The closely knit Irish American community was a place where outsiders of any stripe were eyed warily and those with black skins were viewed with the greatest suspicion.

The glue that gave the neighborhood its cohesion consisted of many elements, not the least of which was South Boston High School, a yellow-tan brick structure atop a hill with a commanding view of the double-decker wooden houses lining the narrow streets below. The children of Southie, as this working-class enclave is known, have attended South Boston High since the turn of the century. Though the quality of education has never been good, they carried with them into adulthood bonds of affection for the old school. Thus, it was probably predictable when an attempt was made to desegregate all-white South Boston High that the sons and daughters of Southie would resist with ferocity. And resist they did. Not only did they deplore the busing-in of black youngsters, they also objected to the busing-out of local students.

Desegregation converted the corridors of the ancient building to avenues of combat, bristling with state troopers watching carefully over each change of class. Metal detectors searched for weapons at the schoolhouse door. City police patrolled the hilly streets around the school and motorcycle escorts with sirens blaring accompanied the buses of black youths to school. Even in the face of such a show of strength, there were racial brawls among the students. Attendance fell to the point that no more than a few hundred of the more than 1,000 students assigned to the school appeared for classes. Finally, the school became so unmanageable that it was closed and placed in receivership by a federal judge, who appointed outsiders to take control of South Boston High.

What happened in the immediate aftermath of desegregation at South Boston High could hardly be called a victory for education. Teaching and learning ceased. Hundreds of young people, black and white, stopped going to school, never returning to complete their education and get diplomas. Eventually, order was restored and the school slowly began functioning again. By 1980, six years after the onset of desegregation, South Boston was probably a better school than it had been. The police were gone and student suspensions had shrunk from 1,660 in 1975–76 to 86 in 1979–80. Schoolwide scores on nationally standardized reading tests placed the school fifth among Boston's eighteen high schools. One-third of the graduating class of 1980 was bound for college.[14] All of this at a school that had historically sent 6 to 8 percent of its seniors on to postsecondary education. But the price of this progress was steep, a reminder of the enormous sacrifice that the young people made for the sake of their elders.

SCHOOL DESEGREGATION VS. HOUSING DESEGREGATION

Ultimately, though, if school desegregation is the most desirable social policy and if the law is to be enforced equally, then the onus of compliance should not rest with the beleaguered school systems of the nation's largest cities. Too much is already expected of them. What is the use of trying to mix black and white students when there are hardly enough white youngsters in some locales to make busing worth the cost of the fuel? The proportion of white pupils in the enrollments of the school districts serving the biggest cities fell steadily during the 1970s. By the 1978–79 school year, the proportion was down to 9.8 percent in Atlanta, 21.5 percent in Chicago, 14.1 percent in Detroit, 25.7 percent in Memphis, 28.1 percent in New York, 14.6 percent in Oakland, 24.9 percent in St. Louis, 20.2 percent in San Francisco, and 3.3 percent in Washington, D.C.[15]

School systems like Atlanta's had taken it on themselves to try to recruit more white students by persuading families to take their children out of nonpublic schools or to move back into the city from the suburbs. Advertisements on the radio and on billboards were aimed at instilling confidence in a school system that was 26.7 percent white as recently as 1972. But such efforts in Atlanta and elsewhere will probably have virtually no impact on the racial composition of the schools.

Social scientists have been arguing for at least a decade about the reasons for the decline of white enrollment in big-city schools. One side says that desegregation, for whatever reasons, was responsible for white families moving to the suburbs or at least transferring their youngsters into nonpublic schools. The other side says that the drop in white enrollment was simply in the natural order of things and that desegregation or the threat of desegregation had little to do with it. In any event, the reasons for the change are not as important as the fact that it has happened. The effect is to make meaningful desegregation all but impossible in many urban school districts.

These are the same school districts that are already beset by difficulties because of the many demands they cannot meet. To continue to require them to carry out a social mandate that the surrounding suburbs are shirking is a mockery. If desegregation is the law for some people it should be the law for all people. What is good for the people of the big cities is good for those of the suburbs. School district lines are artificial barriers, and are not deserving of the sanctity with which they have been endowed.

So far, attempts to penetrate the suburbs with metropolitan school desegregation have been largely resisted. One of the most notable efforts was made in Detroit, where the U.S. Supreme Court overturned a plan to have suburban school systems exchange pupils with the city system. More recently, federal district courts in both St. Louis and Houston rebuffed attempts during the spring of 1980 to extend mandatory plans for citywide school desegregation to the suburbs. "White suburbanization is so far advanced in the urban area," a court-appointed expert, Gary Orfield, argued in St. Louis, "that full compliance with the Court of Appeals order will leave the large majority of black schools untouched by desegregation."[16] The district court in St. Louis, however, was able to order state officials to draw up a plan to promote voluntary school integration between the city and the suburbs.

In the halcyon days before school desegregation moved north, there was a naive hope that housing integration would eventually make mandatory busing unnecessary. That turned out to be like expecting the oil companies voluntarily to sacrifice profits to keep the price of a gallon of gasoline under one dollar. More than good intentions are needed to transfer the title of a three-bedroom house in the suburbs. The preponderance of black Americans have remained captives of the inner-city, hostages to a cycle of poverty. Whatever might have been possible through housing integration has now been pushed aside by inflation and the surge of real estate values. The median price of a single-family home in the U.S. has soared to $67,200 for a new house and $64,500 for an existing house.[17] Suburban housing is too costly for most blacks—even if whites would be willing to sell to them—and the hope of achieving school desegregation through housing integration is as dead as the 6 percent mortgage.

If they chose, state legislatures could abrogate the boundaries dividing school districts, but they refuse to do so. It is as though the lines were drawn by the Lord. The schizophrenic policy of the federal government adds to the muddle. The Department of Education has the authority to combat segregation in school systems found in violation of Title VI of the Civil Rights Act of 1964. This power is seriously limited, however, because since 1977 Congress has forbidden federal education officials from requiring a district to formulate a plan involving busing a student beyond the nearest school. This might imply that Congress would prefer to promote housing integration as the route to school integration, but the Fair Housing Act of 1968 authorizes federal agencies only to mediate complaints without any right to impose settlements or to punish those who discriminate. The Senate refused to join the House in an attempt in 1980 to strengthen the law. It was perhaps in keeping with these inconsistencies that the Democratic Party platform in 1980 proclaimed within a single paragraph: "School desegregation is an important tool in the effort to give all children equal educational opportunity. . . . Mandatory transportation of students beyond their neighborhoods for the purpose of desegregation remains a judicial tool of the last resort." Not a first, second, or third resort, but a last resort. It is abundantly clear that there will be no large-scale school desegregation in the United States of America unless the inviolability of school district lines is erased by the federal judiciary.

BILINGUAL EDUCATION - *SE HABLA ESPANOL*

In a manner only slightly less clumsy, the federal government decided to give schools the job of dealing with language differences in the population. However, Washington could not articulate a clear and consistent policy, leaving the schools with a host of political, nationalistic, and sociological considerations that all but inundated the academic significance of bilingual education. Congress passed the Bilingual Education Act in 1968, an amendment to the Elementary and Secondary Education Act of 1965, so that Washington could aid local programs with seed money. Underpinning the act was the idea that a child whose native language was not English should get the help he needs to learn English and reach his full potential in school.

It was a sound proposition. Millions of immigrant children of generations past were thrown into the educational sea without so much as a few survival phrases from which to fashion a linguistic life preserver. The tendency to romanticize those sink-or-swim days glosses over the fact that tens of thousands of first-generation Americans dropped out of school, confounded by their inability to make progress in the alien tongue of their English-speaking teachers.

But what began as an ostensibly voluntary endeavor evolved during the 1970s into one more required program. The U.S. Supreme Court ruled in 1974 that the protection of the Civil Rights Act of 1964, which banned discrimination on the basis of race, color, or national origin, extended to schoolchildren whose native language was not English. Yet, local school systems received vague and conflicting signals from the federal government as to what they were expected to do about bilingual education. Despite a memorandum drafted in 1970 and a set of guidelines issued in 1975, the former U.S. Department of Health, Education, and Welfare was not able to provide the schools with a definitive mandate. Instead, there was an air of intimidation as representatives of the Department's Office for Civil Rights ruled arbitrarily on what was acceptable.

A look at one community, Saginaw, Michigan, illustrates the awkwardness of the federal policy during the 1970s. Saginaw, nestled in a rich agricultural valley that is one of the centers of the nation's sugar beet industry, is the home of many Mexican Americans whose forebears emigrated to the region several generations ago seeking work as farm laborers. Many remained in the valley, and some of their offspring exchanged the incessant sun of the fields for the heat of the foundries, where at least the pay was better even if the temperatures were no lower. Despite their long residence in the United States, however, a portion of the families continued to use Spanish as the primary language in the home.

When the Saginaw schools implemented bilingual education, the first step was to have teachers take note of those children whose dominant language did not seem to be English. Then, the students were given language tests to find out if English or Spanish was their primary language. But in the mid-1970s the Office for Civil Rights investigated the situation and found that Saginaw's method was inadequate for identifying and assessing the needs of youngsters who might require bilingual education. Saginaw was told that it "must, at a minimum, determine the langauge most often spoken in the student's home, regardless of the language spoken by the student."[18] The school district was also ordered to find out what language the children used in social settings.

The extent of the burden placed on the school system by the federal government was reflected in the further instructions that Saginaw was given for deciding which children belonged in bilingual education. The directive was as follows: "Determine—by observation—the language used by the student to communicate with peers between classes or in informal situations. The assessments must cross-validate one another (example: student speaks Spanish at home and Spanish with classmates at lunch). Observers must estimate the frequency of use of each language spoken by the student in these situations. In the event that the language determinations conflict (example: student speaks Spanish at home, but English with classmates at lunch), an additional method must be employed by the District to make such a determination (for example, the District may wish to employ a test of language dominance as a third criterion)."[19]

Variations of this bureaucratic nightmare haunted school districts around the country in the late 1970s as agents in the regional offices of the Department of Health, Education, and Welfare, emboldened by their growing authority, dangled threats of fund termination in front of local school officials they deemed uncooperative. In 1977, according to the records of the Department, 222 school districts were declared in "noncompliance" with the Civil Rights Act because of what the government said were flaws in their bilingual programs, and the districts were ordered to submit corrective plans.

In 1980, when the new Department of Education promulgated proposed regulations that were finally supposed to clarify the bilingual responsibilities of local school districts, the waters were roiled. State and local education officials charged that the directives were so specific that the federal government would usurp control over instructional policies. The outcry was so loud that Congress interceded with a resolution delaying implementation of the regulations. Then, less than two weeks after taking office, the Reagan administration altogether killed the Carter proposal. "The policies are harsh, inflexible, burdensome, unworkable, and incredibly costly,"[20] said Terrel H. Bell, the soft-spoken, white-haired westerner whom President Reagan had installed as Secretary to preside over the possible dismantling of the Department of Education. The heavy hand of regulation seemed to be lifted, but there was concern among proponents of bilingual education that there might be no commitment whatsoever in the Reagan administration to carrying out what the Supreme Court declared was the nation's educational obligation to the non-English-speaking. The middle ground is a region that sometimes even the best compass cannot locate.

The essence of the controversy over bilingual education revolves around two questions: who is to receive it, and for how long? Some students who did not belong in such classes were included and others who should have been in the classes were excluded. The cause of uniformity was plagued by an inability to develop consistent national standards. Continuing controversy in the 1980s is guaranteed by differences over what tests to use to assess a student's need for bilingual education, how high to set the cutoff mark, and how to interpret the results. The Department of Education conceded in 1980 that it was uncertain what should be done with "comparably limited students," those lacking proficiency in both English and their native language.

Disagreements are also certain to continue over the issue of how long to keep students in bilingual programs. Logic would have it that, as a pupil gains the ability to function effectively in English, he or she will be phased entirely into the regular program. At least that ought to happen if bilingual education is a means to an end, rather than the end in itself. The duration of the programs is a main concern of those who suspect that bilingual education is, in part, a vehicle to promote the establishment of Spanish as an official second language in the United States. And it is Spanish that is the focus of bilingual education, accounting for 70 percent of the participants.

Noel Epstein, who produced a lengthy critique of bilingual education while on leave from the *Washington Post*, charged that some leaders of the bilingual movement did not view the approach as simply a transition to a full program in English. "The critical distinction in their drive," wrote Epstein, " is that they are seeking government-financed and government-promoted ethnic identities through use of language and culture in the public schools, a policy which might be called affirmative ethnicity. They want Washington to sponsor limited English-speaking students' attachments to their ethnic languages and histories. . . ."[21]

In light of such opinions, Alan Pifer, an ardent supporter of bilingual education and president of the Carnegie Corporation of New York, used his organization's annual report in 1980 to issue a warning. He cautioned that "advocates of bilingual education should be wary of advancing rationales for it that go beyond its strictly educational purpose of helping children acquire the intellectual skills they will need to compete successfully in the American mainstream. Such arguments, surely, will simply exacerbate the considerable hostility that already exists toward bilingual education. . . ."[22]

PAPERWORK

Though it means more work for the schools, it is not difficult to appreciate why they have been given such weighty responsibilities as caring for the disabled, integrating the races, and arbitrating the cultural differences inherent in language. No other agency has risen to accept challenges of such magnitude. The schools, like it or not, are stuck with the problems. It should be no surprise, however, that the schools sometimes cease functioning effectively. Nor should parents and other taxpayers wonder why schools are sometimes unable to carry out the teaching and learning mission that is supposed to be at their core. John Sawhill, for instance, suggests that the "prolonged and ill-advised effort to make the educational system the principal tool for social change has contributed to such problems as the sharply increased incidence of functional illiteracy."[23]

Owen Knutzen is among those who are troubled by the pressures being applied to schools as they are prodded to take on more and more tasks. He also happens to be keenly aware of the effects of such pressures because he is the school superintendent in Omaha. "I believe in the necessity of all of these things being done, but I wonder whether the school system is the appropriate agency," said Knutzen. "For the last quarter of a century, society has been turning to the public schools to address a lot of the maladies. Maybe there should be some new agencies invented to tackle some of these problems, or at least some of the problems should be delegated to other agencies." A prime target of Knutzen's complaints is the voluminous paperwork required to comply with federal, state, and local directives. "It becomes monumental and frankly it does not add to the schooling of boys and girls," he said.[24]

School administrators throughout the country speak with frustration of the avalanche of printed forms that threatens to bury them. Teachers and supervisors must squeeze time from their schedules to fill out thousands of forms a year. There were 284 separate programs listed in the Federal Register of February 19, 1980, for elementary, secondary, and higher education, all requiring the filing of forms. San Diego discovered in surveying the workload of its teachers that they were being asked to handle 186 different forms, some once a year and others hundreds of times a year.[25]

The proliferation of forms is one of the results of shifting more of the funding for local education to state and federal authorities. The farther removed the funding source, the greater the likelihood of more paperwork so that distant officials can monitor the expenditures. No longer does most of the money for public elementary and secondary education come from local sources, which now provide 47.6 percent of the revenues. The state contribution has reached 43.0 percent and the federal government pays for 9.4 percent of the total.[26] It would be fatuous to suggest that schools could be insulated from external influences even if the federal and state mandates were wiped out and all control were returned to the local level. Other, subtler forces, would remain to diminish the ability of the schools to control their destiny.

Boob Tubes and Dope

Television may be the most pervasive of these other influences and no amount of local autonomy can shield the schools from its impact. Television respects no boundaries; what occurs within the confines of the classroom can no more be free of the influence of television than children can be free of the influence of their parents during the time that they are not with them. Television is unlike any rival the schools have known. A typical elementary school pupil spends 25 hours and 48 minutes a week in the company of a television set, almost as much time as is spent with his or her teacher.

Every passive hour in front of the tube robs the child of time that might be used to develop other interests and talents, both intellectual and physical. Television opens an international vista to the youngster in the privacy of his home, while denying him time for experiences on his own street corner. Soap opera replaces literature. A spectator's seat on the 50-yard line replaces participatory sports. Unimaginative quiescence replaces creative play. An oration by Big Bird replaces conversation with a parent.

The ultimate challenge is to the schools. Television is

the other curriculum, ubiquitous and always beckoning. Neil Postman made this point noting "television is not usually acknowledged to have a curriculum or to be one, which is probably why parents do not pay as much attention to the television education of their children as they do to their school education. . . . But all of this can be seen in a clarifying light if we simply define a curriculum as a specially constructed information system whose purpose, *in its totality,* is to influence, teach, train, or cultivate the mind and character of our youth."[27]

Television seems to affect the very style by which youngsters learn. An orientation to pictures instead of to words may even condition and stimulate the brain differently. Experts disagree on the effect of television watching on children. Thus, there is growing interest in improving the quality of the programming, at least giving young people better fare since it is assumed that they cannot be weaned from their viewing habits. The Federal Communications Commission in 1980 began considering a requirement that stations broadcast at least 7½ hours of instructional programs each week for children. There was also a move among some educators to start teaching "critical viewing skills," so that time in front of the television set could be more productive.

If, however, the very act of watching television is the issue—regardless of the quality of the program or the sophistication of the viewer—then upgrading content is not enough to combat the problem. Marie Winn's thesis is that what a person watches on television does not matter as much as the watching itself.[28] Common sense dictates that the printed word and traditional teaching methods cannot have the impact they once did in an age when youngsters reach high school having spent up to 20,000 hours being assaulted by rapidly moving images dancing across a glowing screen.

Like so many teachers, Robert Greenman was curious about the pervasiveness of television in the lives of his students. Greenman polled the youngsters in a couple of his English classes at James Madison High School in Brooklyn's legendary Flatbush neighborhood and discovered that 47 of the 57 had television sets in their bedrooms. Twenty-six of the 57 had so many sets in their homes, four or more, that almost anywhere they moved they were not far from the warm, reassuring glow of the tube. "I definitely think I have watched too much television," commented a rueful eleventh-graders, Richard Guarneri. "I watch television at least four hours a day and on Sundays I watch it most of the day. I can't seem to peel myself away from it. I think television does more harm to a person than it does good. Even though there are many educational programs on television, there are many more noneducational shows which most people prefer. I think television has done me more harm than good because instead of using time for studying, I've spent it watching TV."[29]

For today's television-bred generation of young people, learning is half spent absorbing information effortlessly from an entertaining box and half spent deciphering symbols laboriously from pictureless pages. It is obvious which activity is favored. The problems facing schools cannot possibly be separated from the dominance of television in shaping culture. From the time an infant peeks through the slats of his crib and follows the movement of objects across a television screen, he is bombarded with electronic messages that will exacerbate the difficulty of his teachers in commanding his attention. Mr. Chips never had to compete with Brooke Shields peddling her Calvins.

It was probably only a matter of time until an attorney cited the adverse influence of television in defense of a client's transgression. It happened in Miami in 1977, when 15-year-old Ronny Zamora's continual exposure to violence as a heavy viewer of television was the excuse given for his fatal shooting of an 82-year-old next-door neighbor. The youth was nonetheless found guilty of murder, but the case stirred debate across the country about the effects of television. And it turned out to be the precursor of another defense plea 4 years later, when a Manhattan lawyer blamed the depiction of criminal behavior on television for influencing his 9-year-old client to rob a bank in Rockefeller Center. Researchers at the Annenberg School of Communications at the University of Pennsylvania have found that television cultivates a heightened sense of being surrounded by a mean, violent world. Moreover, those who watch the most television, according to social scientists at

Penn, exhibit a higher degree of mistrust and insecurity. In general, though, television's impact on classroom achievement remains uncertain.

If the influence of television on school performance is still a matter of conjecture, the effect of drugs is no mystery to any teacher who has seen students arrive in class so stoned that they can barely recall their birthdates, much less remember a Shakespearean sonnet or figure out an algebraic equation. No discussion today on the role of outside influences on the school would be complete without recognizing drug use among the young. The situation grew worse during the 1970s as the proportion of 12- to 17-year-olds who had used marijuana rose from 14 percent in 1972 to 30.9 percent in 1979.[30] As many as one in four high school students may be regular users of marijuana. An ample portion of that use occurs during the school day. It is a problem that educators sometimes feel they are battling alone. A society in which head shops selling drug paraphernalia operate as openly as the corner candy store cannot expect its schools to run with the naive efficiency of the Riverdale High attended by a perpetual generation of Archies and Veronicas.

A variety of other outside forces exert powerful influences on the schools, just as drugs and television do. An advisory panel that searched for reasons for the decline in scores on the Scholastic Aptitude Test noted, for example, that there is probably more than sheer coincidence to the rising number of young people living in homes with one parent and the falling scores. The panel's report, pointing out that the sharpest drop occurred between 1967 and 1975, also raised the possibility that the trauma of dissension over the Vietnam War, political assassinations, the wave of permissiveness, riots in the cities, and the political corruption of Watergate may have affected the motivation of students.[31]

In such a setting it is no wonder that schools do not always get the most out of their students. Annie Sullivan became a "miracle worker" with only one student and dedicated a lifetime to the project. There are so many students and so many problems with which to contend that schools at times are overwhelmed. Public education has been given a plethora of assignments exceeding anything asked of any other agency. Perhaps there is nowhere else to turn, but society must beware of the implications of its demands.

CHAPTER THREE

MINIMUM COMPETENCY

THE SEDUCTION OF AN UNSUSPECTING PUBLIC

There's something in 't
That is deceivable.

WILLIAM SHAKESPEARE
Twelfth Night

Bill McCurdy was not the sort of young person to make excuses for himself and insisted that it was his fault and not that of the school system that he failed the mathematics section of Florida's State Student Assessment Test. He had to take the test three times. Never mind that he had studied high school mathematics, including algebra and geometry, for four years and had passed his courses without being told that his work seemed deficient. McCurdy enjoyed running the mile on the track team more than he liked sitting in math class and he realized he was not the best student at Hialeah-Miami Lakes Senior High. But he thought he was making satisfactory progress toward graduation and the day when he could go off to a community college to study forestry.

"It's the school's right to come up with a test that you have to pass to get out," said McCurdy, whose older sister had graduated from Hialeah-Miami Lakes, a sprawling monster of a school whose 2,700 students represent the potpourri of ethnicity—black, white, and Hispanic—that is Dade County. Their families span an economic range from the small, modest dwellings of Opa Locka to the opulent symbols of the good life just a few sunny blocks from the school. McCurdy's father was a cable foreman for Southern Bell. "If you tell people you have not passed the test they say to you, 'What's the matter? It's easy,' " said McCurdy, a lean, brown-haired youth in jeans, t-shirt, and sneakers, an outfit that seems to be the school uniform. "It eats you up inside. All the years I put into school and then not able to graduate with my class. It would be a real letdown."[1]

McCurdy graduated with his class in 1980. He passed the test on his third try and, as it turned out, he would have gotten his diploma even without passing it. The test that gave him so much trouble was a portion of a two-part examination that was originally intended to be a diploma requirement throughout Florida. A federal district court, however, had ordered the state to delay implementation of the requirement, helping white kids like Bill McCurdy as well as the black youngsters who had filed the suit.[2] And so it goes with minimum competency.

The idea of minimum competency was born in a burst of civic enterprise. School officials in Denver wanted to counteract the complaints of irate businessmen who said that the city's high school graduates were not mentally equipped to be productive workers. Young clerks were miscalculating figures on sales slips. Young secretaries were misspelling words in letters. Young delivery drivers could not read directions. So, to mollify the captains of industry, the school system introduced tests in four areas—reading, spelling, language use, and arithmetic—that students would have to pass to qualify for diplomas. That was in 1959. The bandwagon called minimum competency picked up momentum slowly during the 1960s and began racing at a furious clip in the 1970s as concern about declining achievement swept across the country like an advertising slogan for a new detergent.

People were alarmed by what they thought was happening in the schools. The media assaulted them continually with vivid descriptions of scholastic deterioration. Finally, any move perceived as an attempt to restore standards was welcomed. After all, society had never abandoned the expectation that the schools would equip youngsters with the fundamentals of learning. The burden of the extra demands was not intended to interfere with the teaching of the basics. Or so some people argued, with good reason. Taxpayers lavish $87 billion a year on the nation's network of 62,600 elementary schools and 25,400 secondary schools, an endeavor that is the largest beneficiary of local taxes. These schools provide employment for 2,190,000 teachers and other instructional staff members. Somewhere along the line, this gargantuan undertaking is supposed to pay dividends in the form of achievement by the 41 million pupils.

Yet, there has been mounting evidence of an insufficient yield from this huge investment. Many young people emerge from twelve years of schooling without skills worthy of employment. The most comprehensive effort by the federal government to assess the skills of the adult population, the Adult Performance Level Study, revealed that more than one in five men and women did not have the functional literacy to handle such tasks as reading a help-wanted advertisement or using available information to locate a needed service.[3]

At the same time, the military is troubled by the low educational achievement of its recruits, and college-bound high school graduates are registering lower scores on the Scholastic Aptitude Test and other college entrance examinations. Once enrolled in institutions of higher education, students are frequently in need of remedial work. In New Jersey, for instance, the Basic Skills Placement Test administered to 47,951 freshmen entering college in 1980 showed shocking deficiencies among many of them. Basic proficiency was lacking among 31 percent in verbal skills, 45 percent in computation, and 62 percent in elementary algebra.[4]

Enter the minimum competency movement. Few educational fads have had so wide an impact so quickly. By the beginning of the 1980s, 36 states had adopted some sort of minimum competency requirement. But the effort to seek redemption through minimum competency smacks of gimmickry. It is a simplistic response to a complicated problem, not unlike the political rhetoric that has enraptured so many, inculcating false hopes of recapturing an era that existed mostly in fantasy. The truth is that minimum competency standards are either so low that they are meaningless or so high that they are unenforceable.

Legislators have coated themselves with a veneer of toughness by enacting statutes on minimum competency. School board members and administrators have assuaged public disenchantment with the schools by creating an illusion of action through minimum competency. And teachers, who would rather blame anyone but themselves for the low achievement of their pupils, have used minimum competency to put the onus for failure on the students. Minimum competency gets everyone except the student off the hook. It is as though teachers, principals, and superintendents had no more to do with the quality of education than the person who drives the school bus.

Like some magic abracadabra, the words minimum competency are supposed to fix all that is wrong. It is not that easy. "Any setting of statewide minimum competency standards for awarding the high school diploma—however understandable the public clamor which has produced the current movement and expectation—is basically unworkable, exceeds the present measurement arts of the teaching profession and will create more social problems than it can conceivably solve," stated a panel of the National Academy of Education that was asked by the federal government to examine the testing of basic skills.[5] The same panel also advised strongly against the creation of any sort of national minimum competency test, a step that some publicity-hungry members of Congress were urging.

What some people would like to see happen under the guise of minimum competency is unrealistic beyond the earliest grades because there is no single set of courses taken by all students after they leave elementary school. Students have varying interests and uneven abilities. They are not all headed toward college, and even among the college-bound the requirements for entrance are not the same. They do not learn at the same rate and they do not confront the same lessons at the same time. They simply do not study the same subjects. A test of ability and knowledge in mathematics, for instance, can not be set on much more than an eighth-grade level because the majority of students never advance into intermediate algebra, geometry, trigonometry, and calculus. It is therefore impossible to have anything like a minimum competency test that sets a high level of difficulty.

An alternative is a much easier test covering only very basic material, an examination of the fundamentals that a capable student should have mastered by the end of the seventh or eighth grade. The mathematics could involve dividing and multiplying fractions and decimals. The vocabulary could be taken from a sixth-grade reader. This is the essence of minimum competency in most states. It is a pretension of the worst sort, a test for a high school diploma that has no more to do with the substance of a high school education than a comic book has to do with literature. It is a sham to use an eighth-grade examination as a qualification for a diploma and then turn around and tell the public that standards are being upheld.

Denver did it first with a minimum competency test that was ridiculously easy. Schools elsewhere have followed suit. In New York State, for example, when the board of regents ordered the state education department to develop a test that high school students would have to pass as a graduation requirement, three of the questions produced for the mathematics section were:

"Fred has four candy bars. If he divides each bar in half, what is the total number of pieces he will have . . . 8 . . . 2 . . . 16 . . . 4?"

"When written as a percent, the fraction ½ is . . . 75% . . . 50% . . . 25% . . . 20%?"

"A basketball is a . . . cylinder . . . cube . . . cone . . . sphere?"

The reading portion of the test was of a similar level of difficulty. There was a reproduction of a notice of church services for various faiths and a multiple-choice question asking the time of the Methodist service. Another page contained a restaurant menu and multiple-choice questions about the cost of a particular meal.

These are so-called survival skills, the rudiments that a person allegedly needs to eke out a daily existence. That is the measure of a high school education in the United States. The student is not assessed on whether he understands Faulkner or knows why the United States did not join the League of Nations, but on whether he comprehends the terms of a lease or can figure out how much change he would have after an excursion to the supermarket. The public thinks it is getting standards. Little do they know.

Education officials in many parts of the country have settled for such tests, but when the board of regents in New York State discovered the result of its mandate, the state education department was directed to design a new, tougher test. It is the more difficult examination that becomes a requirement for a diploma beginning in 1981. Those who enroll in the state's academically oriented regents courses and pass the end-of-the-year examinations will be exempted from the competency tests that the remainder of the state's high school students will have to pass in reading, writing, and mathematics. New York's approach to minimum competency is one of the most rigorous in the country. The state even plans to place a high school on a conditional status if more than 15 percent of its seniors fail to pass the competency test.

But the Regents Competency Tests will not be as difficult as the regular Regents Examinations, and there will not be the single standard for a diploma that the state education authorities would like the public to believe there will be. Furthermore, students will be able to pass the competency tests by answering only 65 percent of the questions correctly. While the mathematics competency test has been made more difficult, it will still have questions like the following:

"Mr. Jones bought a jacket for $15 and had to pay a 7% sales tax. If he gave the clerk $20, what should his change be? . . . $1.05 . . . $3.95 . . . $4.95 . . . $16.05?"

"If carpeting costs $9.50 a square meter, what is the total cost of carpeting an entire room floor which is 3 meters by 4 meters?

. . . $66.50 . . . $114 . . . $133 . . . $228?"

Even in New York, a student will be able to satisfy the minimum competency requirement by the end of ninth or tenth grade and it will hardly be an all-encompassing examination covering the substance of a high school education. The dilemma for schools everywhere is that giving the test too early means making it too easy, while offering it too late means making it too difficult. John Davis, the state school superintendent in Virginia, wondered if it made any sense at all to tie a minimum competency test to a diploma, as the legislature in that state voted to do. "I agree that a diploma should indeed stand for achievement," said Davis, "but, on the other hand, it is punitive to wait until late in a youngster's educational career to advise him that he has been unsuccessful."[6] A test for a diploma administered as early as the ninth grade is too late as far as Davis is concerned. What he preferred was a good testing program, grade by grade, that identifies the skills and competencies that a student has mastered and indicates what ought to be done to make up the deficiencies as he goes along.

It is unfair and demoralizing for a young person to have to wait until he reaches high school, and perhaps even the senior year, to learn that he is not eligible for the diploma he expected. Why was he allowed to advance through the system if he did not have the skills? Why was he not given the opportunity for remediation? "Justice requires that identification of learning difficulties should occur, as in fact is usually does, at much earlier levels, indeed as early as possible, so that remedial measures may be instigated well before the critical time at which a student must manifest competence,"[7] observed Roger T. Lennon, a leading authority on testing.

Minimum competency is fraught with such problems, though many proponents of the movement blithely ignore the consequences of what they are advocating. There is also the risk of the test dictating the curriculum since there is so much at stake. Roger Farr, an Indiana University reading professor and former president of the International Reading Association, fears that minimum competency could point teaching toward the goal of improving performance on specific tests rather than addressing the wide scope of needs that comprise a full education.[8] Moreover, there is the possibility of minimums becoming maximums. Minimum competency is meaningless for able students, but the education of the weaker students might center entirely on acquiring the minimum, just enough to pass the test. Then they could be forgotten and the school system could avoid the embarrassment of having them fail the test.

Two of the states that have restricted the lure of state-wide minimum competency testing, Nebraska and Iowa, decided in 1979 that the concept offered little beyond public relations. Iowa assembled a 20-member task force that studied the issue for a year and concluded that enough tests were being administered to gauge student progress and that the schools simply ought to do a better job of monitoring the available information. In Nebraska, a study commissioned by a legislative committee found that minimum competency testing would be neither desirable nor beneficial to the state. "Such tests are meaningless for most of those who can pass them and devastating to the small percentage who cannot," said Hugh Harlan, head of the instructional services branch in the Nebraska Department of Education.[9] Like Iowa, Nebraska thought that the schools were already doing enough testing to know how students were performing.

Reflecting the shallowness of minimum competency is the fact that in almost all instances students are permitted to take the test as many times as necessary to pass it. Denver administered the test twice a year beginning in the ninth grade and students could keep repeating it until they passed, not having to be retested on the subsections on which they had been successful. The pattern elsewhere is much the same. If Abner Doubleday had applied the same rule to baseball, Mickey Mantle might have swatted 100 home runs a year because he never would have had to worry about striking out.

The question of how low to set the passing mark is another issue that seldom gets a public airing. If the cutoff mark is low enough, almost everyone passes and the school district looks as though it is doing a fine job, though officials neglect to mention that many students being certified as graduates could not answer correctly almost 4 of every 10 questions.

One of the greatest inequities of minimum competency is the practice in some states of allowing each school district to set its own standards. A school system may deny a student a diploma on the basis of a minimum competency score that would be high enough to qualify for graduation in a neighboring district. This is where California is headed. The legislature ordered a minimum competency requirement for graduating starting in 1981, but precluded the state from setting a uniform standard. In other words, each of California's 1,042 school districts is free to comply with the mandate in its own way. In the name of local autonomy, the legislature passed the hot potato of minimum competency to the local school districts, but claimed credit in Sacramento for showing an abiding concern for standards.

Such a pattern in California and other states could spawn a generation of academic Okies, families moving from school system to school system until they found a locale where the test was easy enough for their children to obtain a high school diploma. Parents could also transfer their youngsters into private or parochial schools, which are exempted from minimum competency requirements in California, as well as several other states. Apparently, those who are sufficiently affluent to pay for nonpublic education should not have to be bothered with standards that are applied to the hoi polloi. In addition, there is an escape clause in California allowing school districts to waive the competency test for students who successfully complete a course or set of courses covering material equivalent to that on the examination. It is a clause that could prove to be so big that an entire senior class could be pushed through it without any of them taking the competency test.

Along similar lines in New Jersey, where passage of a minimum competency test will be required for graduation beginning in 1985, schools will be able to excuse students from having to take the test if evaluation and supportive data indicate that the student has mastered material equivalent to that

on the test. Arizona, too, has opened a back door to a diploma.
Though the state insists it is maintaining standards by requiring that no one be graduated unless he can read at the ninth-
grade level, each school district in the state may decide how
to measure for that level. The district may even use the judg-
ment of a teacher instead of a test, if it chooses. In a sense,
minimum competency's claim to uphold standards is a shell
game. Now you see it—now you don't.

California's State Department of Education conducted
a study in 1979 to see how school districts were doing in preparing to implement the minimum competency requirement.
Virtually every school district had a different test and many of
the tests violated psychometric principles. "Many of the locally
developed tests displayed flaws such as inadequate directions
for test takers, poor layout, lack of test item specifications, and
failure to review for bias," the education department reported
on the study.[10] Some of the same material was covered in most
districts. Ninety-five percent of the tests in mathematics, for
instance, assessed addition, subtraction, multiplication, and
division of whole numbers, fractions, and decimals—though
the degree of difficulty varied. But only 5 percent of the tests
examined knowledge of averages, probabilities, and statistics.
On the reading tests, 40 percent assessed vocabulary and 5
percent assessed spelling. Clearly, students would be meeting
different standards, depending on where in California their
families lived.

California, is among certain of the states that gave local
school systems discretion in deciding whether youngsters with
learning handicaps would have to meet the same standards for
a diploma as nonhandicapped students. In an era in which
more and more students are being classified as handicapped,
especially in the category of learning disabled, this is a route
that school districts could conveniently use to boost through
students and to camouflage failure rates.

Wilson Riles, California's popular and politically astute
superintendent of public instruction, acknowledged the many
paradoxes of minimum competency as applied to his state.
Though the state education department was prohibited from
conducting reviews of local procedures, it was given the role

of providing technical aid to local school districts in their effort to design minimum competency examinations. Weighing the question of how difficult the tests should be, Riles said: "It would be politically intolerable for a school board to set the standard so high that only 5 percent of the students are eligible for diplomas. At the other end, the whole thing is meaningless if they set the standards so low that 90 percent qualify."[11] Riles, a tall, expansive man whose resonant voice commands attention, was in such demand on the banquet circuit during the 1970s that he became the nation's best known black educator. He is also a dominant figure in Sacramento, where he takes credit for having helped dissuade the California legislature from ordering a single, statewide minimum competency examination. He thought that such a test in a state as heterogeneous as California would have a shattering effect on a large segment of the school population. The day is gone, according to Riles, when the schools can set a single standard and callously deny diplomas to those who cannot measure up. "This would not have been a major issue in the past, say in 1947, when only the brightest and the most motivated stayed in high school and the rest quit," he said. "But over the years we have made a commitment to educate every youngster to the level of his ability."[12]

A DIPLOMA FOR EVERYONE WHO WANTS ONE

When only a third of the nation's teen-agers finished high school, it would have been easier to talk of common standards and to have imposed meaningful tests of minimum competency, though the need for such examinations was not felt at that time. Students who were less inclined toward academics left school before graduation to go to work, get married, or join the military. There were jobs for high school dropouts and opportunities for them to rise to higher positions.

Today, even Horatio Alger would be stuck in the corporate mail room for his entire career if he did not have a diploma. A diploma is no longer a luxury; it is the key that opens the first lock on the door to the job market. Denying a youngster a diploma today is like handing him a life sentence on the welfare line. There is no way, regardless of the enthusiasm for the minimum competency movement, that schools could get away with holding back legions of students. Political, racial, and social considerations militate against so Draconian a policy. Any attempt as a result of minimum competency to reduce the number of young people getting diplomas would amount to repudiation of the nation's social commitment to universal secondary education. The young person who goes looking for work without benefit of a diploma is usually turned away summarily, hardly given a chance to fill out an application form. Applicants learn quickly that only by falsifying forms to make it appear that they completed high school will they get an interview for even the most menial job.

As it is, high school graduates are finding themselves competing for jobs with the college-educated. The situation is hopeless without a diploma. Positions are not opening in sufficient numbers for college graduates and they are curbing their ambitions to seek jobs that used to go to high school graduates. The competition is so severe that it would be inhumane to withhold a diploma from a youth who persevered through the system for twelve years. "Is American society ready to live with a growing number of young persons who are rejected by the schools between ages 14 and 17 without credentials that will allow them a chance at a job and a decent life?"[13] asked Harold Howe II, a former commissioner of the U.S. Office of Education, who went on to be vice president for education and public policy at the Ford Foundation, a position from which he retired in 1981.

Rightly or wrongly, the idea of every student attending high school—and presumably graduating—has been established as the norm in the United States. The nation is too far into the sea to try to swim back to the shore. As Fred and Grace Hechinger pointed out, "The extension of secondary education to include poor children represented a dramatic egalitarian advance."[14] It is a step that was taken early in the life of the country, but progress was not swift. The venerable Boston Latin School, the nation's first public secondary school, was created in 1635—a year before the founding of Harvard College. As late as 1890, however, Charles W. Eliot lamented the fact that three-fourths of the country's population still had no direct access to secondary education.[15]

At the turn of the 20th century, a high school diploma was still an indulgence reserved for the children of the rich and a few exceptional youths intent on the professions or a life of intellectual contemplation. A proliferation of free public high schools and changing attitudes about education expanded enrollments in high schools and, by the dawn of the 1920s, 32.3 percent of those in the 14- to 17-year-old age group were in school. A decade later, in 1929, 51.4 percent of the age group attended high school.[16] But girls disproportionately outnumbered boys, and a large number of people believed that going to school beyond the eighth grade was unnecessary for anyone with the ambition to get started in the work force.

The unavailability of jobs during the Depression had a profound impact on high schools, impelling young people to remain longer within the protective womb of the classroom since the prospect of employment was dim. The proportion of teen-agers attending high school rose to 73.3 percent by 1939, dropped a little during the early 1940s as male adolescents trooped off to find their manhood in military service, and began inching up again after World War II. In 1949, 76.8 percent of the nation's 14- to 17-year-olds were in high school. The prosperity of postwar America made it unnecessary for families to send their children to work, and the idea was spreading that the good life was linked to education. High school was firmly entrenched as an institution for the multitudes by the 1950s, and in 1969, fully 92.7 percent of the age group was enrolled. The figure climbed slightly and reached a plateau of 95 percent during the 1970s.[17]

Twentieth-century American has tranformed itself into one of the most extensively schooled societies the world has known. Formal education through high school is considered appropriate for all and the disdain toward those without diplomas shows what the country expects as a minimum.

In the rest of the world, the opportunity to attend high school is still largely a privilege. Many families elsewhere have to pay tuition for their children to go to high school in much the way that Americans pay for college. Furthermore, there are not enough high schools to serve the population in many of the world's countries. Survival in the developing world often dictates a lifetime of labor that begins even before childhood has ended. Statistics tell the story. The proportion of teen-agers in high school is 19 percent in Algeria, 18 percent in Brazil, 9 percent in Gambia, 28 percent in India, 20 percent in Indonesia, 38 percent in Iraq, 15 percent in Kenya, 17 percent in Pakistan, and 26 percent in Thailand. A few countries like Japan and some in Western Europe have statistics more closely approximating those of the United States. But the nations that have reached this level are few, and the figures are still low in such countries as Australia (73 percent), Czechoslovakia (37 percent), England (81 percent), and Poland (55 percent).[18]

Where those who continue their education through high school are a homogeneous group, as was once the case in the United States, the possibility still exists of setting and enforcing common standards. After all, until very recently many European countries screened out students with an examination at the age of 11 and allowed only the most promising to continue their academic preparation. What passes as minimum competency for high school graduates in the United States, though, is usually junior high school work. Baltimore, for example, has a package of tests that students must pass to get a diploma. They can take the mathematics examination in the eighth grade and the reading and writing tests in the ninth grade. In the first two years that Baltimore applied the requirement, 1979 and 1980, no more than 2 percent of the seniors were prevented from getting diplomas by their inability to pass the minimum competency tests.

Diplomas Mean Different Things
Perhaps the first step toward shaking loose of the grip of minimum competency comes with the acknowledgment that a high school diploma is not a high school diploma is not a high school diploma. No two diplomas signify the same set of accomplishments. The best response to the public clamor about standards would be for educators to explain that high schools have

different purposes for different students. One graduate meets his English requirement with Shakespeare and Dostoyevsky, while another meets the same requirement with movie star profiles and public speaking. One meets his science requirement with honors physics, while another does it with a modified biology course in which two semesters of work is stretched over three semesters to give him more time to absorb the watered-down lessons. This is perhaps as it must be if a diploma is to be obtainable by all. The only body of knowledge common to most of today's high school students is what they saw on television the previous night.

One example of the ill-advised effort to try to convince the public to perceive all high school diplomas as the same was seen in New York City, where a so-called single diploma was implemented in 1974. Until then, students could earn various diplomas—a commercial diploma for business subjects, a vocational diploma for job training, an academic diploma for college preparatory courses. The single diploma was adopted as an egalitarian device, supposedly eradicating the stigma of the less prestigious diplomas. Suddenly, the single diploma meant that all of the city's high school students would have to take the same number of years of English, mathematics, science, social studies, and other subjects. Simplified versions of the courses were developed for those unable to cope with the regular courses. Moreover, there was no longer sufficient time in the schedule for commercial students to enroll in the number of typing, stenography, and bookkeeping courses they formerly took. They were ostensibly receiving an academic education instead. What it really amounted to, though, was a diluted program that contained neither the rigor of a precollege program, nor the depth of experience that they had previously gotten for entry-level office jobs. The single diploma was an empty promise of equality.

Perhaps high schools are doing no more than following the lead of colleges and universities that try to create the illusion of a single diploma. Actually, college degrees represent no more of a uniform standard than do high school diplomas. If there were a minimum competency requirement for a bachelor's degree and it embodied college-level achievement in such subjects as mathematics, science, and philosophy, chances are that many students would not qualify for graduation. Many never even study such subjects in college and, if they do, they do not move beyond the introductory courses. They all get bachelor's degrees, but their experiences are dissimilar. In many eyes, though, the credential is what counts and often no one asks what the degree-holder did to get it, just so he has it.

As a growing percentage of young people have completed high school, the demand that job applicants have diplomas has increased—even if the work could be performed just as adequately by a high school dropout. Phony obstacles have been erected to force young men and women out of competition and some who would prefer to leave high school have no choice but to remain.

Standards are fine, but if they have no relevance to the task at hand they are superfluous—and possibly illegal. A little-noticed decision by the U.S. Supreme Court in 1971 held that "if an employment practice which operates to exclude Negroes cannot be shown to be related to job performance, the practice is prohibited."[19] According to the case, brought under the equal employment section of the Civil Rights Act of 1964, the Duke Power Company in North Carolina traditionally employed blacks only as laborers. When civil rights legislation was enacted and blacks sought promotions to other jobs, the company decreed that those higher positions were open only to applicants with a high school diploma or a passing score on an equivalency test. The U.S. Supreme Court backed the view of the Equal Employment Opportunity Commission that requiring diplomas of these workers was illegal and that the only acceptable criterion in hiring and promoting them was a professionally developed test that examined the applicant's capacity to do a specific job.

At the same time, the school systems of North Carolina and many other states did not show the kind of support for black youngsters that they did for whites, forcing many blacks —males in particular—to leave school before graduation to look for work. The court ruling stressed that so long as such circumstances prevailed and a higher proportion of whites than blacks graduated from high school, there was the potential of racial discrimination in requiring a job applicant to have a diploma.

But requiring a diploma for a job is more than a racial issue. It is a distortion of the purposes of education and is sometimes a ploy for cutting down the applicant pool. As the U.S. Supreme Court emphasized, the ability to do a job and not the possession of a diploma should be the test of employment. This is especially true in an age in which diplomas have become so plentiful. If young people thought they would receive equal consideration from employers without having the benefit of a diploma, then perhaps more of them who do not wish to be in high school would leave. As long as the nation places a premium on the diploma, though, the rules cannot be changed midway through the game. Failing students on minimum competency tests does them no favor. They are not the ones who decided that having a diploma should be part of the rite of entrance to the job market. What they need is a better education from the very beginning.

This was the essence of the federal district court decision that blocked Florida from applying its graduation standards until 1983. Originally, the state's Educational Accountability Act was to take effect with the high school graduating class of 1979. Students were to demonstrate "satisfactory performance in functional literacy" as a prerequisite for a diploma. But Judge George C. Carr, after a four-week, nonjury trial, held that the "taint of segregation" was still upon the schools of Florida and that it would be unconstitutional to implement such a test without giving students who were already making their way toward the twelfth grade more time to prepare for it.[20] Had the judge not blocked the minimum competency requirement, 4,800 students would have had their diplomas withheld in 1979 and probably even more in 1980. Seventy-two percent of those youngsters were black, though blacks made up only 20 percent of the state's public school enrollment.

The fault was apparently not in the test. It was one of those innocuous examinations discussed earlier, a test calling on the student to read road maps, fill out applications, and balance checking accounts. The judge found the test valid and reliable. Springing it on students whose earlier education did not prepare them for it was the problem.

Melvin Jackson, a black classmate of Bill McCurdy's at Hialeah-Miami Lakes, also seemed for a while to be one of the thousands who might not have gotten his diploma if the district court had not intervened in Florida. He, too, failed the competency test the first time he took it in the eleventh grade and finally passed it toward the end of his senior year. He graduated in 1980, but his experience gave him pause to reflect on his education. "I want to go into TV and radio repair," he said. "To me the diploma means you went through school, that you learned enough to go out into the world and do something with what you learned. You have certain people who look at you differently if you don't have a diploma. They wonder what you were doing in school all that time if you didn't get a diploma in the end. Through the years they should be teaching you the stuff that will be on the test. How did I get to the twelfth grade if I couldn't do the work? That's where it's unfair."21

Chances are that the difficulties of some of Florida's students will not have been resolved when the court's ban is lifted and the state is able to begin using its test as a criterion for a diploma. Unless Florida vastly improves the quality of education in the early grades, a disproportionate number of black children will probably continue to fail the examination. Giving a test is the easy part. Preparing students to pass it is something else.

The only remaining possibility for restoring the integrity of the diploma may rest in the granting of different kinds of diplomas, as used to be done in New York City. Each type of diploma would have a specific meaning. An academic diploma could be reserved for those who complete a prescribed precollege sequence of mathematics, science, a foreign language, social studies, composition, and literature. Other kinds of diplomas could be designated for programs in business, vocational training, fine and applied arts, and various other curriculums. Each program could more nearly represent precise standards of accomplishment—something which just does not exist under the current system. To pretend that all diplomas signify the same level of accomplishment is misleading to employers.

"Few employers ask for a copy of a student's transcript before hiring," observed the National Association of Secondary School Principals. "Employers usually accept the regular high school diploma as though it meant the same thing for every student. The top and bottom ranking students all achieve equal anonymity. The employer is usually pleased or not depending on the skills level of the graduate. Yet the diploma does little to witness to the real difference in skills among the annual crop of graduates."[22]

Admittedly, there is the risk that differentiating diplomas might squeeze students from poor families and minority groups into certain categories. But the disadvantages should be weighed against the present situation in which diplomas often stand for nothing. Pretense could be abandoned if a commercial diploma, for instance, represented the acquisition of entry-level job skills in which the recipient could take pride. The goal of trying to see as many young people as possible graduate from high school would in no way be impeded.

Certificates
Even under this approach, though, some students would not complete the requirements for graduation. Staying in school takes a perseverance that not all young people possess, regardless of their ability to do the work. Theirs is the agony of enduring, not the joy of learning. Certificates could be awarded to these students instead of diplomas. It could be a Certificate of Attendance or a Certificate of Completion. In California, where this idea is getting its most thorough trial, they are called Certificates of Proficiency, and any student who has reached the second half of the tenth grade or the age of 16 may take a test for such a certificate. If he passes, he gets the certificate and can leave school with his parents' permission. Those 18 or older need no one's permission to leave school. The legislature has directed institutions of higher education in the state to recognize the certificate in the same way

they do a diploma. It is the answer for some students. The lives of two young people in Sacramento illustrate the point.

Mark Tyler found high school a steadily disappointing experience. "In a way," he said, looking back on those days of frustration, "I wish I wouldn't have screwed up and fallen behind. It was lack of interest on my part. It was mainly my own fault. I just didn't care."[23] Tyler, a slim six-footer with a crown of red hair, took the test for a Certificate of Proficiency near the end of his junior year and passed. He never bothered returning to the hassle of his senior year. Certificate in hand, he set out to find a job. He knew that the colleges were required to treat the document like a diploma and he hoped that employers would do the same. He was hired as a busboy at Sambo's, a fast-food operation that has gone spiffy with upholstery on the benches and tinted glass in the windows. But for those who clear the tables, scraps are scraps. Tyler's duty was to fill the plastic tub with dirty dishes and scrub the catsup stains from the formica-topped tables. He was not sure what the folks at Sambo's thought of his Certificate of Proficiency. "It was better than going in for a job without anything," he said, "but I think they would have preferred a diploma."[24]

After three months, Tyler decided he had had enough of handling other people's leftovers. His father, a general contractor, gave him a job and, when last seen, Mark Tyler was stuffing insulation into the walls of houses to help make them a little less vulnerable to the vicissitudes of foreign oil supplies. He did not plan to use his Certificate of Proficiency to get himself admitted to college and expected instead to try to build a career in the construction business, hoping for the day when he could begin laying a little cash aside. "I didn't enjoy school very much," Tyler mused. "I kept falling farther and farther behind, but I knew that if I just dropped out without at least getting the certificate I would have nothing and I would have a hard time getting a job anywhere."[25]

Though some employers may be slow in recognizing the Certificate of Proficiency, the power of the state leaves institutions of higher education no choice. Tony Lewis found that his certificate was sufficient cachet to get him into American River College, a two-year community college a couple of miles down the road from the high school he left after his junior year. "My dad was skeptical at first about my taking the test," said Lewis, who thought that what bothered his father was the possibility that young Lewis might use the opportunity to get out of school early as a pretext to avoid college. The father did not know his son's aspirations. Tony Lewis had wanted to be a lawyer since the age of six, when he first became intrigued by his father's work as an investigator for the prosecutor's office. The job did not require a law degree, but it certainly whetted the youngster's interest in matters legal. So, Tony Lewis gradually found himself less and less attracted to the baseball diamond and the boxing ring as he thought about concentrating on his goal of becoming a lawyer. "It takes seven years," he said, "and if the test hadn't helped me skip my senior year of high school it just would have meant one year longer before I could be a lawyer."[26]

Mark Tyler and Tony Lewis are not unusual. There are three separate testing dates—fall, winter, and spring—for the California High School Proficiency Examination and a total of about 35,000 students a year take the test. On the average, just under half of them get passing scores, earning them the Certificate of Proficiency and making them eligible to leave school early. The California Department of Education does not monitor the students to see who uses the certificate as an exit credential from high school, but John Gilroy, who runs the program, estimates that probably about 85 percent leave once they get the certificate.

Wilson Riles thought that more young people did not use the test to leave school because there was no place in the economy for them. "The labor unions wouldn't say it," Riles observed, "but they feel threatened by the test. Youngsters are kept longer and longer in school to keep them off the labor market, where they are not really needed." Nevertheless Riles supported the creation of the Certificate of Proficiency because he felt it was a way to deal more honestly with students. "We set up hurdles and say you should know this or that. So, if they can show they know it, then why force them to stay around?"[27] The test is not academically oriented. Rather, it measures applied basic skills in a real-life context, using reading and mathematics to add up the prices of goods or to read a help-wanted advertisement—problems not unlike those on most minimum competency tests used for high school graduation. There is also a short essay question so that the writing of the students can be judged.

Is this better than minimum competency testing? It is more forthright. The Certificate of Proficiency stands for something quite specific. It is not a claim to a thorough education or to any great academic prowess. It is an approach to credentialing that could be valuable in every state and it will be interesting to see if it is adopted beyond the borders of California, which the rest of the nation tends to regard as an outpost of flaky experimentation. One state that flirted with the idea, Connecticut, followed in California's footsteps with a much heralded announcement that it, too, was going to create a test to allow students to leave school early. Connecticut students were to get the opportunity to win a high school equivalency diploma and quit school at 16 by passing two examinations. Born in fanfare, the proposal perished in quiet anonymity. The state legislature never bothered providing funds for the program and the state education department did nothing to implement it.

One shortcoming of the Certificate of Proficiency, like minimum competency testing for a diploma, is that it focuses on the end of the educational process rather than on the substance of the twelve preceding years. Grade-to-grade promotion and the granting of diplomas have become so automatic that the nation has been lulled into an education-as-a-conveyor-belt mentality. The child is placed on the assembly line at the age of five or six, a little tinkering is done during the ensuing years and he is lifted off at the age of 18, supposedly a full-blown product of the American system of schooling. Feats of magic are presumed to have been performed during those dozen years of movement from grade to grade. But the magic does not always take hold. The magicians, better known as teachers, cannot wield their wands in ways guaranteed to bring the desired results for every child. Seldom, however, is the belt stopped long enough to hold a child at a certain point, making the necessary readjustments on him before letting him complete the twelve-year odyssey. Even a Chevrolet gets repaired on the line if the door is loose or someone forgot to insert a bolt in the engine mounting.

PROMOTION STANDARDS: MINIMUM COMPETENCY GRADE BY GRADE

The best of the fallout from the concern about minimum competency is a fresh examination of the notion of advancing pupils from grade to grade whether or not they have learned the work in the previous grade, otherwise known as social promotion. The "social" part is the belief that the socialization of a child is impaired if he is retained in a grade and forced to sit in classes with younger children, supposedly undermining his self-image and subjecting him to possible ridicule.

One approach to minimum competency involves setting standards for grade-to-grade promotion, as well as for high school graduation. New York City, for example, established minimum standards that pupils must meet to be promoted out of the fourth and seventh grades, starting in 1981. Promotional "gates" were set at these two points to assure that, regardless of what happens during the intervening grades, there would be at least two grades at which learning problems would be caught. The reading achievement of students will have to be no more than a year below grade level in the fourth grade and no more than a year and a half below grade level in the seventh grade. In 1982, there will be an added requirement that pupils be no more than two years below grade level in mathematics. The policy will not be without its problems. Never during the entire 1970s were fewer than 30 percent of the pupils reading a year or more below grade level.

The difficulties posed by New York City's promotion standards are seen in a place like Community School District 8, running along the southeastern shore of the Bronx, from the graceful Throgs Neck Bridge to the burned-out hulks of tenements in the South Bronx. One of every four junior high school youngsters in the district reads two or more years below grade level. In the worst of the elementary schools, P.S. 75, serving a neighborhood where family mobility is so high that more than half of the pupils either enter or leave the school during the academic year, only 10 percent of the children read at grade level. Yet, 92 percent of the students in District 8 are promoted routinely to the next grade each year, riding a merry-go-round that seems to be moving but never gets anywhere.

Confronted by the prospect of holding back a large proportion of the district's entire enrollment, the local school board began to recognize the magnitude of the problem. "These figures are abominable and intolerable," the board declared, going on to take note that the district's administrators were considering sidestepping the issue by certifying large numbers of students as handicapped so that they could be exempted from the promotion standards. "The community school board does not want any wholesale dumping of children into special educational programs because they have not been taught to read," the board asserted.[28]

Not that some districts have not been able to implement similar policies successfully. In the Greensville County Schools in Virginia, about 75 percent of the pupils were reading below grade level in 1973. That was when Sam Owen, the superintendent, decided that something ought to be done to stop turning out high school graduates who were reading at an elementary school level. Greensville County, where cotton was once king, was long accustomed to public schools in which the predominantly black student body took low achievement for granted. School was little more than a holding pattern to keep students busy until they were old enough to go out and work in the peanut and soybean fields or cut timber for one of the plywood companies. Sam Owen had other ideas.

In 1974, 1,312 of the system's 3,500 students were held back. The outcry from their parents forced Owen and his staff to reconsider their plan. Finally, the parents of 800 of the youngsters saw the wisdom of the policy and agreed to let their children repeat the grade they had been in. The schools were also reorganized so that it was possible to give some students a partial promotion. This meant setting up one building as a kindergarten, first grade, and second grade school, another as a third grade and fourth grade school, another as a fourth grade and fifth grade school, and so forth. If a fourth-grader in a building with third- and fourth-graders mastered only part of his work, for example, he would be assigned to spend the next year in a fourth grade and fifth grade school, where he could repeat portions of the fourth grade and begin doing part of the fifth garde. Such a partial promotion would keep him from having to stay in the same school, entirely repeating the fourth grade.

In 1975, Greensville County used these partial promotions for 483 youngsters and made 620 others totally repeat their grades. So effective was the policy that by 1980, the numbers dropped to 122 partial promotions and 376 full retentions. Reading achievement of sixth-graders rose from the 23rd percentile in 1973 to the 48th percentile in 1980, according to Owen.[29] This meant that the school system improved its position from being near the bottom quarter of the nation's districts to reaching nearly the upper half. Mathematics achievement of sixth-graders climbed from the 22nd percentile to the 55th during the same period.

Whether this approach, successful in a rural Southern school district, would have the same results elsewhere is a question that may be asked increasingly during the 1980s as more attention focuses on social promotion. The other side of such a policy is the need for remediation for those students who are retained. Children who fail need special attention and just having them repeat the work they could not handle the first time may not be enough. Why were lessons not learned? What prevented these students from making the same progress as their peers? Holding back students and making it a worthwhile experience costs money. Otherwise, it may be little more than punishment—cruel and unusual at that. Everyone remembers the overgrown kid who flunked the year before and was repeating the grade, still at the bottom of his class. Some students might be held back two or three times if the policy is strict. Is this what school districts want? Is this what parents want? As Mr. Howe notes, "By the time a kid has a beard you ought to put him in high school."[30] Flunking clearly has its limits. Some educators recommend that it should not be invoked without the guarantee of money for smaller classes, more individual attention, and special materials for those who repeat a grade. Furthermore, they stress that the most desirable approach is to provide help as early as possible in a student's schooling and before he or she has been held back.

This caveat was emphasized during a series of four regional meetings on minimum competency during the fall of 1977 under the sponsorship of the Educational Commission of the States and the National Institute of Education. Participants offered evidence that remediation is more expensive and less successful the longer the schools wait to provide it. Reaching youngsters in the primary grades is best—prevention rather than remediation. In addition, spokesmen for some districts were anticipating a backlash by parents of higher achievers against the further allocation of resources to marginal students, who already had the benefit of compensatory funds. "Many feel that if the legislators believe that minimum competency testing will improve achievement, they should also be willing to finance the entire program since their decisions will directly influence the spending patterns of local districts and possibly cause some disruption to ongoing programs," the report stated.[31]

Even if extra money is available for remediation and steps are taken to strengthen minimum competency, the blame for failure still ends up being placed on the pupils. The thrust of minimum competency, after all, is to fix blame. Dispensations go to everyone but the kids. They are the ones who are not promoted. They are the ones who do not get diplomas. They are the ones who do not get into college or do not get jobs. They are the ones headed for society's scrap heap.

Don't Blame the Kids

How can this be? How can students fail to learn on so massive a scale and yet no one else bears any of the blame? It is as though the sky fell on Chicken Little and he was told that he was at fault for standing beneath. What about teachers who do not teach their lessons effectively? What about administrators who do not monitor their students' progress? What about school board members who do not bother finding out what is going on in the classrooms? What about the parents who do not provide a home environment supportive of the schools? What about the taxpayers without children in the schools who refuse to approve an adequate tax rate? What about the legislators who mandate programs for the schools, but do not provide the funds to pay for what they demand?

It is no wonder that the courts have ruled against the various malpractice suits that have been filed against school districts around the country. "The ultimate consequences, in terms of public time and money, would burden them—and society—beyond calculation," a California court said in ruling in favor of the San Francisco schools.[32] The city school district was sued by the pseudonymous Peter N. Doe, a high school graduate, who maintained that he had not been taught to read at better than a fifth-grade level. Judges know that if they rule otherwise there will not be enough money in the public coffers to indemnify all the worthy litigants.

So far, the courts have tried to deny any such wrong as educational malpractice. While physicians and lawyers can be sued successfully, teachers and school administrators cannot. The case of Edward Donohue appeared to be one of the strongest. He was graduated from a Long Island high school in a blue-collar suburb of New York City after failing 7 of his 23 courses and receiving barely acceptable grades in the courses he did pass. His reading ability at the time of his graduation was apparently on a low elementary school level. A lower court dismissed the case after finding no legal precedent for Donohue's suit. Then, in 1979, a state appeals court also rejected the suit with the observation: "To entertain a cause of action for 'educational malpractice' would require the courts not merely to make judgments as to the validity of broad educational policies—a course we have unalteringly eschewed in the past—but more importantly, to sit in review of the day-to-day implementation of these policies."[33]

Whether or not the courts acknowledge it, schools are failing in their obligation to educate students. Denying diplomas to the victims of the system is not the answer. Minimum competency tests for graduation are after the fact; children have to be reached much earlier. No minimum competency test for graduation would help a person like Daniel Hoffman, who was assigned to a class for the mentally retarded soon after he began kindergarten in New York City and was kept in such classes for the balance of his education. It was not until he was eighteen years old that it was determined that he was not retarded. The Hoffman case almost broke through the hard surface to establish a precedent of educational malpractice. He won $750,000 in a lower court decision that was later modified to $500,000 by another court. But in 1979, New York State's highest court overruled the earlier decisions with the opinion that "the court system is not the proper forum to test the validity" of education decisions nor the place to "second-guess" such decisions.34

If there is a positive upshot to the minimum competency movement, it is the implicit admission that students have been permitted to reach commencement without the skills and knowledge they will need. America's young people have been betrayed by a blizzard of statistics that covered the ills of the educational system with a pristine blanket of numbers and that allowed their elders to take smug satisfaction in showing that the nation was coming within reach of its goal of universal high school education. That accomplishment has the hollow ring of superficiality.

CHAPTER FOUR

INNER-CITY SCHOOLS

EMPTY PROMISES
AND
UNFULFILLED DREAMS

A child miseducated
is a child lost.

JOHN F. KENNEDY
First State of the Union Address

The symbolism was difficult to escape. In the classroom, with its scuffed oaken floor and old-fashioned hanging globe lamps, tenth-grade students were straining to perform arithmetical computations more suitable to the fifth grade. And through one of the windows, the white marble dome of the Capitol was gleaming in the distance. Seldom were the two Americas so poignantly juxtaposed as that morning on the third floor of Washington's Cardozo High School, high on a bluff overlooking the grandeur of the nation's capital. This was a high school that in a self-study a few years earlier described its immediate neighborhood as containing thirty-nine percent of the city's crime, with more than one of every three people living below the poverty level, and the area of origin of half of the cases brought before Juvenile Court.

As irony would have it, the imposing brick and stone structure opened early in the century as Central High to serve

65

the white half of Washington's racially segregated, dual school system. It was reassigned for use by black students in the 1950s as whites streamed over the district line to the suburban enclaves of Maryland and Virginia. Now, Cardozo had become a typical inner-city high school, a place where an entirely minority student body trailed the rest of the country pathetically in every possible category of student achievement.

On this particular day in Emily Foster's mathematics class only 6 of the 25 students had bothered showing up. Some of the rest were probably perched on the concrete wall on Clifton Street, near the school's main entrance, where youngsters often sat and whiled away time whenever they felt like cutting a class. There was no telling where the others may have been. The six who had attended class were at their desks trying to figure out how much an item could cost if the price were listed at $498.75 with a 15 percent discount and a sales tax of 5 percent. The entire 43-minute period was devoted to working six such exercises as Miss Foster moved from student to student, answering questions and reviewing figures.

The very fact that a student enrolled in math was thought remarkable at Cardozo. The District of Columbia required no math after the ninth grade. The results of this policy were devastating. Scores on the Everyday Skills Test, a nationally standardized examination, showed that the average eleventh-grader at Cardozo performed math calculations at the level of a seventh-grader. In measuring mastery of computing skills, the test found that 16 percent could figure sales tax, 13 percent could determine discount rates, and 11 percent could calculate interest rates.

Progress takes strange forms at Cardozo. The school's administration in 1980 could take satisfaction in the fact that the school was no longer the hell-hole it had been in previous decades. No one was shooting craps in the corridors, a stabbing the previous year had been an anomaly, and threats to teachers had diminished under a policy of summoning the police immediately. Most everyone said it was safe even in the lavatories. But Cardozo was still the last stop on the journey of hopelessness known as inner-city education, the culmination of years of apathy in elementary school and junior high where little was taught and even less was learned.

There was no calculus taught at Cardozo because no one was prepared to study it. Only five students were enrolled in precalculus. There were 24 in physics. Because the Board of Education of the District of Columbia had decided that just 17½ credits were needed for a diploma, most students found they could graduate by taking only two courses a year as juniors and seniors. And even if the school made them sign up for additional courses, the youngsters knew they could refuse to go and still have enough credits for a diploma.

There is a school like Cardozo to be found in every sizable city in the United States. The biggest of the cities— New York, Los Angeles, Philadelphia, Chicago, Detroit—have many such schools. The statistics, whether they deal with achievement, dropouts, vandalism or crime, are about the same in each of the schools.

The minority children of America's inner cities are forgotten souls. Theirs is a legacy of failure, year upon year of crushing failure. The chapters of this story unfold annually in the form of statistical reports chronicling scores on standardized achievement tests. Each year, as the children grow older and move up through the grades, they fall farther and farther behind the national averages. By the time they reach the upper elementary grades it is not unusual for them to be reading two years below grade level, and when they get to high school some still read at the fourth- and fifth-grade level. The same tragic fate awaits them in mathematics and each of their other subjects. Minimum competency requirements for graduation are too late for them.

It is a phenomenon almost universal among the black and Hispanic children of the nation's urban school districts. In a city like Newark, for instance, the word "despair" might as well be inscribed as the municipal motto. Achievement levels in the schools of New Jersey's largest city sink with frightening regularity as youngsters move into higher grades. The school system has become more than 90 percent black and Hispanic as whites have fled to the suburbs. Newark has been left to suffer the ravages of high unemployment, a soaring crime rate, and a crumbling financial base. Department store sales tumbled by more than 20 percent in a single decade as suburban shopping malls stole away Newark's commerce. Even one of the city's two daily newspapers has perished. This is a city so woebegone that it does not have a television station of its own in the regular frequency, leaving its neglected residents to pirate errant signals from the transmitters of New York and Philadelphia.

Newark, third oldest of major American cities, founded in 1666 by the Puritans, epitomizes the collapse of the industrial Northeast. It is a demise that has cut deeply into Newark's school system as its population has dwindled to what it was at the turn of the century. Virtually every family that could escape has done so. This is Newark, the city of Stephen Crane and Philip Roth, the city of Jerome Kern and Sarah Vaughan, the city of Charles Evans Hughes and Peter Rodino. This is the Newark of the 1980s.

Now it is a city where the percentage of schoolchildren reading at or above the national norm reads like the temperature on a winter thermometer. In 1978, which was as typical as any other year, the proportions in reading—which would have been 50 percent in each case, if the city had been at the national average—were 42 percent in the second grade, 24 percent in the third grade, 18 percent in the fourth grade, 13 percent in the fifth grade and 12 percent in the sixth grade. The figures in mathematics were equally depressing: 38 percent in the second grade, 28 percent in the third grade, 30 percent in the fourth grade, 23 percent in the fifth grade, and 17 percent in the sixth grade.[1]

THE TRAIL TO DROPPING OUT

There are few exceptions to this pattern among the minority students of the nation's big cities. As the proportion of minority students has increased in city after city, the problem has grown worse. It is a gradually debilitating process that may not be so obvious when a child is in the second or third grade because it is not yet possible for him to trail very far behind. But the damage compounds with each passing year. Soon, the student does not have the educational tools to keep pace. Reading is a device for exploring social studies, science, and other subjects, and the inability to read effectively holds the youngster back in every area. Similarly, each year of mathematics builds on what was taught previously and the learning lapses of the past assure the failures of the future.

School districts across the country use a wide variety of standardized tests, making it difficult to comment on the cumulative impact of the problem of low achievement in the big cities. However, one set of tests offers a window through which it is possible to glimpse a portion of the tragedy. The tests that provide this view of the country at large are sponsored by the National Assessment of Educational Progress, the federal government's program for monitoring school achievement in the United States. Examinations in a cross-section of subjects are given to students when they are 9, 13, and 17 years old.

In science, for example, the National Assessment showed that 9-year-old white students were 2.5 points above the national average and black students of the same age were 12.8 points below the average. Among 17-year-olds, the disparity was even greater, with white students 2.6 points above the national average and black students 15.7 points below the average. In social studies, the pattern was the same. Nine-year-old whites were 2.2 points above the average and blacks of the same age were 8.6 points below. Seventeen-year-old white youngsters were 1.6 points above the average and blacks of the same age were 9.4 points below the average. Every test in every subject revealed the same kinds of differences between the two races.[2] All black students, of course, are not in inner-city schools, but the majority of them are. One may view the statistics under every light—the starkness of the disparities always shows through.

Behind the anonymity of statistics is the human story. The low scores represent the inability of minority children to make adequate progress in school. Ultimately, low achievement means the embarrassment of being unable to handle work that can be done by another youngster, even by some who are younger. And before long, self-esteem becomes shaky, which inevitably gives way to anger. The child would rather be anywhere but in school. First, he starts skipping part of the schoolday, as happens at Cardozo High, and then is absent for entire days. It is just a short step to truancy and, finally, the teen-ager drops out altogether, fleeing from the place that has become a symbol of his failure.

This pattern is worse in the city than in the suburbs and it is usually worse for blacks in the city than for whites in the city. An illustration of just how striking the differences can be is seen in the dropout rates of blacks and whites in a city like Cleveland, where blacks dropped out at a rate of 43.2 percent, compared with 29.3 percent for whites.[3] The significance of such statistics is best appreciated in the context of a report from the U.S. Civil Rights Commission that identified Cleveland as one of the ten most segregated school districts in the country.

Only in 1979, under the compulsion of an order by a federal district court, did Cleveland begin a busing program to break the rigid color line that historically divided its schools. The polluted Cuyahoga River, an open sewer to Cleveland's industry, was a stagnant Mason-Dixon Line, separating the white West Side from the black East Side. Only two of the city's twelve regular high schools—one on the East Side and one on the West Side—were truly desegregated before the 1980s. Five of the other six East Side high schools were more than 99 percent black and the sixth was 96.3 percent black. Three of the six had dropout rates exceeding 50 percent and two of the three remaining black schools had rates of more than 45 percent. The highest dropout rate among the white high schools was 32.9 percent.[4]

The pattern of low achievement, once established, is seldom reversed. Thus, it should come as no surprise that the daily frustration of being intimidated by words on paper eventually persuades young people to leave school. It is the only relief that some youths can find. Many of those who do not leave school direct their anger at convenient targets within the school, making life miserable for their teachers and fellow students. Troublemakers can bring learning to a halt for everyone in an inner-city school. The educational climate is poisoned and everything surrounding the potential dropout becomes a hated reminder of his own failure.

Children who do not learn become adults who do not know. The foundation of a democratic society is undermined by this failure of the schools. "We all pay a price in terms of safety in our streets and our homes; in terms of heavy social costs for unemployment, law enforcement and prisons; and in terms of the social malaise that stems in part from the recognition that we are not meeting the problems of many of our youth," stated the Carnegie Council on Policy Studies in Higher Education.[5] Almost all the work of the Council, which ended business in 1980 with the retirement of Clark Kerr, its chairman, had been devoted to an examination of higher education. It is notable that the focus of the panel's next-to-last report was shifted to youth who were not bound for college. It was as though the Carnegie Council were stepping back to say that all the good done for higher education might be for naught if the needs of the non-college-bound are left unattended.

The 1960s and 1970s comprised a period during which access to colleges and universities was expanded to include many of the sons and daughters of low-income families previously excluded from higher education. The black enrollment in the nation's colleges and universities almost quadrupled between 1965 and 1980, from just over a quarter of a million to more than one million, rising from less than 5 percent of the total enrollment to 10 percent. This achievement was noteworthy, but by the beginning of the 1980s there was a tendency to ignore the multitude of youths—black, white, and brown—whose education amounted to something less substantial—the dropouts and high school graduates who completed their formal schooling without the ability to earn a living. According to the Carnegie Council, dropout rates from high school were 23 percent overall and even higher for minorities: 35 percent for blacks and 45 percent for Hispanics. Those youths not heading for college are now falling between the cracks, unnoticed until they appear in police lineups or on welfare lines. They are the fodder for what the Carnegie Council bluntly termed a "lumpen proletariat."[6]

An additional problem in the inner-city, one that outsiders often overlook, is the transiency of the families. Life on the edge of poverty is life without stability. If there is not enough money to pay the rent, it may be easier to move. If the landlord refuses to make needed repairs or will not supply sufficient heat, it may be easier to move. If drug addicts take over part of a building and threaten the tenants, it may be easier to move. The effect on educational continuity can be disastrous. Some schools find their rolls turning over more than 100 percent a year. Not every child leaves, but enough do as some desks end up being assigned to three or four different pupils between September and June.

Educational research has tended to give little attention to this problem as a factor in school achievement. There is, however, at least one study that documents the startling impact of pupil turnover. Jacob Abramson examined the reading achievement scores of 25,037 fifth-graders in ten separate community school districts in New York City, comparing the performance of those who entered their schools before the third grade with those who transferred into their schools after the third grade. Invariably, those who were enrolled longer did better.[7]

On the average, the stable group read one month below grade level, while the transient group read a year and two months below grade level. Furthermore, 45.2 percent of the stable group read at or above grade level, compared with 21.6 percent of the transient group. The differences also held up among children from the same economic background. In looking only at economically deprived youngsters, the ones whose families had moved into the neighborhood before they began the third grade did better on tests than the others. They averaged only eight months below grade level in reading, while lower-economic-group children from transient families were one-and-a-half years below grade level. In addition, 28.7 percent of the stable group was reading at or above grade level, as compared with only 14 percent of the transient group. Similar differences were discovered between groups of students from affluent families when they were compared on the basis of family transiency.

In light of transiency and a host of other adverse influences, the big cities with their heavy concentration of minority children from underprivileged backgrounds face a difficult challenge in trying to raise achievement. An indication of the problem is contained in the results of New York State's Pupil Evaluation Performance Program, one of the most respected of the statewide assessments. When the program began in 1966, the State Education Department established a minimum score, now called a statewide reference point, to identify youngsters needing remediation. Every student in the state was tested in reading and mathematics in the third grade, the sixth grade, and the ninth grade.

Year after year, the relative outcome was the same. New York City students did the worst. Students in village and suburban school districts did the best. There was some encouragement for New York City during the late 1970s as its percentage of low achievers shrank at a faster rate than the rest of the state, but the city was so far behind to start that the remainder of the state did not have as much room for statistical improvement. By the 1978–79 school year, the statewide reference point in reading for sixth-graders was surpassed by 58 percent of the students in New York City, 64 percent in the state's other big cities, 77 percent in the smaller cities, 82 percent in the rural regions, and 84 percent in the villages and suburban districts. In mathematics, the percentage of sixth-graders above the reference point was 51 percent in New York City, 70 percent in the other big cities, 73 percent in the small cities, 77 percent in the rural areas, and 81 percent in the villages and suburbs. It was a pattern not unlike that throughout the United States.

Struggling in Suburbia

In the suburbs, which also happen to have the fewest minority students, the schools are largely successful in teaching the basics in the early grades. Students move into the upper elementary grades and into secondary school able to handle the work in most of their subjects. This does not mean that there are not some students lagging behind even in the highest achieving suburban school systems. But the problems of low achievement do not bring the entire learning process to a halt in the suburbs as happens sometimes in the inner city. Low achievement in the suburbs is of manageable proportions. The youngsters who are struggling do not take up so much of the teacher's time that no one else gets taught. Most importantly, the rest of the class can keep moving ahead while low achievers get the attention they need.

A look at the schools in Weston, a rustic suburb west of Boston, shows how a wealthy community is able to aid its low achievers. Weston is a place of comfortable homes in sylvan settings, where highly educated parents take it for granted that their offspring will perform well. The average IQ of a second-grader in Weston is 116, and elementary school students rank from the 80th to the 90th percentile in all of their reading and mathematics skills, outscoring all but 10 to 20 percent of the students in the country. While the rest of the nation experienced a precipitous drop in scores during the 1970s on the Scholastic Aptitude Test, Weston's seniors actually improved their scores. Ninety-five percent of the graduates go on to college and at least a third of them attend Ivy League schools and a handful of other highly selective institutions.

Many of the students who get special help in Weston would rank in the upper portion of their class if they were in some other school system. Weston simply identifies the 10 percent of the pupils who are more than one year below grade level on standardized tests as being in need of special education, which in most districts is a designation for the handicapped. In other words, for many such students in Weston, being "handicapped" merely means falling a little below the national average.

Each of Weston's three elementary schools has a learning center to which these special education students are assigned for 40-minute periods two or three times a week, receiving attention individually and in small groups. A team consisting of a special education teacher, a counselor, a nurse, and a speech therapist meets weekly to discuss each child. At Weston's junior high, there is a resource room staffed by a director and a tutor for each of the school's two grades, seventh and eighth. The two rooms serve a total of 40 of the school's 400 pupils, providing from four to eight periods a week of special instruction to each child.

The unusual form that special education takes in Weston can be seen in the skills center in the high school, where some of the supposedly "handicapped" students work on such sophisticated tasks as footnoting their term papers and improving their writing style. The high school also has organized a compensatory mathematics class for ninth- and tenth-graders, using federal assistance for which the district never bothered applying before 1979. A teacher and an aide spend a year instructing the youngsters in algebra and geometry, going slowly enough to allow them to fill in gaps that developed during junior high. In addition, the students in the class go to the skills center for individual tutoring.

Inner-City Blues

The luxury of being able to help slower students the way Weston does is unknown in the big cities, where so many youngsters are below the norms that special attention is needed for the masses. The depth of the problem is illustrated by the plight of many of New York City's 32 community school districts. Since the city's budget crisis in 1975, local boards that run the community school districts have found that their main responsibility has been to set priorities for cutbacks. District 5 in Harlem is one of those 32 local school systems, reaching across the waist of the island of Manhattan, from the Harlem River to the Hudson River, to embrace one of the nation's most famous black communities. Fewer than 100 of its 12,000 pupils are white, and 90 percent of the entire enrollment is from families eking out a poverty-level existence, barely surviving in a city in which it took an income of $6,662 to keep a family of four from falling below the poverty line in 1978. There is just one elementary school in Harlem in which the achievement level is as high as the national average. In 13 of the 17 elementary schools and all 5 of the junior highs, more than 60 percent of the pupils were below grade level in reading. All of the junior highs had at least 20 percent of their youngsters reading at least two years below grade level.[8]

Failure is endemic in District 5. Children build their futures on educational sandpiles that erode a bit each year. Pupils never accumulate enough skills to shore up the edges and by the time they are teen-agers much of what they were taught earlier has washed away. If this miserable record of low achievement were peculiar to Harlem it might be a localized problem that could be addressed by a modest mobilization of resources. But District 5 is emblematic of a failure so widespread that black America is in jeopardy of seeing the aspirations of an entire generation destroyed. Most white Americans have no idea of the pervasiveness of the educational difficulties in the schools attended by minority pupils.

There is no escaping the conclusion that the nation's schools are not teaching minority children to read, write, and compute on a level they will need to function in society. What is most dangerous about this failure is that it has engendered a widespread attitude that there is virtually nothing that can be done to change the situation. In other words, failure in the inner city is taken for granted. The prophecy fulfills itself These children will not learn, say some of the people responsible for their education. Low expectations lead to few demands, and they do not learn. It is supposedly the fault of the students, not of the schools. As in most instances when students do not learn, little of the blame is ascribed to the teachers, the principals, the superintendents, the school board members, and others who are entrusted with making schools work. This dismal situation is justified and reinforced by the contentions of some social scientists that urban schools can do almost nothing to overcome the effects of poverty on educational achievement. Family background and home environment are viewed as creating an inalterable climate in which the seeds of learning are doomed to wither on the hard soil of socioeconomic reality.

In the wake of the passage of the Civil Rights Act of 1964, the federal government sponsored a study to examine the differences among school resources allocated to black and white students. The idea was that by pinpointing the advantages available to whites, federal policy could be directed toward replicating those opportunities for blacks. But James S. Coleman, the principal author of the study issued in 1966, concluded that inequities in the educational support of blacks and whites were not all that great and probably did not account for the differences in educational performance between the races. "Schools bring little influence to bear on a child's achievement that is independent of his background and general social context," the report stated.[9] Coleman put his emphasis on the effects of social class and cultural influences. He left room for the possibility of offsetting some of the differences by bringing together in a single classroom children from a wide range of backgrounds, a notion that underpinned the integration efforts of the late 1960s and early 1970s.

The idea that schools are helpless to improve the lot of the downtrodden was reinforced by Christopher Jencks and his colleagues, who observed in 1972 that "none of the evidence we have reviewed suggests that school reform can be expected to bring about significant social changes outside the schools." Jencks concluded that redistribution of income, not innovations in the classroom, was the key to making an impact on the lives of the poor. "We cannot blame economic inequality on differences between schools since differences between schools seem to have very little effect on any measurable attribute of those who attend them," Jencks stated.[10]

Then, in 1979, Jencks reaffirmed in another volume that family background, not schooling, was the instrument of success in the United States. He did concede this time, however, that the credentials bestowed on one by schooling—diplomas, and, especially, college degrees—were helpful in opening the door to a better life.[11] The cause of schooling was dealt a further setback in 1979 by Richard N. DeLeone, who produced his work in connection with the studies of the Carnegie Council on Children. "Class, race and sex are the most important factors in determining a child's future," DeLeone asserted in a volume with the pessimistic title *Small Futures: Children, Inequality, and the Limits of Liberal Reform.*

Whatever the limits to schooling and whatever the

shortcomings of the schools, it is alarming to think that the futures of inner-city children might not be made more promising. Admittedly, the challenge confronting schools in a Harlem is a sick joke compared with what schools face in a Weston. The backgrounds of many inner-city students seem designed for failure. They come overwhelmingly from homes in which the parents—and very often it is only the mother who lives with them—are without jobs and of limited educational background. The youngsters suffer disadvantages that begin in the womb and get worse, rather than disappear, when they reach school. In the big cities, with their large concentration of such children, the problem is at its worst.

School officials in the urban centers of New York State, recognizing these obstacles, joined together in 1976 to participate in a suit initiated by the Levittown public schools on Long Island to compel the state to create a more equitable method of school finance. Levittown, a bedroom community, contended that its low property wealth made it unable to pay for its schools in a way that could be done in neighboring suburbs with their expensive homes, shopping malls, and small industry. At first, New York City seemed an unexpected ally in such a quest for fairer treatment. On its tax rolls the city has hundreds of magnificent cooperative apartment buildings lining Park Avenue, Fifth Avenue, Central Park West, and Riverside Drive. It has the sleek corporate headquarters of many of the Fortune 500. It has the industries, large and small, of the five boroughs. New York City has what seems to be a bountiful property tax base from which to finance its schools.

But unlike the school systems in other cities, New York's does not have autonomous taxing power. The money to keep the city's almost 1,000 schools running is drawn from the same pot as the funds that provide welfare payments for 875,000 people and sustain a municipal hospital system that consumes $1.258 billion a year, $334 million of it from the city's tax revenues. It is the same source that pays for a police force of 22,292 men and women and supplies a host of services to a population that includes between 500,000 and 1.5 million illegal aliens, ghosts whose unofficial presence places further strain on the city.

In sum, it is called municipal overburden. What it means is that the ability of a big city to pay for its schools is not what it appears. Revenues must be stretched much further than the comparable per capita revenues of a suburb or small town that is not called upon to provide such a wide array of services. New York City's police, for example, must protect not only the city's taxpayers, but also the Pope, Fidel Castro, Ronald Reagan, or any other dignitary whose presence warrants massive (and expensive) protection. The city's 8,300 sanitation workers must retrieve 22,000 tons of garbage and litter a day, produced not only by those who make their home in the city, but also by the more than 600,000 suburbanites who earn a living in the city while paying a fraction of the income tax assessed against residents. Furthermore, the city's schools, like other urban schools, serve a heavier proportion of students who are the most costly to educate—the disabled, the bilingual, and the economically deprived.

A lower court in New York agreed that the state's method of school finance was unfair, taking note of the plight of the big cities and the problem of municipal overburden. The state appealed the decision to a higher court. In the meantime, this vivid description remains, given to the court by a prekindergarten teacher in the South Bronx who spoke of life in the big city for her pupils:

Willie could curse fluently but did not know what a red circle was or where his eyes or toes were, nor could he follow verbal directions. With five brothers and sisters, including an 11-year-old partially blind deaf-mute, the family lived in four rooms and was twice forced from apartments by fires during the year. Because the third apartment lacked heat and electricity, Willie's hands were swollen from the cold and he was frequently absent. Although he made some progress in the class, he finally moved again and is no longer in preschool because programs in his area are full.

Another child, Johnny, slept in a bed flush with a third-floor window without guards. The kitchen in his apartment was swarming with flies, plaster was falling in the bathroom and there was no furniture in the living room. There were no toys, no books and frequently no food (Johnny suffered from malnutrition). At the end of every school day he had to be coaxed from the top shelf of the closet, apparently because he feared physical abuse from his mother. During the year, his building burned and he disappeared from school and when at his mother's request several months later, the school authorities looked for a place for him in a new prekindergarten program, none was available.[12]

SCHOOLS HELPING STUDENTS—HIGH ACHIEVEMENT POSSIBLE DESPITE RACE AND BACKGROUND

Possibilities for Improvement

A growing number of educators, concerned about the low level of achievement in inner-city schools, are challenging the idea that improvements are impossible without the reordering of society. They maintain that enough is known about how to upgrade the education of minority children to bring about changes on a wide scale. One such person is Ronald R. Edmonds, a faculty member at the Harvard Graduate School of Education, who took a leave of absence to serve as senior assistant for instruction to the chancellor of the New York City schools.

"If your argument for pessimism and inaction derives from your reading of social science, then I have an alternative," said Edmonds. "Schools know now and always have known what they need to know to teach the children we are talking about. But social services are provided for those society thinks it must serve and when society thinks it needn't serve, it doesn't. There are no penalties for failing to serve people who are poor or are of color. Left to their own devices, those who provide social services will do next week what they did last year. We know what makes schools effective, but we are not using what we know in the schools that are least effective. To be effective, schools have to avoid failure. We are reaching the point at which a lot of people are persuaded that public schools are on fragile ground. It is clear that schools cannot go on as they have. So, there are initiatives under way and some are showing results."[13]

One such initiative is the School Improvement Project, launched in New York City in 1979 to cultivate the development of the characteristics that Edmonds said contributed to a successful school, regardless of the home background of the pupils. The formula concentrates on upgrading the leadership of the principal, teachers' expectations for their students, emphasis on basic skills, monitoring of student progress, and the school environment. A group of public schools numbering fewer than 20 are the sites of this pilot project. One of the participating schools—it is strictly voluntary—is P.S. 155 in Brooklyn, mentioned earlier, where Al Kisseloff is the principal. The project has helped the school stress basic instruction by providing coordinated sets of basic reading books for each grade, a necessity that could not be obtained on the meager allowance furnished by the Board of Education. The school has also gotten testing materials that make it easier to monitor pupil progress.

Inside Mr. Kisseloff's cramped office there is now a large gray wall chart on which he keeps track of the month-by-month progress of all the reading groups in each classroom in the school—blue for those in English and yellow for those in Spanish. In addition to enabling the school to keep closer tabs on its students, the chart is a device for raising expectations, a visible symbol of achievement in front of which Kisseloff can stand with a teacher and plot out hopes for the future. A squarely built man with streaks of gray in his bushy beard, Kisseloff was already a strong leader, perhaps too powerful in the opinion of some of his teachers. Through the project, the school has become more democratic, establishing an improvement committee on which each member including the principal has a single vote. Morale, which was already high, has soared. An improvement plan, incorporating Edmonds's concepts, has been written by the committees at each of the schools, letting those who work in the schools decide how best to carry out the implementation. Furthermore, a specialist has been assigned to each school by the Board of Education to work with the principal and teachers in helping the school circumvent the bureaucracy to get what it needs to make the plan succeed. The specialist has no authority over the school itself and can give those at the school advice and candid assessments without his intervention being perceived as a threat.

Regardless of the outcome of the School Improvement Project, such attempts to raise achievement merit serious consideration. If inner-city students were incapable of learning the skills of literacy then none would reach the national average. This is not the case. There are many instances, in school after school, of individual children exceeding the national averages, overcoming disadvantages that are supposed to doom them to failure. There are also entire classes within otherwise low achieving schools that have made remarkable progress. Most convincing, however, is what has happened in entire schools serving some of the poorest families in the most blighted areas of some cities.

Such bursts of achievement are testimony to the tenacity of dedicated teachers, committed principals, and involved parents who refuse to surrender in the face of adversity. Some are like English teacher Maxine Crump, upholding standards to seniors at a school like Washington's Cardozo High, where many young people have learned to take failure for granted. Ms. Crump, a small, coffee-skinned woman in slacks and a shawl, races through a lesson on 18th-century Britain. This honors English class really is a blend of the disciplines. Literature in the hands of Ms. Crump is an excuse for teaching history, politics, economics, and anything else she can squeeze into the lesson. Students keep arriving in the basement classroom up to 20 minutes after the beginning of the period. She continues delving into the history of English kings and prime ministers, gradually working her way into the literature of the period, ignoring the late arrivals and expecting them to pick up the train of thought. Walpole, Disraeli, and Gladstone give way to Swift, Addison, and Defoe.

The students have already been asked to write research papers on the development of the governmental process in England and now she is assigning the satire "A Modest Proposal" to study overnight. She pulls out editorial cartoons by Herblock and Oliphant to explain satire to them, though they cannot seem to grasp the nuances of Swift. Next she is reading from Buchwald and even though only a couple of the students seem responsive to her questions, she continues pushing ahead. Only one member of the class seems to know that Defoe wrote *Robinson Crusoe.* She tries to win the interest of others by quoting snippets of Defoe and Pepys, but there is no response. Ms. Crump is undeterred in her mission. "They are reaching for a level for which they have not been asked to reach before," she said to a visitor after the class, removing her tinted glasses and holding them while balancing an attendance book in the other hand. "They are capable, but little has been demanded of them. I force them to try to work harder. Teachers who don't place demands on them are letting them down."[14] She will not believe that teaching and learning should be an occasion for great celebration in the inner city when they are part of the routine of the suburbs.

It is a feeling shared by Kenneth B. Clark, the psychologist, who grows angry thinking about the way a generation of black children is being written off as unable to learn. He recollects his own experience:

I went to school in Harlem and I remember my teachers in Junior High School 139. I knew Miss McGuire insisted that I respect the structure of a sentence and she explained to me what a sentence was. Those teachers had standards that we knew we had to meet. Why is it that that could be done in the late 1920s and the early 1930s and not in the 1970s and 1980s? Why?

All of them—Mr. Deegan, Miss McGuire, Miss Smith, and Mr. Mitchell—never asked whether I came from a broken home. They weren't social workers; they were teachers. As far as I recall, for five or six hours, five days a week, the universe was what was happening in that classroom. Mr. Ruprack kept me after school if I didn't get those equations and there was respect for us that was indicated by the standards to which we were held and by the sense of achievement that we felt. If we had thought that Mr. Ruprack thought that we couldn't have done algebra then we would have felt badly. Public education is a cornerstone of the stability of this democracy. If that isn't maintained there is no solution to the urban crisis. The public school system in this country can't be sacrificed on the altar of race. The only thing resisted more than desegregation is increasing the quality of education in predominantly minority schools.[15]

There are still a few such minority schools. Public School 91 in Brooklyn's Crown Heights section was one of them during the 1970s. It was an island of hope in a sea of despair, an inner-city school with an enrollment exclusively of impoverished minority youngsters who knocked the hell out of the national averages. Often, it was the only school in all of Community School District 17 to surpass the national average; other times, two or three schools climbed above the average along with P.S. 91. In the 9 annual standardized reading examinations given from 1972 through 1980, the school led its district every year but one. Half the time it had not just 50 percent of its pupils at the national average—which would be acceptable almost anywhere in the country, let alone in the midst of deprivation—but almost two-thirds of its students at that level. The figure climbed to 72.9 percent in 1980. Meanwhile, the rest of the schools in the district averaged about one-third of their pupils at the national average. About one of every four of the district's 26,788 students was reading more than two years below grade level. The achievement of Public School 91 was remarkable by any standard.

It was a school in which 88 percent of the students were black and most of the rest were Puerto Rican. Two-thirds of all the youngsters in the school were from families poor enough to qualify for free lunches. One-third of the 1,200 students were from homes receiving Aid to Families with Dependent Children.

The exterior of P.S. 91 gave no hint of the miracle occurring behind its fortress-like walls, erected in 1902, just four years after the five boroughs were amalgamated to form New York City. The desolate neighborhood around the school was swathed in decay. Crumbling tenements and boarded-up storefronts provided the backdrop for this educational drama. Vandals and thugs roamed the streets and had no respect for the sanctity of the school, invading the building on occasion to rob teachers in their very classrooms.

P.S. 91 mobilized every resource at its command to start the difficult job of counteracting the deficits of the students almost as soon as they toddled into kindergarten. In the mid-1970s, it was a place where the highest priority was given to the lowest grades. Larger classes were tolerated in the upper grades in order to free more teachers for smaller classes in first grade and second grade, the delicate stages of beginning reading. In a typical kindergarten at P.S. 91, a portion of each day was devoted to equipping the children with the rudiments of the basic skills in reading and mathematics. The familiarity with letters and numbers that was given to five-year-olds at P.S. 91 was something that white suburban youngsters got at home even before they entered school. Being able to provide pupils at P.S. 91 with individual and small-group attention in kindergarten was possible because the school's personnel were reshuffled during these skill-building sessions. Kindergarten teachers were aided by paraprofessionals, student teachers from Brooklyn College, and even by the security guards from the hallways, who were asked to leave their posts to read to the children.

P.S. 91 had no secret formula and its approach was mostly traditional. The key element was the leadership of the principal, Martin Schor, now retired, who placed a high value on organization and who paid close attention to details. He gave the teachers strong support, for which they praised him lavishly. The progress of each pupil was monitored by the teachers, and reports were turned in regularly to the principal, who reassigned pupils as their reading skills grew stronger. There were several classes at each grade level, all grouped homogeneously—the best readers in one class, the worst in another, and gradations in between.

Grouping pupils the way it was done in P.S. 91 is contoversial. The schools of this country have a long and bitter history of trying to identify the least promising students when they are young and pigeon-holing them with other children who have already had the "unpromising" label applied to them. The rationale of this approach is that students make the best progress when they are taught with others of like ability. Furthermore, many teachers argue that they can do a better job if they do not have to address too wide a disparity of abilities within a single class. More often than not, though, minority children end up in groups at the lowest end of the spectrum and white children are placed in the highest groups.

Because of the tendency of grouping to lead to racial segregation, the question of whether to group by ability remains one of education's dilemmas.

In any event, the decision to group students according to achievement at P.S. 91 was made for reasons of efficiency. Since minority children comprised the school's entire enrollment, racial segregation was not an issue. The principal also tried to soften the impact of grouping by shifting pupils into higher groups during the school term if their work improved. No child, however, was ever moved to a lower group during the school year. Disruptive children at P.S. 91 were assigned to a single class, relieving their regular teachers of the distraction of having to deal with them. This was a tough approach to be sure, but the teachers appreciated any move that left them free to devote their energies to teaching. A few of the school's best teachers were freed from regular duties and became full-time reading teachers, spending their time with small groups of pupils who were having trouble with reading.

Role of the Principal
Scratch the surface of any successful school like P.S. 91 and what quickly appears is a good principal. There are bad schools with good principals in the inner city, but there are no good schools with bad principals. In the suburbs, children from affluent families may achieve academic success regardless of the quality of the school principal, but a first-class principal is the sine qua non of a good inner-city school. All evidence points to leadership as the single most important ingredient in lifting the quality of education in such schools.

One of the studies that helped most in demonstrating the value of leadership was a report by the Ford Foundation on the $30 million Comprehensive School Improvement Program that it had sponsored. The project, similarly named, but different from the one in New York, was aimed at promoting innovations in teaching and the curriculum in school systems around the country. In reviewing the results, the report concluded that "the success or failure of a project probably was determined more by the performance and continued service of the project director than by any other single factor."[16] Not only good leadership, but continuity in that leadership was deemed essential. Frequent turnover at the top proved almost fatal for some of the efforts.

Recognition of the role played by the principal has been slow in coming. Not long ago, the fashionable view was that schools ran themselves. The premise was that almost anyone could be appointed principal and it would make no difference to the operation of the school. People were appointed as principals who did not have the leadership ability even to guide a pack of lemmings into the sea. Former gym teachers were considered especially well prepared to preside over schools because they were accustomed to coaching teams and as principals would be able to flex their muscles to intimidate rowdies and restore discipline if things got out of hand.

There is obviously more to being a principal than controlling troublemakers. The position is full of complexities that some principals never master. But preparation for the job has not kept pace with the demands of the modern principalship. "Most higher education institutions continue to offer substantially the same training programs for principals as they did a quarter of a century ago," notes Ann Kurzius.[17] Perhaps the biggest change among those being elevated to principalships now is that more of them have advanced degrees. In 1968, 20.1 percent of the nation's elementary school principals had no credential beyond the bachelor's degree, but by 1978, this figure had shrunk to 3.6 percent. This is an impressive difference, except that there is little evidence to show that those with master's degrees and doctorates are any better qualified to run schools. Institutions of higher education have reaped a tuition windfall from the trend toward graduate degrees for educators, but no body of research exists to demonstrate that the schools in which those men and women work have benefited. Furthermore, some of the education programs producing advanced degrees for school personnel are little more than fast tracks to credentials, offering academic credit for courses of questionable substance.

The enormity of the challenge facing the principal of an inner-city school requires something more than a talent for accumulating academic credits. Pupils, teachers, and parents must be able to respect the educator placed in charge of a school. Pupils must know that the principal has authority. Teachers must know that the principal will support them in their best efforts. Parents must know that the principal can make a difference. The principal has to be able to organize and monitor the entire educational enterprise. The Council for Basic Education, a no-nonsense group that holds to traditional values, offers this observation: "A good principal needs to be a liberally educated person, preferably an experienced teacher, with a coherent philosophy of education that he can translate into defensible goals and realistic objectives for the teachers and students he is given to lead. He must have authority that will encourage teachers and students to follow his leadership."[18] But even having these skills and attributes may not be sufficient if a principal is not able to cope with the forces that conspire to limit his power. Teachers' unions, superintendents, school boards, and legislatures all have their own agendas, sometimes shackling the creativity and ingenuity of all but the most resourceful principals.

Successful principals in inner-city schools are those who can kindle the interest of parents in their children's education, getting mothers and even fathers involved in the school. Caring parents breed sons and daughters who realize that someone is concerned about their progress in school. At P.S. 335 in the vast Bedford-Stuyvesant ghetto in the heart of Brooklyn, parents are asked to visit the school on a regular basis to get instruction in what they can do to help their children overcome their individual weaknesses in reading. Philip Finkelstein, who retired as principal in 1979, kept the school above water at a time when the other schools in the district were sinking. Community School District 16, which serves the area, draws an enrollment in which three-quarters of the 15,000 students are from families so poor that they are eligible for free lunches. There are virtually no white students in the district. P.S. 335 ranks at the top of the district's 16 schools in reading, with 64.4 percent of its students achieving grade-level scores or higher. Like P.S. 91, it is a school where students know that someone cares.

Principals and teachers in such schools have faith in the

possibility of improvement, warding off the temptation to despair. One of the leading exponents of this attitude is Arthur Jefferson, the superintendent in Detroit. He said:

> If we are making progress, it is due to a combination of factors, one of them being that we have begun challenging our students with higher levels of expectation, both academically and behaviorally. Correspondingly, that places a higher level of expectation on the staff. We have also been working very hard to get parents and others in the community directly involved in the learning process. Paraprofessionals in our middle schools have been assigned to go into the students' homes with information they have gotten from the teachers and to provide the information to the parents so that they will know what we are trying to do for their children and what they can do to help.
>
> There is no question but that there is still an attitude problem to face with a lot of the professional staff and with the community at large, people who think that once a school district becomes predominantly black less should be expected of the students and that achievement is going to decline. You have to attack this notion and let the kids know that you expect them to achieve and that you are going to hold them responsible. We're trying to do new things in America today. Kids don't drop out of school the way they used to so we have to educate more kids and we have to do it at a time that the urban areas are becoming more homogeneous economically. Our challenge is to learn how to educate the poor.[19]

In Mr. Jefferson's district and in other urban school systems there was a glimmer of progress as the 1980s began. It was seen in Detroit as students raised their average reading scores in every grade from the first through the seventh, and in Newark as students increased their reading scores in seven of the first eight grades. In New Orleans, students in every grade from kindergarten through twelfth got higher scores in reading and mathematics, and in Philadelphia students in the middle and upper grades generally reached their best performance levels since the start of that city's testing program in 1967. New York City's schools recorded better reading scores in 1980 than in 1978 or 1979 and actually exceeded the national norms in many grades in 1981.

Though the modest rise in achievement still leaves big-city schools far behind those in the suburbs and in small towns, even a small reversal of the inexorable decline is welcome news to weary urban educators. They are showing fresh determination to confront the problems of low achievement as their school districts come to serve populations that are increasingly made up of minority students. Educators in the big cities credit the new gains to the adoption of competency-based curriculums, the introduction of management by objectives to their classrooms, and the teaching of test-taking skills. The problem of low achievement in urban schools is of such magnitude, though, that only deep-reaching, long-lasting remedies will solve it. Hopes have been dashed by too many false panaceas. The 1980s will show whether the optimism born of short-term solutions will last.

A BETTER CHANCE

Ultimately, improving the education of minority youngsters means changing lives, raising achievement levels, and giving young people the hope that they can attain what their parents have dared to dream for them. No program in the country has done this better than A Better Chance. Seldom has an educational undertaking altered what might have been the way ABC has. Its graduates have risen from the most abject of conditions to form the core of a burgeoning generation of black and Hispanic professionals. A systems analyst for IBM, a surgeon at New York University Medical Center, a corporate attorney, a deputy bureau chief for *Newsweek* Magazine, an accounting supervisor in San Francisco, a nuclear engineer with Babcock and Wilcox—all are products of ABC.

For all its impact, little is heard of ABC. It carries out its quiet revolution by finding teen-agers of academic promise and steering them into 130 participating secondary schools, mostly private boarding schools and a few public schools, where they live with neighborhood families. The program began in 1963, when several boarding schools wanted to boost their minority enrollment. By 1981 almost 6,000 youngsters had participated. The best measure of ABC is what has become of those participants. At least three out of four have stayed in the program, earning diplomas at the secondary schools at which they were placed. Then, 90 percent have gone on to college, many attending the nation's most selective institutions of higher education. Harvard, for instance, has enrolled more ABC students than any other school, admitting 104 of them between 1965 and 1979. During that period, 93 went to Dartmouth, 91 to the University of Pennsylvania, 82 to Carleton, 62 to Columbia and Barnard, 62 to Brown, and 56 to Williams.

The impact of the program is stunning when one considers the difference it has made in bringing minority students into the nation's most prestigious educational institutions. Jesse Spikes, the tenth-born in a family of Georgia sharecroppers, is one such person. Spikes, who was a waterboy in the cotton fields, attended the public schools of his native McDonough through the tenth grade. At that point, a guidance counselor at his high school referred him to ABC. Spikes spent the summer of 1966 at Dartmouth College sharpening his skills so that in the fall he could enter the eleventh grade at the public high school in Hanover, New Hampshire, where the college is situated. All of his expenses were absorbed by the program, and he lived with seven other teen-agers in an ABC student house with a teacher's family and two Dartmouth students who helped tutor the ABC youths.

Gradually, young Jesse Spikes blossomed and his academic promise won him acceptance at Dartmouth, where he majored in literature and became a student leader. Recognition of his accomplishments came in 1972, when he was graduated from Dartmouth and awarded a Rhodes Scholarship, one of the academic world's most coveted honors. During his two years at Oxford University in England as a Rhodes Scholar, Spikes got a second degree, this one in politics and philosophy. He returned to the United States to attend Harvard Law School and after graduation won a clerkship with a federal court of appeals judge in Detroit. His clerkship completed, Spikes returned to Georgia, settling in Atlanta, less than thirty miles from the central Georgia hamlet where he was raised and a world apart from the rural poverty he knew as a child. He was accepted into practice with one of the city's most distinguished law firms.

ABC stands out as no other program in the country in what it has done for minority students. The program has demonstrated what is possible under the best of circumstances. Admittedly, those accepted into the program have already displayed unusual potential, having ranked in the top ten percent of their classes and having maintained averages of at least 85 in order to be chosen. The tragedy is that the young people who participate must be yanked loose from their native soil, sent to live among strangers, attending classes with few youngsters with whom they share a cultural heritage. Furthermore, an expensive undertaking like ABC can reach only a relative few. There are hundreds of thousands of promising students in inner-city schools who will never be touched by anything like ABC.

"Clearly, ABC provided me with an educational opportunity and a chance to learn about other people," said Jesse Spikes. "But the number who can participate in ABC is limited and the program cannot be a solution. Always at the end there is the question of those who were left behind. The solution is not to send people away from their homes in search of better educational opportunities. There is a far greater number for whom something has to happen to help them where they are."[20] And where they are is in the classrooms of the inner city.

CHAPTER FIVE

TEACHING THE FUNDAMENTALS

THE THREE R'S AND THEN SOME

The line of life, that beautiful developing
structure of language that he saw flowing
from his comrade's pencil, cut the knot in
him that all instruction failed to do, and
instantly he seized the pencil, and wrote the
words in letters fairer and finer than his
friend's. And he turned, with a cry in his
throat, to the next page, and copied it
without hesitation, and the next, the next.
They looked at each other a moment with
that clear wonder by which children accept
miracles, and they never spoke of it again.

THOMAS WOLFE
Look Homeward, Angel

They stand erect as soldiers, their right hands over their little
hearts, carefully mouthing each syllable of every word of the
Pledge of Allegiance. The flag they face is suspended horizon-
tally from the molding just below the ceiling, hanging down
almost to the blackboard, a tableau that repeats itself in each
of the classrooms in Oakland Park Traditional School. The rite
of patriotism echoes through the corridors as all the teachers
begin the school day in the same manner.

Oakland Park Traditional School in Columbus, Ohio, is an anachronism, William Holmes McGuffey in the 1980s. Such schools are springing up throughout the country as parents seek the reassurance of a bygone era. It is a school where respect for country means following the Pledge with the singing of George M. Cohan's "Grand Old Flag" and then a rousing rendition of "America" to the teacher's piano accompaniment. God is with them, acknowledged in a prayer that is part of the opening ceremony and again in a blessing before lunch. Discipline means walking the halls in silence when going to the library, the gymnasium, or anywhere else, treading an imaginary line down the middle of the corridor in single file.

The public school system in Columbus operates two such schools as alternatives to conventional schools. Students throughout the city are eligible to apply for entrance, and the waiting list is so long that a lottery has been used to fill the openings. Oakland Park, the traditional school serving the northern end of the district, is housed in a one-story, red-brick building in a middle-class neighborhood of small, single-family houses. Eleanor C. DeLoache, the principal, a meticulous, matronly woman, presides over her 400 pupils and 14 teachers with a benign despotism that sets the tone for the school. Parents both white and black send their children to Oakland Park because they want them in a place where teaching and learning do not have to compete with misconduct. Even though the school has more than 30 children in a class, a teacher can turn her attention to one child at a time without fear that others will disrupt the lesson. There is a paddle waiting in DeLoache's office for the behinds of those who misbehave. The worst offenders are suspended for a day or two. Even transgressions on the buses that carry the youngsters to and from school can bring severe penalties. "They must respect themselves and other children,"[1] said DeLoache, summing up her standard for behavior.

Drill, memorization, and rote learning are de rigueur at Oakland Park. Though geography has disappeared from the curriculums of many other schools, there are globes and pull-down maps of the United States and Ohio in every classroom at Oakland Park. Ms. Kiser's third-graders can, in a glance, name the river forming the southern boundary of Indiana. Grammar and sentence structure are stressed in every grade, beginning with Ms. Robinson's first-graders identifying "telling" sentences and "asking" sentences and continuing through the sixth grade, where Ms. Lacey's students diagram sentences by parts of speech. Ms. Brown's fifth-graders can manipulate fractions in a way that might win them a passing grade on the minimum competency tests that some states require of high school graduates.

High expectations at Oakland Park begin in kindergarten, where the pupils sit on a braided rug balancing small chalk slates on their laps, not unlike the hornbooks carried by children in colonial America, copying alphabet letters from the board in front of them. Other youngsters are at their seats, cutting, pasting, and coloring pictures of objects whose names begin with the letters they have just copied. Ms. Jackson moves about the room, checking with each child. The youngsters work with quiet intensity; the only sounds are those of the chalk clicking against the slates and the scissors snipping through the paper.

The absence of chatter in a building filled with children is striking at Oakland Park. Even in the lunchroom they barely talk to each other, stiffly waiting in front of their tables until every student is at his place and then sitting down in unison after a joint prayer. Free play in the schoolyard follows lunch and all prohibitions save one are lifted: no youngster at any time may push or strike another. The serious mood of the school is restored during the first twenty minutes that they are back in their classrooms from lunch. It is a silent period throughout the school and each child sits at his desk reading. A visitor strolling through the spotless, linoleum-tiled corridors, passing the open doorways of the classroom, hears only the turning of pages. The remainder of the afternoon is a replay of the serious mission of the morning.

This is back-to-basics at its purest, an approach to schooling unadulterated by what the basics people would consider the permissive notions of starry-eyed Deweyites and their indulgent disciples. Reading, 'riting and 'rithmetic—the traditional fuel that has kept the fires of education burning. And to embellish the R's, throw in the three D's: discipline, dress codes, and a dash of jingoism. Entire schools like Oakland Park have been reconstituted in this stern image of an earlier America. If the Gallup Poll is an accurate reflection of the popular attitude, this is the nostalgic brand of schooling that the public is seeking. In nine out of ten years, from 1969 through 1978, people who were surveyed said that discipline was the number one problem of the schools.[2] They said they wanted a return to the schooling of a previous era, when good manners, respect for authority, and obedience were integral to all that happened in the classroom.

Indeed, many schools have waned in their commitment to fundamentals and would do well to bolster their educational fiber. The question, though, is whether this requires shrouding the effort in the cloak of patriotism, whether it is necessary to beseech the Lord's imprimatur on the day's activities. Singing the national anthem every morning does not help a child learn to read better; wearing a dress instead of jeans does not help a child improve in long division. What the schools need more than ever is a curriculum that prepares students for the fullness of life. The argument is not whether reading, writing, and mathematics ought to be emphasized. They should. All too often, however, back-to-basics is a crude excuse for denuding the curriculum of depth, a subterfuge to save money. It is a reminder more than anything else of the fragility of the curriculum during the formative years when children are so susceptible. What is happening at Oakland Park Traditional School and at similar places bears close scrutiny; it is an approach to education admirable in its respect for what is basic to learning, but perilously close to a rigidity that builds strong backs and weak minds.

THE THREE 3R'S AND NOTHING BUT

If back-to-basics is permitted to lapse into a simplistic approach to knowledge it can become dangerous. It should not give youngsters the idea that some subjects occupy a second-class status and lead them to the opinion that those areas of learning are worthless. It is a matter of approach and attitude. Like the Dutch boy who put his finger in the leaky dike, some teachers, including many of those dedicated to the basics, are trying to stem a public tide of know-nothingness that would have them distort the curriculum. Twelve national groups of teachers of subjects spanning reading and math to music and foreign languages banded together to voice their concern in a joint position paper. "A definition of the essentials of education should avoid these easy tendencies: to limit the essentials to 'the three R's' in a society that is highly technological and complex; to define the essentials by what is tested at a time when tests are severely limited in what they can measure; and to reduce the essentials to a few 'skills' when it is obvious that people use a combination of skills, knowledge and feelings to come to terms with the world," the statement said.[3] It called on educators to resist pressures to concentrate on easy-to-test bits of knowledge and to go beyond short-term objectives of training for jobs or producing citizens who can perform routine tasks.

Back-to-basics can be destructive if all else is considered fluff. Art and music are most vulnerable to the vicissitudes of the movement. Even social studies and science sometimes get pushed beyond the pale of respectability. "The social studies have felt the impact of the emphasis on 'basics'," declared the National School Boards Association, going on to state: "Money spent on materials and equipment and time allotted to social studies are down as schools reallocate resources to the three R's."[4] The enthusiasm that raised the teaching of science to a high priority in the wake of the Russian sputnik shot of a generation ago has ebbed, and schools have allowed the teaching of science to slip at both the elementary and secondary levels. "There is ample evidence that the schools in recent years have neglected science education; at best, it has remained a stagnant area of the curriculum. When we realize that science is often not even considered one of the 'basics,' we can see clearly the damage done by faddishness and a misunderstanding of the relationship of curriculum to society," stated an editorial in *The National Elementary Principal*, a magazine directed to the heads of elementary schools throughout the country.[5]

As it is, science and social studies each get 20 minutes a day in the typical elementary school. In some high schools, the sciences are becoming as obscure as foreign languages. Fewer than four of every ten students enrolls in chemistry and fewer than two in ten take a physics class. An American Albert Einstein growing up in the last quarter of the 20th century might be lucky to understand how his aunt is related to her father-in-law, let alone have any idea of what the theory of relativity suggests. The scientific knowledge and abilities of the nation's high school seniors is deteriorating, according to the National Assessment of Progress Education. The pattern for this dismal trend is set in elementary schools, when science instruction is declared unimportant and science is seldom presented to youngsters in ways that spark their interest. The National Assessment discovered that the greatest decline in scientific knowledge and abilities occurred among older students, but there was slippage among younger children, as well. On questions asked in three successive assessments—in 1969–70, 1972–73, and 1976–77—the proportion of correct answers dropped 2 percent for 9-year-olds, 3.6 percent for 13-year-olds and 4.7 percent for 17-year-olds.[6]

Reading and mathematics are, of course, fundamental parts of the curriculum, but they are so closely allied with other subjects that it is foolish to view the basics in isolation. How is social studies learned if not by reading? How can the physical sciences exist without mathematics? Art and music, too, are complementary parts of a sound curriculum. A wise administration recognizes this interrelatedness and does not compel teachers of the humanities to justify their right to be represented in the curriculum. There should never have to be a choice between the three R's and music, for instance.

It was sad to see what happened to teachers like Ara Zerounian during the 1970s. After spending 25 years teaching music to elementary and junior high school students, he lost his job when Detroit's voters turned down a tax increase for the schools, bringing an end to all music instruction below the high school level. The system's music teachers were forced to become substitute teachers in other subjects if they wanted to remain employed. Ara Zerounian, who had seen three of his pupils go on to occupy first-chair positions in major American orchestras. Ara Zerounian, who had music in his fingertips and was the American String Teachers' 1977 music teacher of the year. Here he was, shuffling back and forth as a substitute, filling in one day as a mathematics instructor, another as a gym teacher, and sometimes as a kindergarten teacher. "A person without music is not educated any more than a person who cannot read or write," Zerounian said.[7] But music was expendable in Detroit. And in lots of other places.

Teaching 'Rithmetic

Banishing other subjects from the curriculum is not going to improve the teaching of the basics. Mathematics, for instance, is rooted firmly in the curriculum. Yet this is a nation of mathematical illiterates. People who are apparently well educated are stymied by all but the simplest arithmetic. Intellectuals able to discuss political theory or art history stumble over calculations performed in sixth-grade classrooms.

The origins of this deficiency lay in the earliest arithmetic instruction. Many elementary school teachers, like people generally, lack confidence in their mathematical ability. Their queasiness is transmitted to their students; generation after generation of schoolchildren grows into adulthood to keep the cycle going, some as elementary school teachers trying to teach mathematics to their own pupils. Television advertisements offer relief for nervous tension and for that achy, upset feeling. But there is no pill to pop for math anxiety. You just live with it. Unfortunately, the worst sufferers are women, cut off from "male" careers because of a high school mathematical background so limited that they cannot hope to major in college subjects involving mathematics. In a typical high school calculus class, for example, boys outnumber girls three to two.[8]

Many proponents of the basics would cure the malady by drilling students in computation. It is an approach that the National Council of Supervisors of Mathematics rejects. The mathematics supervisors warned against defining mathematical literacy so narrowly that many critical skills are neglected. The organization identified ten areas in which a good mathematics program should develop the skills of every student:

problem solving; applying mathematics to everyday situations; alertness to the reasonableness of results; estimation and approximation; geometry; measurement; computer literacy; using mathematics to predict; reading, interpreting, and constructing tables, charts, and graphs; and computational ability.[9] In other words, the basics of adding, subtracting, multiplying, and dividing should get attention, but not to the exclusion of other skills.

Spending more time on mathematics instruction in the early years is not enough. Even using the entire school day for mathematics would not be sufficient if the teacher were ill-prepared. And that is the problem. "A basic ingredient of an instructional psychology in mathematics is a solid knowledge of the mathematics appropriate to the grade levels and ability levels of the students," said Vincent J. Glennon, director of the Mathematics Education Center and Clinic at the University of Connecticut's School of Education. "Teachers cannot teach for understanding that which they have learned associatively. They cannot teach what they do not understand," he said.[10] If clocks were built by people who knew as little about clockmaking as some elementary school teachers know about mathematics, no one would be on time for an appointment.

The responsibility for mathematics instruction in the elementary school is often in the hands of a person whose ability in the subject is modest by any measure. In general, elementary school teachers who attended college before the 1960s took, on the average, only one course in the teaching of mathematics—a methodology course in how to teach the subject. They probably took no course in which they actually studied the content of mathematics. All of the nation's teachers over the age of forty fall in this category, and there seems to be no way of determining how much further training they have had in mathematics since they began teaching. Even in the mid-sixties, the most prevalent requirement in colleges of education for future elementary school teachers was no more than the equivalent of two mathematics course. Remarkably, 8 percent of those preparing to become elementary school teachers were not required to take a single mathematics course. Sending these men and women into classrooms to teach mathematics is like sending someone to cut down a redwood with a butter knife.

One possible answer? Do not ask them to teach mathematics. Let others teach mathematics. Make better use of the time devoted to mathematics instruction in elementary schools by turning over the teaching responsibility to specialists. There is a precedent for this approach. Specialists often handle instruction in art, music, and physical education in elementary schools. Surely mathematics is as important as those subjects and as deserving of special attention. There is nothing sacred about having regular classroom teachers provide mathematics instruction. The approach has failed and it is time for a change.

Teaching Reading
While it might be possible for elementary teachers to delegate mathematics instruction to specialists, one task they must be able to handle on their own is the teaching of reading. It is a skill that cuts across the curriculum, and a teacher who cannot take responsibility for reading instruction might as well not accept a job in an elementary school. And yet many teachers have only the slightest preparation in the mechanics and philosophy of reading instruction. A society that turns to specialists to fix automobile transmissions thinks nothing of entrusting to amateurs the most important lesson schools have to offer.

The situation is worse at the secondary level. If a student has not made substantial progress in learning how to read by the time he reaches junior high school, he may never attain an adult proficiency in reading. Teachers in secondary schools are trained in the content of their subjects—science, social studies, mathematics—and usually have little interest or background in teaching reading. Even English teachers are not necessarily prepared to teach reading. They are oriented toward literature, although some of the more well-rounded teachers can also provide instruction in composition.

In recognition of this problem, the Carter administration proposed a $2 billion education and employment program for youths. Half the money would have been directed toward remedial programs for secondary school students whose skills were lagging. These are young people for whom school has become a nightmare of frustration. Moreover, there is little prospect of their finding jobs to liberate themselves because they have few skills to sell. The problem is that students who have not learned how to read proficiently by the time they reach junior high school may never get much additional help without some sort of new initiative from Washington. Separate reading instruction ends for most students after the sixth grade. Mr. Carter's bill, the Youth Act of 1980, fared no better than he did in that fateful year.

What is still needed in the nation's schools is some attention for students in secondary schools who have slipped through the grades without acquiring the basic skills needed to do the work in junior and senior school. Bringing about change means a massive effort to teach reading at the secondary level, using virtually all subjects—social studies, science, and even mathematics—as vehicles for reading instruction. "What goes on in an English course has to be reinforced in every classroom," according to Constance J. Cuttle, an English teacher at Brooklyn's Clara Barton High School, who has worked with teachers in other subjects to show them how to incorporate reading instruction in their content area. "This is an age in which kids are nonreaders at home because they watch TV," she said. "If we don't reinforce reading in their other subjects, then they will not get it. If people in this city could smell a rotting mind the way they can smell rotting garbage, they wouldn't hesitate to pay more money for programs to teach reading at the secondary level."[11]

Ms. Cuttle and an associate spent the summer of 1980, paid by a grant, poring over a widely used ninth-grade social studies textbook, figuring out ways that social studies teachers could use their courses to help students improve their reading. One thing they did was compile lists of vocabulary words that the social studies teachers could teach as an introduction to each new section of the book. Ordinarily, without such lessons in vocabulary, many youngsters never really understand the material and stumble through the subject matter. Other lessons that they developed dealt with such reading skills as finding the main idea in a paragraph, understanding the relationship between cause and effect, and drawing conclusions. These are higher level skills—really thinking skills—without which it is impossible for anyone to read at an adult level. The International Reading Association, the most important professional group for reading teachers, has increasingly recognized the need for reading instruction in the content areas in high school. The organization has published booklets to assist teachers of mathematics, science, and social studies. As if to demonstrate the universality of its message, one of its latest publications is "Using Sports and Physical Education to Strengthen Reading Skills."

Remedial Reading Instruction

One need not look further than the nearest inner-city high school to see why such a commitment is needed in reading instruction beyond the sixth grade. The magnitude of the problem can be seen, for example, at Louis D. Brandeis High School on Manhattan's polyglot Upper West Side, where 60 percent of the 3,500 students read two years or more below grade level. This renders them incapable of handling the kind of work common in the courses at a good suburban high school. Despite a remediation program larger than that at most high schools, the 19 teachers in the program must measure their successes in tiny increments. One reading teacher estimated at least 100 students were virtual nonreaders. Many of them were first assigned to classes in a so-called annex a mile away, down the block from the famed Juilliard School of Music, distant by several thousand psychological blocks from most of Brandeis's annex students. Signs of progress had to be shown by the youths in the annex before they could be reassigned to the main building. Some never made it, stagnating in the ninth grade until they were 17 or 18 years old and finally dropping out of school, lucky to read as well as a third-grader. Ann Williamson, a remedial reading teacher who began working at the annex in 1973, felt the frustration of not being able to help such students break through the reading barrier that prevented them from knowing the fullness of life. There is just not enough time in class for Ms. Williamson or any other teacher to give such students the individual attention they need. So Ms. Williamson gave up her lunch hours to work with students on a one-on-one basis. It is the approach that every educator knows such youngsters ought to have, but which the schools can not afford.

Throughout the school, in the main building as well as in the annex, conversations with youngsters in remedial reading classes were a curious experience. The students tended not to acknowledge that they were having problems. One young man, James, an eleventh-grader, said that he did not expect to need remediation as a senior. Later, a look at James's records showed that he scored slightly below a fifth-grade level in reading in February, 1978, fell to a month above the fourth-grade level in January, 1979, and was at the fifth-grade level for the first time in January, 1980, when he was interviewed. Some of the teachers explained that many of the students might truly believe they had no serious difficulty, being surrounded as they were by a majority of youngsters whose low reading levels were no different from their own.

Reading is a complex process, and even the experts are uncertain of how the camera called the eye and the computer known as the brain coordinate the various impulses that enable a child to ascribe meaning to squiggles on paper. In the beginning, the incipient reader is the agent trying to crack an enemy code. Access to written knowledge must await the glorious moment when he associates sounds with letters and groups of letters. Eureka. The sounds become words and the marvel of protoplasm that is the human child is suddenly elevated to an exalted place above God's other creatures.

Without this breakthrough, there can be no advance to further achievement. Many young readers fail to move very far beyond the threshold. Only in its most rudimentary form is reading limited to the decoding of words. As the results of reading tests in the big cities have shown, respectable scores in the early grades fade like numbers inscribed on a moist windowpane as the children reach the upper elementary grades. Reading becomes reasoning ability. The student who is unable to derive inferences from the phrases and sentences is not really reading even though he may be able to sound out the words. Reading skills at higher levels are, as mentioned earlier, thinking skills. If schools do not help students learn how to reason, then their reading ability will not grow to its fullest potential.

Teaching 'Riting

One way that some schools have helped develop these skills is by having youngsters write, honing the ability to reason by having them commit their thoughts to paper. It is amazing even in these days when the shibboleth of back-to-basics is on so many lips that writing continues to be regarded as a bastard kin of the fundamentals. Of course, to some of the basics boosters, writing means penmanship. They are more interested in the curve of a child's S's than in his ability to propound ideas in proper syntactical and grammatical fashion. Penmanship, not composition, is what was meant by the second of the three R's when the slogan was coined, but what is needed today is more emphasis on teaching students to express written ideas.

Marjorie Kirrie, who has invested many years in reading the work of students as an English professor and director of composition at Portland State University in Oregon, offers an eloquent description of writing: "Writing cannot be casual or desultory and succeed. There are bothersome matters like clarity and logic. Words have to be selected carefully, spelled properly, and make their appearance in sentences that parse. These sentences, in turn, have to be punctuated, contain connectives and transitions, and participate in the structure of developed and unified paragraphs. The paragraphs must make logical contributions to the larger unity of the essay as a whole. Facts, figures, and quotations have to be presented accurately in contexts which preclude distortion and misinterpretation."12

The organization and presentation of ideas that becomes writing is a craft that schools are not teaching adequately. Students not encouraged to reason and to marshal their arguments are not likely to become strong writers. The college employment market for young philosophy professors is bleak these days. Perhaps some of these people should be hired to help teach schoolchildren to think and reason so that the young people could read and write better.

Something also ought to be done to stimulate all teachers to get more writing out of their students, who do not write much in school anymore. Thomas C. Wheeler says that one of the reasons is that multiple-choice, true and false, and short-answer tests are widely preferred to essay examinations.[13] It looks like the problem has come full circle. The College Board's Test of Standard Written English, administered by the Educational Testing Service as a measure of writing ability, is a multiple-choice examination.

There is no mystery as to why multiple-choice and short-answer tests have become so popular in the schools. Grading essays takes time. In the same way, teaching students to write is terribly time-consuming because papers must be read, evaluated, and discussed with the students if the lessons are to take hold. If compositions are not handled this way, students do not have the benefit of feedback and what could be a learning experience is reduced to an exercise. Some teachers would like to give the teaching of writing the time it deserves, but they do not have the time. Others have the time, but do not want to give it. And still others do not recognize the importance of teaching writing. "Writing instruction in the elementary curriculum has been accorded a status so low that teachers are often uncertain whether they are supposed to teach writing," said Timothy Shanahan, a reading expert at the Chicago Circle campus of the University of Illinois.[14]

If, indeed, teachers do not have the time to mark compositions, this need not mean that students should not be asked to increase their writing output. The Pittsburgh Public Schools dealt with this problem in the early 1960s by going outside the regular staff to hire lay readers. College graduates who had majored in English were tested and interviewed before being hired to work with high school English teachers. Most were homemakers eager for an outlet for their pent-up academic skills; others were graduate students at universities around Pittsburgh. They were given the responsibility of reading compositions written by the students, inserting appropriate comments and affixing grades. The teachers retained final authority over the process and sometimes had the lay readers write the grade in pencil so that it could be changed if the teacher disagreed. Each teacher was assigned a specific lay reader who would come by the school to pick up the papers and to return the previous batch, conferring with the teacher about the assignments. Lay readers occasionally sat in on classes to get a better sense of the assignment. They were paid about $3 an hour and limited to a maximum of $2,000 a year.

But the lay reader program was deemed expendable when Pittsburgh's school budget got squeezed in the mid-1960s. Items without strong constituencies are always the first to be cut by schools when money gets tight. And there has never been much of a lobbying group for good writing. Someone found some money again in the early 1970s and the program was reinstituted, giving each of the city's almost 200 high school English teachers the opportunity for assistance by a lay reader. Some teachers chose not to participate in the program because they thought that evaluation in the hands of a lay reader was too remote from the classroom. Also, a few teachers dropped out because they found themselves frequently disagreeing with the assessments of the lay readers.

On the whole, though, the program was as successful in the 1970s as it had been in the 1960s. The lay readers generally took the work seriously and looked forward to reading the revised drafts of corrected papers that had been returned to the students. Ultimately, what was most important was that the students wrote and wrote and wrote. The availability of lay readers meant that students were turning out a theme every other week. But, when a budget crisis struck again in the late 1970s, writing was once more on the hit list and the lay reader program was among the first of the "frills" to fall under the ax.

Without a lay reader program or some other way of assisting teachers, it seems that many students will not be asked to do as much writing as they should. There must be a person, the teacher or someone else, who can give enough time to reading compositions so that the students will be encouraged to get in the habit of drafting and redrafting their work. James B. Conant once suggested that high school English teachers be given lighter class loads so they would have more time to read student compositions. Too many young people in schools and colleges feel that the first words they apply to paper are etched with the same finality as the words that were engraved on the stone tablets. Few students are imbued with the sense that continual revision is essential to good writing. Perhaps this is to be expected in an era of instant gratification, when even some of the ablest students lack the patience needed for good writing. Young people grow accustomed to turning in papers in which they have neither challenged their original thoughts nor weighed their methods of expression. They take no time to search for the metaphors that inject life into their prose. They eschew the tedium of refining their phrases. Their work is without precision or clarity. The pity is that there is no one to point out the shortcomings.

Writing is too important to be left solely to English teachers, regardless of how well they teach it. Like reading skills, writing skills ought to be stressed in every class—science, social studies, and even mathematics, when possible. Such an approach requires secondary teachers to abandon the egocentrism with which so many approach their subjects. A student who writes an essay in social studies that is insightful in its comprehension of the teachings of Gandhi should also be marked on the literary quality of his work. He must be made to understand that he undermines his achievement whenever he neglects to convey his insights through writing of high quality.

But there is nothing inherent in being a schoolteacher that automatically confirms on a man or woman the ability to help students become proficient writers. Teachers themselves may be poor writers. Their own experiences may have done little to cultivate among them a fuller appreciation of form and style. James Gray came to recognize this as an English instructor at the prestigious Berkeley campus of the University of California. Berkeley skims the cream off the top of the graduating classes of the state's high schools to assemble its freshman class. Yet, professors at Berkeley were astonished and dismayed during the late 1960s and early 1970s to discover that incoming students were seriously deficient in their writing abilities.

Mr. Gray wisely concluded that the best way to attack the problem was to help raise the quality of writing instruction in the school systems that yielded most of Berkeley's students. His conception grew into the Bay Area Writing Project, an ambitious program aimed not directly at the students who would eventually be coming to Berkeley, but at the teachers in whose classes they would sit in elementary and secondary schools. The program reached into the California counties surrounding the Bay Area, north, east, and south of San Francisco.

What began as a local endeavor expanded to 74 sites in 37 states, accounting for combined expenditures of about $500,000 a year and drawing extensive support from the federal government's National Endowment for the Humanities. Despite its growth, the program, now called the National Writing Project, has remained essentially unchanged in concept as it has been replicated around the country. Teachers from elementary and secondary schools attend summer workshops for five weeks. They write compositions and read them to each other for criticism. They learn to draft and perfect their work. And they talk to each other about their methods of teaching writing, borrowing and sharing ideas. On several afternoons each week throughout the five-week session, visiting speakers, often authorities on writing, address the teachers. Frequently, the guests are graduates of the workshop who have gone on to sharpen techniques with their own students. Teachers in the workshop are encouraged to arrive at common standards of evaluation by using a "holistic" approach to grading. This involves having several people read and evaluate a composition, usually on a scale of one to four. In the process of reading a consensus the teachers discuss the merits of the papers, clarifying their thoughts about how to assess a piece of writing. Finally, they go back to their schools to apply what they have learned, disseminating the ideas of the project among their colleagues and continuing to reassemble for periodic refresher workshops.

Time in Class

Schools can always fall back on the excuse that the day is too short to teach writing as well as to do everything else that is expected. The shortage of instructional time is a problem, but a persuasive case is made by some studies that schools compound it by not making the best use of the time available. One such study of 25 elementary school teachers in urban and suburban schools around Los Angeles showed that teachers were devoting only 20 percent of their morning classtime to instruction.[15] "It may come as a surprise to some to be told that the schools may allow less than adequate time for learning any task, but second thought will make one realize that this is very often the case,"[16] John B. Carroll, an eminent figure in educational research, concluded in a now classic study of the time devoted to instruction. This finding has been reinforced through the years by other researchers.

Researchers have found that what counts most if learning is to occur is the amount of time spent on the learning task itself. Time in the classroom is of scant value if not used productively. A teacher who is a poor manager of time robs the students of precious minutes of instruction. One study found that in the average elementary school classroom the organizational activities between subjects—having students put away one set of materials and take out another—consumed 34 minutes a day.[17] Furthermore, even when the teacher uses time efficiently, the student's attention may not be engaged. Distractions abound in the classroom. A slow-moving fly sauntering across a page in an open book. A pencil dropped and rolling on the floor. Thoughts of an after-school dental appointment. Such distractions compete with the lesson and win 30 percent of the time, especially among low achievers, who will more readily allow themselves to be distracted.

Considering how much time is squandered one way or another during the school year, it is a wonder that the school calendar is not lengthened. Imagine the objections from families if they were told that the schools were too crowded and that every child, in turn, would have to be kept home for half a term each year to make room for someone else. Would families be agreeable to such a proposal? They are already doing it. The time at home is called summer vacation, and it means two and a half months away from the classroom for each child every year.

Many students would be better served by spending much of this time at school. It makes little sense for an urban society edging toward the 21st century to cling so tightly to a school calendar geared to the needs of the agrarian communities of the 19th century. Is it not time to think about a change in the school calendar? "Egalitarians should probably concentrate on changing the distribution of time spent in school, rather than concentrating primarily on what happens to different kinds of students while they attend school," Christopher S. Jencks suggested in the foreword to what is perhaps the most thorough examination of the issue, *Summer Learning and the Effects on Schooling*, by sociologist Barbara Heyns.[18]

Talk about wasted opportunity. Nothing beats society's indifference to public education during the summer. Buildings are shut. Teachers do something other than what they have chosen as their life's work. Many youngsters forget how to open a book, let alone how to read one. Not only do most of them not progress educationally over the summer, but some actually fall backwards, showing lower achievement test scores in reading and mathematics in October than they had the previous April. What is most pathetic about this is that the greatest setbacks over the summer are suffered by the pupils who can least afford it: the economically disadvantaged, who are already trailing others their age. The National Advisory Council on the Education of Disadvantaged Children favored formal summer programs as a way "to reduce fallback in regular school practices."[19] Congress, in theory, has endorsed the philosophy of year-round school as a way of sustaining school gains among low achievers. Yet, it remains harder to find an open school building in July than to find a Baptist in the Vatican.

INDIVIDUALIZED INSTRUCTION

Using time well should also involve letting a student advance through the work at his own speed, rather than holding him back and wasting his time until the slowest members of the class are ready for the next lesson. Teaching one lesson for the entire class and expecting the slow students to keep up and the fast students to hold their ability in check makes as much sense as manufacturing suits or skirts in a single size. This does not mean that a teacher should never address a lesson to the entire class. It is just that the lesson, once presented, can be the basis for each student to pursue learning at his own rate. Nor does this mean that the teacher is no longer needed once youngsters begin advancing on their own. The teacher must monitor their work and provide the constant feedback that is essential to progress in school.

The importance of the teacher's role was underscored by an extensive study sponsored by the federal government in cooperation with the California Commission for Teacher Preparation. The results challenged the wisdom of individualizing instruction if it is not monitored and accompanied by regular one-on-one interaction between teacher and student. Individualization is not a license for the teacher to abdicate responsibility. If anything, it requires a better-organized teacher than is needed for traditional, whole-group instruction. Indivdualization calls for providing each child with materials appropriate to his achievement level and making certain that he understands the work before continuing to the next level. Individualization is not a matter of leaving students on their own.

As it happens, the Education of All Handicapped Children Act recognized the need for students to be treated as individuals long before some of the schools acknowledged this necessity. One provision of the statute calls for an Individual Education Plan to be written for each disabled youngster. The parents have a right to demand a hearing if they do not concur with the objectives of the plan and ways detailed for reaching those goals. Yet, so-called normal children cannot be guaranteed a right so basic. An estimated 10 percent of all youngsters are afflicted with minor neurological difficulties that impair their ability to learn in the usual fashion. There are idiosyncracies in the manner in which their brains process information.

One out of every ten kids. Yet, they have to be called "learning disabled" and classified among the handicapped before schools pay attention to their special needs. "Why is it necessary for a child to be labeled—in effect, called a derogatory name— before help can be offered?" asked a special education director.[20] The Valley School District, serving an Omaha suburb, is one of the few that wrote an IEP for every student during the 1970s. The diagnostic-prescriptive approach to teaching grew more popular as schools claimed to be paying more attention to individual needs. And there is considerable merit in the idea of diagnosing a youngster's learning condition in much the same way that a physician might diagnose the same child's physical condition. Tests, interviews, and class performance enable teachers to get a firmer notion of what the child has and has not learned, as well as his strengths. The prescription includes a list of the lessons that will address the student's shortcomings and allow him to use his learning style to advance to higher levels of achievement.

Benjamin S. Bloom of the University of Chicago believes that giving more attention to each student could trigger a transformation unlike any that the schools have known. Bloom's theory is embodied in an approach called "mastery learning." He thinks that it is reasonable to expect as many as 80 percent of the pupils, given sufficient time, to learn what is taught, mastering the work at a level equivalent to that at which teachers usually award A's. Under most circumstances, only 20 percent of a class reaches this level. This can be accomplished, according to Mr. Bloom, through a continual process of feedback and corrective strategies. To show what is possible when a teacher is intent on every student learning the lesson, Mr. Bloom cites the example of a mother instructing her children in how to cross the street. "No mother is satisfied if only a third of her children learn the lesson well," Bloom observed. "Mothers are concerned that each child learns the lesson thoroughly."[21]

In the same way, the responsibility can be vested in the school to make certain that each youngster learns every academic lesson before going on to the next one. The value of such an approach in reading and mathematics, which require the student to build on previous knowledge, is obvious. When the earlier learning is faulty or incomplete, it is unlikely that subsequent lessons can be mastered. In mastery learning, a child is tested to see how much of the lesson he has learned. The test results show the gaps in his learning and further teaching is aimed at filling in those holes in his knowledge. Then, he is retested to see if he has finally mastered the material.

Thus, from the time the pupil enters the first grade, mastery learning demands that each lesson be learned thoroughly so that knowledge can build on knowledge with no faulty underpinnings to give way when the accumulated weight of learning grows heavier in later grades. But mastery learning also depends on a motivated student and a well-prepared teacher; this means that, like other educational theories, it is not fool-proof. It holds as much promise for improving education in the 1980s, however, as any idea on the horizon at the beginning of the decade.

Whether through mastery learning or any other philosophy, the notion of students progressing at a rate diminished only by their inability to learn the material seems crucial to the renewal of the schools. It means a rethinking of the organization of elementary schools so that grade demarcations no longer act as artificial barriers to block the progress of pupils along a continuum of learning. There is no guarantee, for instance, that third grade is the proper place for every 8-year-old. One possibility is to send a child to the fifth grade for reading and the fourth grade for mathematics. Perhaps grades could be eliminated altogether, since their function is largely to reassure anxious parents that their children are indeed being promoted each year.

The Modern One-Room Schoolhouse
When grades are no longer an issue and students are assigned to classes that cut through several age groups, the emphasis can shift to giving every youngster work in each subject that corresponds to his achievement level and may or may not correspond to his age. The East Silver Spring School in Montgomery County, Maryland, at the end of the subway line from Washington, offers one of the best examples of interage, con-

tinuous progress education. A red-brick structure built into the side of a hill, the school is entered from the second floor. Inside, there is a surprising feeling of spaciousness—a two-story open area of classrooms without walls, all facing into a central area from which every class can be seen. The two levels, fully carpeted, are connected by a ramp with a media center crammed with books and visual materials halfway up the ramp. The sound of children's voices is always in the air, an incessant drone that distracts but seldom disrupts.

Upstairs are four kindergarten classes, fairly ordinary groups of 5-year-olds. Downstairs is another matter. The 6-, 7-, and 8-year-olds, who in other schools would be called first-, second-, and third-graders, are mixed together in seven classes. Each teacher's post is called a teaching station, and the youngsters move among them, continually regrouping according to achievement level, not grades or ages. Mathematics, reading, and language arts are studied in this way, and children go from teacher to teacher for the corresponding level of instruction. Only for social studies are they grouped by age. Most instruction can generally be tailored to a pupil's level of performance and there is nothing to keep a youngster from progressing through the curriculum just as fast as he is able.

For a student like Eurina, who was 7 years old, the system had the kind of flexibility that she would not have been likely to find in an ordinary second-grade classroom. She had begun the year reading as well as an average first-grader, but by the end of the year was starting to use a reading book commonly given to third-graders. Her mathematics performance had been at the level of a first-grader when the year started and she was at the level of a beginning second-grader by the end of the year. "It takes a great deal of planning and work by the teacher," said Claire Serabian, one of Eurina's teachers. "We evaluate them every afternoon to see where they are."[22] If a pupil is not making reasonable progress, the school's educational management team takes a look at the case. The team—a diagnostic-prescriptive teacher, a reading teacher, a speech pathologist, the child's teacher, and the principal —meets one afternoon a week to see which children need special attention.

Sixty-two percent of the country's adults say they favor a continuous progress plan that permits students to progress through school at their own rate of accomplishment, but many schools are loathe to break with the tradition of expecting everyone of the same age to be doing the same work. In the early elementary grades, when children are still developing at a very uneven rate, it makes sense to organize classes around interage groups so that all levels of achievement are acceptable. Furthermore, it permits a youngster whose progress is slower than average to remain in the group for several years without the school having to make a decision about whether or not to promote him. Attempting to inflict minimum competency promotion standards on pupils who do not reach certain standards in the early grades makes no more sense than expecting every infant to walk at the same age.

Recognition of the advantages of interage grouping can prepare the way for appreciating what the elementary schools can gain by also giving up the practice of putting marks on a report card to represent the progress of each student. During the wave of protests that rolled across college campuses during the late 1960s, students carried posters proclaiming: "I am a person. Do not fold, spindle or mutilate me." How different is it really to try to transform the worth of a 6-year-old child to a series of numbers or letters on a report card? It implies a precision in assessment that is ludicrous in the early elementary grades. There is time enough for awarding marks in secondary school. More school systems might follow the lead of Great Neck, a New York suburb on Long Island, which has abandoned the practice of giving report cards with marks to elementary schoolchildren. Instead, parents are summoned to regularly scheduled individual conferences with the teachers, and narrative reports on the youngster's progress are written by the teacher and sent to the family.

PRESCHOOL INSTRUCTION

In light of the difficulty of getting schools to treat students as individuals it is perhaps not surprising that the schools altogether ignore children during the period when they might most benefit from attention. The prekindergarten years are nonexistent as far as most schools are concerned. Other than the participation of the schools in some poverty programs providing services to children 3 or 4 years old, most schools make no attempt to reach youngsters during the crucial years before the age of five. It is as though they have been vacationing on Mars until their fifth birthday, when the schools deign to admit them to kindergarten. Yet, educational psychologists say that a disproportionately large part of a child's mental development occurs before the fifth or sixth birthday. Burton L. White, a developmental psychologist at Harvard, says that a child's intellectual future may be decided by the events in his life even before the age of three.[23] For many youngsters not in a setting with adequate stimulation, this apparently means a loss that schooling cannot recapture because they reach school too late.

One of the better attempts to ensure that the preschool years are spent productively is the Parent-Child Early Education Program in the Ferguson-Florissant School District, outside St. Louis. This is a school system that feels it owes something to children even before they enter kindergarten. Thus, the district starts serving youngsters when they turn 3 years old, administering screening tests to find potential learning problems. The one in five with serious difficulties begins receiving weekly home visits from teachers.

Every child in the school district is eligible to participate in the home visit program starting at the age of four, when all are again tested to make individual assessments. Then each child is visited once a week at home for the entire year by a fully certified teacher, who meets with the youngsters in small groups that may include one or two other 4-year-olds from the neighborhood. In addition, every Saturday for two or three hours, the children assemble at a school in groups of about 20 to meet with the same teacher who visits them at home. The instructional activities of Saturday School and the home visits are coordinated so that one builds on the other. Furthermore, after each home visit, a copy of the weekly Parents' Home Activity Guide is given to the parents by the teacher to stimulate learning projects in the home. The program is an unusual effort to combine systematically play and education. It is done without the kind of pressure that may be applied to some children when they reach the regular classroom. It builds both confidence and learning readiness, while offering the additional dimension of extensive parent involvement: the parents assist the teacher in both the home visit and Saturday School, as well as using the activities guide the rest of the week.

Tommy Immer is typical of the 4-year-olds who have participated in the program. The day that the teacher came to his house was one of the highlights of the week for young Tommy and he was invariably at the door, waiting for her. On one particular crisp spring morning, Tommy, in stockinged feet and wearing his Spiderman sweatshirt and plaid slacks, had the door open and was peering through the storm window as his teacher, Judy Brown, arrived. Next door, Ethan Hayden, a blond, blue-eyed smaller version of Tommy, was also watching for Ms. Brown's arrival. He and his mother, Mary Ann, were already crossing their lawn toward the Immers' house as Ms. Brown, toting a tape recorder and three satchels crammed with toys and teaching materials, was getting out of her car.

Ms. Brown, a small, dark-haired woman, who joined the program in 1972, the year after it began, greeted the children and their mothers and quickly settled onto a spot in the middle of the small living room. Kristi, Tommy's 2½-year-old sister, had joined the group—younger brothers and sisters are welcome to participate in the home visits—and Ms. Immer was in a bedroom attending to Jeffrey, 16 months. "Today we're going to talk about listening," said Ms. Brown, sitting cross-legged on the shag carpeting. She was holding a book, *Good Morning, Mouse,* and the children were attentive as she guided them through the lavishly illustrated pages, encouraging them to imagine the sounds of the objects to which the mouse was listening. "It trains their ears to discriminate so that they will be able to recognize the sounds of the letters that will come up next year in reading," Ms. Brown explained in an aside to Ms. Hayden, who was on the floor next to Ethan.

The book about sounds was followed by a rhyming game, a further attempt to cultivate the phonic skills so important in learning to read. "I'm going to give you two words, ape and banana," Ms. Brown said to Ethan, who had by now peeled off his baseball jacket to reveal a St. Louis Cardinals sweatshirt. "Do they sound the same?" After a few such questions, the rhyming activity continued with Ms. Brown emptying a bag of objects on the floor so that the children could match the items that had similar sounding names. A cork and a fork. A hook and a book. A block and a sock. A pan and a figure of a man.

And so it went for the hour session. At first, Ethan was shy and occasionally Tommy was cranky. Ms. Brown, a thorough professional, knew how to steer the lessons through rough spots. There were hopping and throwing activities for the large muscles, and there were objects to cut with a scissors for the small muscles. And there were measuring and counting games to get the children ready for arithmetic. The mothers played an active role, taking turns working with their children as Ms. Brown concentrated on one youngster at a time. Some portions of the lessons would be repeated on Saturday, when the children went to one of the district's schools for either a morning or afternoon class with Ms. Brown, who each week scheduled a few parents or older siblings to remain at the school to help her. On Saturday, the youngsters would move around the room, in groups of five or six, from activity to activity, spending about twenty minutes at each under the supervision of Ms. Brown or one of the volunteers.

Though the children have fun, the Parent-Child Early Education Program is serious business. Its value can be seen in the results, which have been the subject of extensive research. The mental, perceptual, and language development of the youngsters, on the average, far exceeds what would normally be expected during the year between the ages of three and five. The program has existed long enough to discover that the gains have been maintained during the early years of elementary school. Of special importance, the children whose test scores originally ranked them in the lowest third appeared to get the most out of the program, showing the greatest percentage gains in their development.[24] Getting school districts around the country to bring children into their instructional programs at the age of four would not solve all of the nation's educational problems, but it certainly would end the wasteful practice of ignoring the learning needs of youngsters at this critical period of their development.

Before schooling for 4-year-olds becomes universal, however, school systems throughout the country will have to start serving all their 5-year-olds. Though it is difficult to believe, tens of thousands of children are kept out of school until the age of six because only eighteen states have mandatory kindergarten programs.[25] Many school systems in the rest of the states choose to save money by not offering kindergarten to all children. People who are willing to sacrifice kindergarten at the altar of fiscal austerity would be aghast at proposals to do away, instead, with twelfth grade. But, given a choice, it might be a more constructive step. Schools would do well to tip the scale of their priorities toward the youngest children. The idea of choosing between the oldest and the youngest students is not offered as hyperbole. Financial constraints are forcing cutbacks and early childhood education is almost certainly going to get low priority. It should be the other way around. As will be discussed in the next chapter, the twelfth grade is often duplicative of what follows in college. Seventeen-year-olds might be better served by internships with employers, by vocational training in community colleges, or by starting their higher education a year earlier.

This is not a plea for the schools to surrender responsibility for high school seniors. Rather, it is a matter of recognizing that there are other avenues that with slight modifications could speed such youngsters toward adulthood. The resources freed by such an innovation could be diverted to the youngest children, not just to install kindergartens where they do not exist, but to start formal schooling at an even younger age. It is time for schools to be moving toward universal education beginning at the age of four. Too much is lost, never to be reclaimed, by leaving the early development of children to happenstance. What is done for a youngster in the year before the age of five is far more crucial than what is done for him in the year after the age of sixteen.

The 1980s are an ideal time for a change of this sort. The enrollment decline that began in the 1970s will continue well into the decade. Finding sufficient classroom space to allow the schools to absorb 4- and 5-year-olds would be no problem. The days of overcrowding in the schools, when split-shifts were used because the only way all students could be accommodated was to have them attend for less than an entire school day, are long gone in most districts. The dwindling enrollment also creates the possibility of adding 4-year-olds to the schools without a commensurate expansion of staff. Paying more attention to early childhood education could be the most important contribution of the schools during the 1980s.

CHAPTER SIX

THE HIGH SCHOOL–COLLEGE CONNECTION

TIES THAT DO NOT BIND

When I think back
on all the crap I learned in high school
it's a wonder
I can think at all.
And though my lack of education
hasn't hurt me none
I can read the writing on the wall.

PAUL SIMON
Kodachrome R

They show up for only two or three periods a day, spending the remainder of the schoolday as they wish—roaming the corridors, sitting in their cars in the school parking lot, loafing on nearby streetcorners. Some of the more ambitious ones hold part-time jobs during the hours they would normally be expected to attend classes. They are high school seniors, a group caught in the grip of ennui, watching a pause in their academic life lapse into an empty, time-serving experience. It is a purposelessness born of the leniency that enables students in many school districts to complete almost all of their graduation

123

requirements by the end of the junior year or midway through the senior year.

THE ELECTIVE CURRICULUM

A generation ago, when most high schools had a prescribed curriculum, each student had to take a full set of courses during the senior year. Now, students may satisfy requirements early and coast down the beginners' slope to a diploma. The introduction of more and more electives, one exchangeable for another, helped create the current situation in which a student can meet graduation requirements without a rigorous senior year. They no longer have to pursue courses in a sequence that assures that English VII and English VIII, for instance, will be taken in the senior year, after the first three years of high school English are completed in set order. They may now take such electives as the Detective Novel and Sports Literature as extra English courses in the tenth and eleventh grades, leaving them without English requirements in the twelfth grade. Or, as in New York State, English may be the sole requirement in the senior year.

There is nothing inherently iniquitous in the elective system; the problem lies in the sort of electives that have been developed and in the willingness of educational authorities to accept those electives in lieu of the regular program, rather than in addition to it. There is too much of what Dennis Gray, a staff member of the Council for Basic Education, calls "a patchwork; an accretion of watered-down requirements, flabby electives, and slapdash mini-courses, altogether lacking in coherence."[1]

In the widespread effort to pinpoint reasons for the decline of scores on the Scholastic Aptitude Test during the 1970s, some educators began to suspect that a possible cause was the proliferation of elective courses. A lower proportion of students in many high schools was enrolling in the basic English, history, science, and mathematics courses that traditionally prepared students for college. This was happening even though a higher percentage of graduates was going on to college. The consequences for higher education will be discussed at greater length. It may well be that the drop in scores occurred because the SAT tests asked questions about material that had not been covered in the optional courses that many students had substituted for the mainline curriculum. Fred Hargadon, the admissions dean at Stanford and chairman of the College Board, was among those registering concern about the effects of this course-swapping. "We are no longer as concerned as we once were that an English course is in fact an English course and not simply a course devoted to one or another social policy question," Hargadon told high school guidance counselors. "Similar doubts haunt us regarding the content of many history, sociology and government courses."[3]

Other forces, as well, influenced the trend toward electives. The idea of a diploma for everyone implied the existence of a curriculum that most anyone is capable of completing. When the schools found that the traditionally prescribed courses were too difficult for some students, those youngsters were given alternatives so that they could avoid such courses. Perhaps it did not occur to educators to provide better preparation in the early grades so that students would be able to handle the demands placed on them in high school. Instead, the common core of the curriculum was abandoned like some outmoded clothing fashion. The goal was to confer more diplomas, and it has been realized. But to what avail?

Colleges' Weaker Demands

Institutions of higher education, too, must bear some of the blame. Had they not eased requirements, it would not have been so simple for the high schools to collapse in their educational resolve. "A lot of the confusion in the high school curriculum reflects the confusion that began in the college curriculum 10 or 15 years ago,"[4] said Ernest L. Boyer, president of the Carnegie Foundation for the Advancement of Teaching. Boyer, one of the most astute of educational observers, had the chance to view the confusion from two important perspectives, first as president of the State University of New York and then as the last commissioner of the U.S. Office of Education before it was raised to Cabinet-level status. One of his first acts with Carnegie was to start a two-year study of high schools, emphasizing relationships with higher education, that is to be completed in 1982.

An example of the influence of colleges and universities on the high school curriculum is seen in the study—or should one say the lack of study?—of foreign languages. Perhaps it was not for the best of reasons that secondary youngsters pursued foreign language instruction in large numbers. Their impetus was the entrance requirements of higher education. It was a bludgeon, but at least many a reluctant student was prodded into Spanish or French class. Seldom have students relished the opportunity to twist their tongues around foreign phrases. They need a push. But the nation's high schools lost this hold on their students during the 1960s, when the rush of colleges to rescind foreign language requirements, both for entrance and graduation, resembled nothing so much as state legislatures hurrying to repeal the Prohibition Act in 1933. By the middle of the 1970s, only 11 of the 148 large state universities mandated the study of a foreign language for a bachelor's degree.[5]

As the 1980s began, the study of foreign and classical languages had almost disappeared from many high schools. It is no wonder that the President's Commission on Foreign Language and International Studies declared that "Americans' incompetence in foreign languages is nothing short of scandalous, and it is becoming worse."[6] Fifteen percent of American secondary school students were studying foreign languages in 1978, a proportion less than half that of 1915. Even the 15 percent figure tended to mislead, however, because six of every ten students were enrolled in first-year courses and most of them would go no further. Only 1.8 percent of all the country's high school students pursue a foreign language for three years or longer, a period essential to attain proficiency. In this entire country, only 3,500 public high school students are enrolled in Russian classes beyond the second year. Just 2 of the almost 100 public high schools in New York City offer regular courses in Russian. Do not bother asking what happened to Latin, which 51 percent of the nation's high school students took in 1905. Today, the figure is 1 percent.[7]

The President's commission proposed that language requirements be reinstated, but the outlook for this happening is not favorable. Few high schools would make the change independently and institutions of higher education are not apt to promote a change of this sort at a time when they are growing desperate for students. They do not want to do anything that might diminish rather than enlarge the available number of applicants.

The problem of foreign language study hints at the paradox of the curriculum reform movement under way in colleges and universities. Institutions of higher education blithely embark on their journey of change, often oblivious to the effects on the nation's high schools. It is an attitude fecund with arrogance, implying that college freshmen are born into this world with no previous schooling. Few institutions of higher education bother finding out whether their prescriptions for reform will make good medicine for the high schools. For example, the highly publicized core curriculum at Harvard College, developed over a period of five and a half years, might as well have been fashioned in a vacuum so far as the secondary schools were concerned. James Q. Wilson, the Harvard government professor who was chairman of the curriculum task force, confessed at a meeting he addressed in the fall of 1980—just after the changes had been completed—that it was his first opportunity to speak to representatives of the college preparatory high schools about the new requirements. In the room were superintendents and high school principals from such high-achieving suburban school systems as Greenwich, Westport, Beverly Hills, Highland Park, Lexington, Newton, Scarsdale, Great Neck, Shaker Heights, and Walnut Hills, districts of the sort that Wilson said provide Harvard with "the bulk of our best students."[8] Yet, Harvard had never bothered asking any of those superintendents or principals what they thought of the proposed changes and how their curriculums would be affected.

The cavalier approach of institutions of higher education permits no serious consideration of the concerns of high schools. Principals and teachers are seldom consulted, and students in the high schools are never asked for their opinions, though the impact of curriculum changes will influence their lives for at least the four years they spend in college. High school, however, is not the separate world that higher education would like to pretend it to be. If anything, interdependence is increasing. Fewer students will be graduated from the nation's high schools each successive year during the 1980s, and this will mean a smaller pool into which colleges and universities can cast their nets as they search for students. The imperative for forging bonds with high schools is no longer a matter of altruism. Colleges and universities will be especially affected by the manner in which incoming students have been prepared for postsecondary education.

Ultimately, the existence of a core curriculum like Harvard's depends on students arriving on campus with the skill and ability to cope with the courses they will be required to take. Students would be more likely to reach this level if institutions of higher education got more involved in elementary and secondary schools. "It is incomprehensible that the colleges and universities have maintained a scornful disinterest in what happens in the schools during the 12 years that precede college," Boyer commented. "If colleges are concerned about their future, the first place they should turn is to the institutions that are supplying that future. They should intervene early in the educational process."[9] Only recently have some institutions of higher education begun acknowledging the possibility of such a responsibility. One indication of this awakening interest was the move in the spring of 1981 by the Association of American Colleges, an organization of hundreds of small liberal arts colleges, to start exploring avenues of cooperation with high schools. At about the same time, the California Roundtable on Educational Opportunity was established by leaders in higher education to give closer attention to the state's secondary schools.

COLLEGE-SCHOOL COOPERATION

What would be helpful, whether initiated by organizations or by individual colleges, would be some integration of efforts with secondary schools in subjects like mathematics and science, where learning is sequential—a student who falls off the track finds it virtually impossible to climb back on at some point down the line. The planning ought to reach to the junior high school level and even lower to help provide the background essential for advanced studies. Consider the child who is not properly taught how to manipulate fractions in the fifth and sixth grade and try to envision him in a high school calculus class or, even worse, as an engineering major in college. Thus, institutions of higher education can do themselves a favor by giving attention to students while they are still in junior and senior high school. "Why should colleges and universities go on expending their shrinking dollars in remediation and developmental programs to compensate for the inadequacies of student preparation? Why can higher education not work more directly and intimately with elementary and secondary schools to assure levels of literacy and competence that rightfully should be achieved in the first 12 years of schooling?"[10] asked Robert Kirkwood, a top official of the Middle States Association of Colleges and Schools, a group with the authority to accredit schools and colleges.

Remedial Education vs. Prevention
Testimony to this lack of cooperation was the birth during the 1970s of a new subject in the nation's colleges and universities. It is called "remedial education," and some professors now devote their entire schedules to such activities. There is even a new field of Ph.D. studies in remedial education, preparing young academics to teach others how to teach remedial education in college. Professors, deans, college presidents, and trustees deplore this turn of events, but few of their institutions have done much to help strengthen the education of students in elementary and secondary schools, where the seeds of academic failure are sown. Michael W. Kirst, the Stanford professor who is president of the California State Board of Education,

blames the University of California for contributing to the decline of high school standards in his state. He charged that by reducing the number of years of study that it expected of incoming students in various subjects, the university opened the way to softer diploma requirements in the high schools.[11] Apparently, Kirst was not alone in his view because the University of California plans, beginning in 1981, once again to require of its applicants four years of high school English, replacing the three-year minimum it instituted a few years ago.

The extent of the problem of inadequate preparation is enormous. Few colleges and universities have been able to escape it. In the 1980–81 academic year, the City University of New York spent $32 million of its $285 million instructional budget on remediation. Seventeen percent of the classes attended by the institution's 165,000 students were classified as remedial.[12] The need for such courses has altered the character of the university, giving it the role of high school as well as postsecondary institution, and making the teaching of basic skills almost as important a mission as the pursuit of advanced knowledge.

Smith College, one of the esteemed Seven Sisters, began a three-year program in 1980 to help students understand that language is a precise tool of writing and not merely a medium of self-expression. "Like the other highly selective colleges in the country, Smith can no longer take for granted the sound basic skills of its students,"[13] said Jill Conway, the president of Smith at the time. A $135,000 corporate gift is being used at Smith to train faculty members in the skills of teaching logic, an underlying essential in good writing. The professors are also learning how to work with students who need remedial help in language skills.

On many campuses there are similar difficulties in mathematics, as well. At Ohio State University, mathematics professors said they were seeing students with gaps in their skills going all the way back to elementary school, young people confounded by fractions and percentages. As many as half of the university's entering freshmen were being diverted to remedial classes in mathematics during recent years. Harold L. Enarson, the president of Ohio State throughout the 1970s, wondered in his outspoken style whether it was time for the state to reevaluate its policy of requiring Ohio's publicly supported institutions of higher education to accept all high school graduates who applied for admission. "If we want to continue the policy of open access," Enarson said, "then let us do so with our eyes open, knowing that it will be costly, inefficient, and a doorway to disappointment for some young people."[14]

Ohio State has not left student development totally to chance, however; at least one program was launched to combat the blight of remediation that threatened to engulf the campus. It began as a pilot project in 1976 and was extended to 100 high schools in central Ohio by 1980. A modified version of the mathematics placement test for freshmen was produced and administered to eleventh-graders at the participating high schools. Professors at Ohio State hoped that by telling students early enough of their weaknesses in mathematics there might be sufficient time for the youngsters to upgrade their skills and avoid remedial classes in college. Along with the test, the high school students fill out a questionnaire indicating their prospective field of study. What they get back from Ohio State is a computer printout that starts, "Greetings from Hal, your friendly computer. . . ." Based on the test results contained in the report and what they have indicated about their expected majors, the students are told what courses in mathematics they ought to take in the remaining year of high school to heighten their chances of succeeding in college.

Since only one year of mathematics is required for a diploma in Ohio, enrollment in advanced high school math courses has been minimal in some schools, and many seniors take no math. The Early Mathematics Placement Testing Program sponsored by Ohio State has helped boost the enrollment of seniors in high school math classes. A student knows that if he can strengthen his background and get a high enough score on the placement test, he will not be assigned to remediation at the university. "It saves the students time and money if they can get high enough scores," said Colin Bull, dean of Ohio State's College of Mathematical and Physical Sciences. "It also increases their morale and enhances the professional atmosphere at the university."[15]

Not only has the university seen improved placement scores by students from participating high schools, but their scores are higher, as well, on nationally standardized tests. The extra year of mathematics as seniors is what has obviously made the difference. At Westland High School, the suburban Columbus School that was the site for the original pilot project, even scores on the mathematics portion of the Scholastic Aptitude Test have risen. The improved results reinforce the belief of those who contend that requiring more years of study of a subject is one of the best ways to improve skills. Westland High is so satisfied with what it has seen that it is contemplating the adoption of a similar early testing program in the language arts to help its students avoid remedial college courses in English.

Freshman Classes of the Future

If colleges and universities had a wider range of choice in their selection of students, then perhaps the problem of inadequate preparation would not be so troublesome. But most institutions, particularly those that are publicly supported, take the vast majority of applicants, and this means that the difficulties experienced by the institutions are bound to grow worse. The size of the nation's high school graduating class peaked in 1980, and it will not increase again until the 1990s. In only ten states, most of them in the Far West, will high school enrollments expand. The declines will be most severe in the Northeast and in the Midwest, which happen to be the regions with the greatest concentration of privately supported colleges and universities. Those institutions will be under intense pressure. In Michigan, for example, the number of students coming out of high school, 132,759 in 1978, is expected to drop to 84,669 by 1994.[16] Many colleges and universities are not going to be able to be choosy about whom they accept. The desperation of admissions offices has profound implications for high schools across the country.

Advertising: One Born Every Minute

Some higher educational institutions are already beset by panic, and more than a few are turning to the ways of Madison Avenue, peddling their wares like shameless hucksters. Think back a decade. How often did a college or university advertise for students? Now they promote their product—higher learning—alongside blurbs for automobiles, underwear, and hemorrhoid relief medicines. Some schools even pay head hunters for each student they recruit; other schools award tuition discounts to upperclassmen who convince high school seniors to attend the institution. William Ihlanfeldt, a vice president of Northwestern University in Evanston, Illinois, who has watched marketing supplant admissions standards in the minds of many of his colleagues, tells of an acquaintance who represented a small college with a tiny stream on its property. The man unabashedly led prospective students to believe there was a lake on campus on which they could sail, an activity that would have been as likely under the circumstances as floating a sloop in a bathtub. The recruiter had to eat his words one September day when a new freshman showed up with a 30-foot sailboat on a trailer attached to his car.[17]

Colleges and universities showing such callous disregard for high school students, treating them like suckers waiting to be hoodwinked, do not enhance relations between secondary and higher education. The National Association of Secondary School Principals has been growing increasingly concerned about what the threat of falling enrollments is doing to recruiting practices. In the fall of 1980, the organization issued a warning on the "Priniciples of Good Practice in College Admissions and Recruitment."[18] Officials of secondary schools were urged to refuse inducements from higher education institutions for placing students with them. Also, the group condemned such unethical practices by colleges and universities as the use of pictures showing students working with scientific equipment that was not actually available at the institution or claims by institutions that certain programs would unfailingly lead to high-paying jobs.

Blacks and Hispanics
While high school enrollments are dropping, another demographic change is also occurring in the form of an expanding black and Hispanic population. Inevitably, this will mean that these two minority groups will comprise a larger percentage

of the nation's high school graduating class. Institutions of higher education already find these two groups in need of the greatest remedial attention. In other words, the difficulties of having to deal with inadequately prepared students are bound to increase, not diminish. Like an abandoned, unwanted infant, the problem is in the vestibule of higher education. There is now probably more incentive than ever, though, to take on the responsibility, since many colleges and universities will need whatever students they can get to offset enrollment losses produced by a lower birthrate. For Hispanics, in particular, the prospect of being welcomed into institutions of higher education is an advance long awaited. Americans of Spanish heritage constitute 7 percent of the nation's population, but only 4.8 percent of the postsecondary enrollment.

Increasingly, educators are going to have to ask themselves whether policies adopted for black and white Americans of English-speaking backgrounds are appropriate for Hispanics, whose dropout rate is one of the highest of any minority group. The growing prominence of Hispanics in the school population and the need to face up to their difficulties is evident in cities like Miami and Los Angeles, where they are now the largest single group in the public schools. In New York City, the overall proportion of Hispanic pupils rose from 23 percent in 1973 to 29.8 percent in 1979 and their representation in the lower grades was even higher. It is vital that institutions of higher education work more closely with high schools to promote the transition of these Hispanic youngsters from one level of education to the next.

In a state like California, where more than one of every five people are Hispanic, the issue of absorbing young Hispanics into higher education is of great significance. Recognizing this, the University of California started earlier than most institutions of higher education to enter into collaborative efforts with secondary schools. In 1976, the system's eight undergraduate campuses launched the Partnership Program with 104 junior high schools throughout the state. The program, now expanded to 250 junior and senior highs and 12,000 students, is aimed at students of all minority groups, trying to reach them while they have most of their secondary schooling ahead of them and there is still time to motivate them academically. The field workers sent into the secondary schools by the university are the key to the program. They work with students directly and through the school personnel to prod them to enroll in the courses they will need to get accepted by the university and to succeed in its highly competitive atmosphere.

Students are discouraged from taking electives that could detour them from the main line of courses leading to the university. Visits are arranged to the university's campuses and students meet with professors, particularly minority members with whom they might identify. Sometimes the professors and other representatives of the university speak to them at the junior and senior high schools. Parents are drawn into the program by the field workers, who may even visit the homes of the students, doing whatever can be done to get mothers and fathers to add their voices to the effort to encourage the youngsters in their studies.

Participation in the Partnership Program is usually limited to about 30 students in a school so that there are not more young people than can be seen personally by the field workers. The schools recommend students for the program. At least half of them have averages of B or higher; 35 percent have B− averages; and 15 percent have lower averages, but high potential. They all enter the program as seventh-graders and continue to participate through the eleventh grade. Academic politics being what they are, the twelfth grade has been omitted not for educational reasons, but because of the rivalry of the state college system. The thought was that if students were not as heavily under the influence of the University of California during their senior year, when they are making their college selection, they might be more inclined to consider other institutions. In any event, the impact of the program cannot be assessed yet, because the first group, those who were seventh-graders in 1976, will not be graduated from high school until 1983. Enough has been seen, however, to indicate that early intervention is an improvement over the former policy of ignoring students until they reached the twelfth grade, when it was too late for them to begin thinking about the courses they needed to attend the University of California.

Adopting High Schools

There is a kind of justice in the involvement of institutions of higher education in trying to build up the quality of schooling in the early years. Colleges and universities, after all, are culpable in the deficiencies of elementary and secondary schools, those lowly levels of education that professors sometimes hold in disdain. Did not the higher educational institutions train the teachers who contribute to the failings of the public schools? It is reasonable that colleges and universities should now be expected to turn whatever expertise they possess to the advantage of the nation's beleaguered public school systems.

One way that colleges and universities might do this is by "adopting" high schools. If each of the 3,130 institutions of higher education in the country took responsibility for one or more of the 17,389 high schools it could lead to a collaboration with far-reaching effects on the quality of education. The opportunities for working together are unlimited. If college students were available to assist high school teachers it would be possible to provide more individual attention to students in large classes. College students also could tutor high school students in various subjects, gaining greater understanding of the material themselves by having to explain it to others. A college could coordinate its schedule with that of a nearby high school so that able juniors and seniors might attend some courses on campus more conveniently and begin accumulating credit for work they are capable of handling, rather than being bored. Furthermore, some of the expensive facilities and equipment at the college could be shared with the high school, giving the secondary students access to materials that a school distrct might not ordinarily be able to afford. Scholars at institutions of higher education are a largely untapped resource for high schools, both as teachers and as consultants on curriculum matters.

A major effort in this direction is being carried out by the National Humanities Faculty, based in Concord, Massachusetts, which has enlisted some 800 professors from institutions throughout the country to accept brief assignments, mostly in secondary schools, but also in elementary schools and in community colleges. Typically, a professor spends three or four days at a site, giving lectures, for example, on Shakespeare to the school's teachers so that they can incorporate into their own teaching what they learn from the visiting scholar. The $800,000 that the National Humanities Faculty spends each year on expenses and fees for the professors—who continue in their regular full-time positions—has been provided by the National Endowment for the Humanities and several large foundations. Future funding, however, has been thrown into question by the proposal of a severe cutback for the National Endowment.

Such endeavors as the National Humanities Faculty could point the way toward other experiments. An exchange of teachers with the proper backgrounds and sufficient interest in each other's activities could be of benefit to both levels. Putting a high school course in the hands of a college teacher, for instance, could give that course a new dimension and, at the same time, force the college teacher to think more deeply about teaching techniques, which get all too little attention in higher education. For the high school teacher working in a college classroom, the confrontation with more mature students could be a refreshing challenge, as well as a source of professional gratification for a person who has learned to find satisfaction in teaching skills.

In Boston, it took a desegregation order by a federal district court to get colleges and high schools to talk to each other about teaching or about anything else. The outlines of cooperation were sketched into the desegregation plan by the court with the agreement of the colleges and universities, which could not actually be compelled to join the effort. Institutions of higher education were paired with individual schools to work together to find ways to lift the quality of education, which historically has been abysmally low in the Boston Public Schools. The idea of building the collaboration into the desegregation plan was an ingenious stroke aimed at combining school improvement with a more equitable racial mix. While the Boston area probably has a greater concentration of colleges and universities than any other metropolis in the country, a tradition of cooperation was as absent there as in most other places.

W. Arthur Garrity, Jr., the federal district judge, invited the presidents of higher education institutions to a breakfast one morning in 1974 to present his ideas for the venture. The presidents quickly realized, as if they were characters out of a page of Mario Puzo's *Godfather,* that it was "an offer they could not refuse." One president, slow to give his approval, was subsequently asked by someone close to the court what he thought the reaction in the black community might be if it were known that his institution, on the edge of the Roxbury ghetto, was not willing to join the cooperative plan. He quickly decided to lend his institution's participation.

The citywide results of the effort have been uneven, but at its best it has produced pairings like that between the Massachusetts Institute of Technology and the Mario Umana Harbor School of Science and Technology. The school opened in 1976, giving MIT a stake in it from the beginning. The Harbor School owes its existence to the court, because the judge ordered the Boston School Department to create the school as a magnet to attract students from throughout the city, thereby promoting voluntary racial integration. The school was established in a building that was scheduled to be a new neighborhood middle school; it was reclassified to meet the court mandate. It is a gray concrete structure, hunched along the shore, directly across the harbor from the shining skyscrapers of downtown Boston. Now, as a school of science and technology, serving students from the seventh through twelfth grades, it draws an enrollment of such geographic diversity that more than 900 of the 1,000 youngsters must be transported by bus from distances as far as an hour away. This in-gathering brings together a heterogeneous student body—47 percent black, 36 percent white, 9 percent Asian American and 8 percent Hispanic—that roughly equates the representation of each group in the citywide school enrollment. The proportions are maintained by a computer that selects the students from among some 3,000 who apply each year to enter the school at either the seventh or ninth grade.

At first, students applied to the school mainly because their parents thought it would be safer than most other schools, freer of the racial strife that characterized desegregation in Boston. Not that East Boston, with its largely low-economic, Italian American population, is a cradle of tolerance. But being in a new building, the Harbor School, unlike South Boston High School, for example, had no tie to its neighborhood and was not likely to be viewed as an institution severed from its constituency.

What caught on as a haven is now attractive to students principally because of its academic program. Students of junior high school age are presented with a curriculum in which, in addition to the usual courses, there is an introduction to each of the school's five special sequences—computer science, aviation, electronics, medical technology, and environmental protection. On reaching the high school level, the student selects one of the five areas as a major field to be pursued along with the normal secondary curriculum. MIT has played an important role in developing the technical courses, helping also to train teachers and aiding in the acquisition of equipment and material. An MIT staff member spends his entire time coordinating the activities involving the Institute and the school, and MIT students tutor at the Harbor School. In addition, one of MIT's graduate students is assigned to the school as an aide in the computer room.

The Harbor School would undoubtedly exist even if MIT had not offered its assistance, but the collaboration has made the school better than it would have been. Furthermore, MIT's imprimatur has helped draw students and has pushed open doors throughout the community that might have remained closed. "Just the influence of MIT's name on the phone gets the School Department to do things,"[19] said Gustave A. Anglin, a tall, soft-spoken former math teacher, who became headmaster of the school in 1977.

MIT and other colleges and universities aiding in the desegregation plan are paid by the state for the expenses they incur in connection with the contracts they have with the schools. But in a relationship such as the one that has evolved between MIT and the Harbor School, a great deal happens voluntarily and spontaneously. The monthly meetings at which MIT faculty members gather with teachers and administrators from the Harbor School are possible only because the professors, who normally get up to $100 an hour as industrial consultants, donate their time to the school. MIT also sends volunteer lecturers to the Harbor School and has cut red tape to allow students from the school to participate in a Saturday morning program and in seminars at the Institute's campus in Cambridge, on the Charles River.

A basic problem addressed by the collaboration is the same as that confronting the Partnership Program of the University of California, namely, making certain that a youngster gets a proper grounding in math and science so that he does not cut off his career options early in life. The need for such an approach is seen in statistics such as those showing that in 1973, among the nation's 51,920 freshman engineering students, 1.5 percent were Hispanics and 4.1 percent were blacks. The Alfred P. Sloan Foundation has zeroed in on the problem through its Minority Engineering Program, which began in 1973 and will end in 1983 with a cumulative expenditure of $13.1 million. In its unspectacular way the program has been one of the nation's better attempts to help minority members in a specific academic area. The effort has also reinforced the notion of having to reach down into the junior and senior high levels if progress is to be made at the collegiate level.

No magic wand is going to enable minority students or any other kinds of students to cope with an engineering curriculum if they have not been adequately prepared in the early grades. What Sloan did was sponsor the creation of six regional consortia across the United States. Engineering colleges, public school systems, industrial corporations, and community organizations merged their efforts in each of the endeavors. Typically, the programs have included counseling, tutoring, field trips, clubs, and motivational activities, often involving parents and teachers along with the junior and senior high school students.

Another major phase of the Sloan project has been the development of curriculum materials aimed specifically at minority students. This has been achieved through the foundation's support of the National Coordinating Center for Curriculum Development at the State University of New York at Stony Brook, on Long Island. The materials are concentrated on the junior high school level, emphasizing once again the need for early intervention. A measure of the effectiveness of the Sloan program is the increase in the number of black and Hispanic youths going into engineering. For both groups, the numbers receiving bachelor's degrees in engineering doubled between 1973 and 1980. On the other hand, figures indicate that members of minority groups are still more likely than white students to drop out or not complete their engineering studies. There is clearly much that remains to be done if the nation is to produce a steady flow of minority engineers in numbers approaching their proportion of the population. Perhaps one of the most valuable functions of the Sloan program has been its role as a model for demonstrating that certain educational problems resist solution until colleges and secondary schools work together.

A similar educational lesson is being taught in a converted industrial building tucked in among the factories and warehouses of the dingy manufacturing section of Queens known as Long Island City, just across the 59th Street Bridge from Manhattan. There, within sight of the graceful art deco spire of the distant Chrysler Building, is one of the nation's most unusual educational ventures, Middle College High School—an institution operating under the combined sponsorship of the New York City Board of Education and LaGuardia Community College of the City University of New York. Middle College admits its students directly from the ninth grade, providing them with a high school diploma and the option of continuing through the first two years of college and earning an associate's degree, all in one locale.

This is one of the best examples of a high school and a college merging their efforts in ways that cut to the core of each institution. The building housing most of the classes for the 440 high school students, a structure in which the Sony Corporation repairs appliances on the top floor, is an integral part of the college campus, directly across the street from the renovated factory (where precision craftsmen once fitted together Norden bomb sights) that has become the main building of LaGuardia Community College. High school students are issued college identification cards and circulate freely through all the facilities. The populations of both institutions are served by the same library, cafeteria, and gymnasium, for example. Because of the sharing, the students at Middle College High School take their laboratory science and studio art courses in college classrooms, affording them sophisticated settings to which they would not otherwise have access.

The idea underlying Middle College High School has to do with more than making better use of facilities, however. It is a high school for high-risk youngsters with college potential, students who in elementary school and junior high have not fulfilled their promise. Two-thirds of them enter Middle College High School reading two or more years below grade level and, if left to the vicissitudes of normal school life, would probably not complete high school, much less go to college. But being in the company of college students, who, by and large, come from the same backgrounds as the high school students, provides inspiration to the younger group. They come to realize that they, too, can aspire to higher education. College is a less forbidding place as it grows to be part of their everyday life. Middle College has few of the behavioral problems that would normally be expected in a high school with its kind of enrollment. The youths want to fit in and be accepted by the college students and they behave appropriately, eschewing the sort of misconduct that would brand them as juveniles unsuited to such an environment.

The arrangement between the two institutions has also helped to get high school teachers and college professors to accept one another, however hesitantly, an accomplishment akin to getting India and Pakistan to sign a friendship pact. In many parts of the country, the mutual distrust between those who teach at the two levels is a chief stumbling block to institutional cooperation. But LaGuardia Community College and Middle College High School have done better than most institutions. Arthur Greenberg, the high school principal, sits in academic meetings as an equal with department chairmen of the college. Teachers from the high school have adjunct appointments to the college faculty and college professors teach occasional courses in the high school.

All of the college level courses are open—with academic credit—to those high school students who have advanced far enough in their own curriculum and are able to handle the work. This means that the high school, not having to mount a wide array of advanced offerings, is able to concentrate a large part of its resources on remedial education for those at the lowest end of the spectrum. Thus, students often fill in gaps faster than they would in an ordinary high school, where their weaknesses would not get as much attention. The results of these efforts are on display at LaGuardia Community College, where graduates of Middle College High School turn out to be far less likely than graduates of other city high schools to need remediation.

Student services, too, benefit from the collaboration. The high school has only two counselors of its own because the 14 counselors at the college readily give their attention to students at the high school. Having access to the placement office of the college also helps the high school students in finding jobs and in applying to colleges. Since LaGuardia is a two-year college, and many of its graduates go on to four-year institutions, the advisers have a familiarity with higher education that is especially helpful to high school seniors choosing a college. The high school has, as well, modeled its cooperative career education program after the version fashioned by the college. Both institutions send their students to jobs and internships for at least a term each year, thereby stimulating student motivation by linking schoolwork to the work of making a living. This has helped produce at Middle College High School a dropout rate one-third the size of that at other high schools in New York City. The rate of daily attendance at the school also exceeds the city average even though Middle College's students are supposedly high-risk.

Being affiliated with an institution of higher education makes Middle College High School more sensitive to the academic demands that await its students in college. The goal of the high school is to ensure that its graduates are at least at a level that will enable them to cope with the LaGuardia Community College curriculum. "I want to make sure they are good representatives or I will hear about it,"[20] said Greenberg, an easy-going, bearded man, who, unlike most high school principals, has daily contact with the professors who teach the students he has been responsible for preparing for college. Eighty-five percent of Middle College's graduates go on to postsecondary education, about half to LaGuardia Community College, a progression that seems perfectly natural to them after constant exposure to the place. One of the advantages such college students enjoy is that of being able to continue to rely on the support system of friends and teachers that they have established in the high school.

Joseph Shenker, the entrepreneurial president of La-Guardia Community College, who was instrumental in organizing the high school in 1974, maintains that closer cooperation between secondary and higher education is the only way to attack the difficulties of inadequate academic preparation. "In the educational community, everyone blames everyone else," Shenker said. "The kindergarten blames the home. The elementary school blames the kindergarten. The junior high blames the elementary school. The high school blames the junior high and the college blames the high school. Let's stop the blaming and see what we can do about it. The division between high school and college is arbitrary. The reason one stops at the twelfth grade when students are seventeen and the other starts at the thirteenth grade when students are eighteen is more historical than educational."[21]

While Middle College High School is designed for the student who is not ordinarily considered college material, two other ventures at opposite ends of the country attempt to blend secondary and higher education for the benefit of the more academically inclined, students who might otherwise languish in the typical high school. One of them, Simon's Rock in Great Barrington, Massachusetts, began as an independent enterprise in 1966 and became a division of Bard College, across the state line in New York, in 1979. The other, Matteo Ricci, is a program operated by Seattle University and Seattle Preparatory School, two Jesuit institutions.

Students usually enter Simon's Rock directly from the

tenth or eleventh grade, going right into college-level work and earning an associate's degree in two or three years, allowing them to reach the junior year of college a year or two early. In 1980, Simon's Rock began accepting students from the ninth grade into a Transitional Studies Program that strengthens their background before they embark on college-level work. Virtually all of the almost 300 students at Simon's Rock are early college entrants, making the institution profoundly different from a typical college or university that simply submerges a few youngsters in a sea of older students. Unlike such institutions, Simon's Rock is able to make early entrance its raison d'être, addressing the special needs of the early entrance group. Counseling and advising, which usually get short shrift in higher education, have high priority at Simon's Rock, where members of the tiny faculty are accustomed to doing double duty as surrogate parents to youths living away from home at an age when most of their peers are still ensconced in the protective womb of the family. Officials at Simon's Rock devote considerable energy to juggling a set of rules that recognize both the need for self-reliance and the need for limits. One year recently it meant trying to keep good faith with the students while implementing a regulation banning overnight room visits by members of the opposite sex.

But imparting knowledge, not sexual mores, is the primary mission of Simon's Rock, and the school attempts to provide the intellectual stimulation that many of its students fled high school to seek. "I didn't like high school; I wasn't challenged at all," said Gina Wolf, a tall, black-haired 17-year-old who entered Simon's Rock in the fall of 1980 directly from the eleventh grade of her parochial school in Altoona, Pennsylvania. "I played sports in high school—volleyball and tennis—and that held my interest, but the teachers were teaching for a job, not to give knowledge. Kids were just staying in school because they didn't have anything else to do, not because they wanted to be there. At Simon's Rock, the teachers expect more, so you do more. There is something to work for."[22]

Simon's Rock is a place of rugged natural beauty, sprawled across 280 rolling, pine-covered acres in the foothills of the Berkshires in western Massachusetts, where its founder,

Elizabeth Blodgett Hall, hoped to provide young people with "a curriculum in line with the breadth of their intellectual interests and abilities."[23] The interdisciplinary approach is organized around seven major fields of study: arts and aesthetics, environmental studies, intercultural studies, literary studies, premedical studies, quantitative studies, and social science. It is a bold attempt to give teen-agers like Gina Wolf who find their needs unmet in high school a fresh way of pursuing their education. But because it has few models to follow and must learn from its own mistakes, Simon's Rock has still not succeeded in putting together a general education curriculum that satisfies its critics. Classes are small, but this is because the overtaxed faculty, burdened by the heavy responsibilities of counseling and advising, spread themselves thin as they each teach a wide variety of courses. Even with its imperfections, though, Simon's Rock, especially since its amalgamation with Bard College, remains a bright spot of innovation on a bleak horizon.

One reason Matteo Ricci College does not have some of the problems that still plague Simon's Rock is that, rather than being a separate, free-standing institution, it is a program of coordinated studies sponsored by two long-established institutions with sizable faculties that assist the program. Forty teachers from Seattle Prep are assigned exclusively to the lower division of the program and an equal number of university professors, borrowed for one to three courses a year, rotate through the upper division. About 20 percent of the entire faculty of Seattle University has taught in Matteo Ricci since it began in 1975. Students enter out of the eighth grade, following a closely prescribed curriculum that compresses the four high school years into three. Upon successful completion of what is known as Matteo Ricci College I, they are accepted virtually automatically into Seattle University for Matteo Ricci II, where they again pursue a curriculum that condenses four years of study into three. Most of the courses at both levels were created specifically for the interdisciplinary program, written from scratch by faculty from the two institutions.

Matteo Ricci and Simon's Rock are among the most comprehensive and far-reaching of the programs addressing the needs of students in the crucial years when high school blends into college. There are other ventures, more limited, that in their own ways also confront the challenge of making this period more productive for students. Project Advance of Syracuse University enables students to earn college credits in their high school classrooms for courses, taught by specially trained high school teachers, in seven different subjects. Each course follows the curriculum and uses the tests identical to freshman courses on the Syracuse campus in upstate New York. The academic credits, like those earned from any institution of higher education, can be transferred elsewhere. In northern Ohio, Kenyon College and six private preparatory schools are linked in a similar effort called School College Articulation Program. Like their counterparts at Syracuse, faculty members at Kenyon help train and supervise the secondary teachers who handle the courses to their specifications.

These programs are more ambitious than most. What passes as cooperation in most places is often no more than a high school letting the appropriate students leave the building for a couple of hours to take a course or two at a nearby college. This is fine, but it should not be confused with a carefully designed collaboration that is carried out with the commitment of both institutions. For the most resourceful students, it may be enough, though. Gard Clark took so many courses at Jamestown Community College while he was a student at Frewsburg High School in rural upstate New York that he was scheduled to receive both his high school diploma and his college associate's degree in 1981 at the age of 17. "When I started, I had it in mind that I might enjoy taking a college class and filling some time during the summer, but soon one course led to another," he said. It all began with a college algebra course that Gard took during the summer after he finished eighth grade. The next spring, while he was in the ninth grade, he took another college math course at night, and then in the summer after completing the ninth grade he enrolled at the college for courses in calculus and computer science. While attending the tenth and eleventh grades, he continued his college education at night and over the summers, reaching the point by his senior year in high school that he was able to divide his time during the day between the two institutions. "Doing it that way," Gard said, "I was able to keep my old friends in high school while making new ones in college. And I didn't have to miss the senior year, which is a pretty big thing."[24]

The nation's largest program offering college-level work to high school students is not affiliated with any particular institution of higher education and carries no guarantee of college credit. It is the Advanced Placement program of the College Entrance Examination Board and, in one way or another, most colleges and universities extend some sort of recognition to students who get high enough scores on the tests given at the end of the courses. If the students do not actually receive academic credits, they do often get certain requirements waived or proceed directly into sophomore-level courses. Advanced Placement began in 1955, allowing students to pursue college-level work in their high school classrooms at a time when high schools were still very leery of the idea of letting their students break out of the academic lockstep. What won credibility for the program and ultimately made it successful was the use of nationally administered tests that imposed a single standard on all students. Advanced Placement is now so well established that 119,918 students in 4,950 high schools sat for the examinations during the 1979–80 academic year, when the results were submitted to 1,868 institutions of higher education.[25] Tests are administered in eleven fields—biology, chemistry, English, French, German, history, Latin, mathematics, music, physics, and Spanish—and portfolios are evaluated in art. Most important of all, a student's education is enriched and needless duplication may be avoided.

HELPING THE GIFTED

All of these programs—Advanced Placement, Project Advance and even Simon's Rock and Matteo Ricci—are for able, motivated students. Some of the participants are gifted, but most are not; they are high achievers who are not served fully by the regular high school curriculum. The situation is more troublesome for the gifted, who need enrichment earlier and in a more organized and deliberate fashion than is available in most schools. For gifted children, knowledge is its own reward. Creativity is often their hallmark. From the very beginning, they are unlike other children in the classroom. Their attention span is longer, their learning rate is faster, their potential for abstraction is greater, their sensitivity is keener, and their need for exploration in depth is overwhelming. Their drive for perfection makes them fearful of mistakes and they are discomfited by their own mental capabilities, which they do not yet comprehend.

New and challenging educational approaches are needed for teaching the gifted, but innovations are slow in coming. The gifted continue to be banished to seats at the back of the educational bus. Mythology has it that they will thrive regardless of whether or not they get special attention. There are all too many indications, though, that this is not true; giftedness unnurtured can wilt like a flower without rain. Champions of increased funding for the gifted face formidable obstacles, the most stubborn of which is the charge of "elitism." Egalitarianism is the order of the day, and the idea of giving extra help to those who are already ahead of the pack strikes critics as akin to allowing 7-foot Kareem Abdul-Jabbar to wear stilts on the basketball court. Many parents of gifted children, intimidated by this mood, are resigned to making few demands.

The shortcomings of high school for the ordinary student are multiplied for the gifted. A student like Rachel Davis had given up on high school by the end of the tenth grade. She was an oddball in Mount Olive, a little tobacco-raising town in central North Carolina, where intellectual isolation was a special kind of torture. It was so bad for her that she stopped trying, failing five of her six tenth-grade subjects, and was ready to drop out of school. "I had a reputation as a smart aleck," said Rachel, a sweet-faced young woman with straight brown hair. "Agriculture was the most popular course in the school and there I was with all those ideas in my head. The other kids just weren't interested in what I was interested in. I was a freak."[26]

Fortunately for Rachel Davis, she got the chance in the fall of 1980 to attend a unique high school, where she discovered other young people with the same ideas bouncing around their heads. She was among 150 teen-agers brought together from cities and villages throughout the state to form the first class for the new North Carolina School of Science and Mathematics. It is the nation's only state-sponsored, residential public high school for the gifted, a place where students are provided with room and board and no fees are charged. It is a school at which young people like Rachel can pursue the sort of programs that the high schools in their hometowns cannot afford because they do not have enough advanced students to warrant the expense. Moreover, the climate breeds an air of common purpose that could not exist at a typical high school with a more representative enrollment.

The school was created by the legislature on the site of a former county hospital in Durham. It is a quiet, wooded spot, a natural place for a campus, where nursing wards and operating rooms have been converted to classrooms, laboratories, and dormitories. All of this has been done so that the students —eventually there will be 750 to 900 of them—could be assembled and confronted with the challenge of a curriculum capable of stretching them to the limits of their ability. "It seemed like my high school was for the mediocre," said Marshall Mauney, who grew up in the mountainous western part of the state. "The level of the courses didn't compare with what we were given here and there was no incentive. Instead of studying, I played the guitar with a band and my grades were on the borderline."[27] But his score on the Scholastic Aptitude Test, which he took as a tenth-grader as part of the entrance test for the School of Science and Mathematics, was 1,410, more than 500 points above the typical high school senior and good enough to get into the Ivy League.

Without such an opportunity as they are getting at the school for the gifted, students like Marshall Mauney and Rachel Davis might never realize their potential. Many of the students at the school tell of having been able to slide through their hometown high schools without studying. Usually, they were bored and restless. When Carolyn Knowlton, another of the students, was in junior high in Fayetteville, she wanted to take algebra, but was told she would not be permitted to enroll in the course because she was too young. There are no such barriers at a school for the gifted, where youth is not seen as an impediment in the search for knowledge. Students at the North Carolina School of Science and Mathematics have the advantage of a faculty that has voluntarily committed itself to work evenings and weekends to exploit the school's residential character.

"At a regular high school," said Dwaine Raiford, one of the 25 percent of the students at the school from minority groups, "you go to classes from 8:15 till 3:30, you go home and you don't study much. Here, the teachers are right on hand and there is no problem finding someone to help you at night. We had an advanced program at home, but compared to this, it was slight. The teachers there were good, but they didn't have this kind of an environment to work in."[28]

At the School of Science and Mathematics, the milieu is one in which disruptive behavior in class is virtually unknown. Students are attentive and teachers, who share a sense of dedication with the students, use a patient, probing style, lecturing extemporaneously and leading students on explorations that take them far beyond the borders of their textbooks. "Our goal is to let these kids have fun in science and be enthusiastic about it,"[29] said Rufus Owens, a chemistry teacher with ten years of classroom experience and a doctorate from Duke University. Owens, a small, bespectacled man with thinning brown hair, keeps his class engaged in the lesson by directing a steady flow of questions at them. Often, it gets the students asking their own questions, opening new avenues of inquiry. "It's only recently been possible to count molecules," Owens tells the students as he paces among them. "How do they count molecules?" a student asks. Owens responds with a brief description of the workings of Geiger counters and electrical currents. Then, in his soft Southern drawl, he is introducing the students to Avogadro's law, the theory of a 19th-century Italian scientist that equal volumes of gases, measured at the same temperature and pressure, contain the same number of molecules.

This is what can be done for gifted students when they

are not numbed into inattentiveness. It can be accomplished in North Carolina and anywhere else that educational institutions are willing to commit themselves to the task. What students of all levels of ability need is a willingness by policy makers to unclog the rivers of possibilities that ought to be opened to young people when they reach their middle teens. The waters should be stirred so that a natural flow connects high school, college, and the world of work, permitting youths to move back and forth as they progress into adulthood. There should be formal mechanisms, for instance, to make certain that community colleges readily and eagerly admit high school dropouts with poor academic records, giving them combined high school–college programs so that they are no longer penalized for what went wrong in the early years of their education. It means support by high schools for students who feel constrained by the curriculum.

There is no place in the 1980s for the kind of thinking exhibited by officials of Hamilton Township High School in southwestern Ohio as recently as 1977, when they reluctantly agreed to let Kimberly Clark complete her diploma requirements early, but refused—until ordered by a court—to allow her to participate in the commencement ceremony. After all, she had entered the school with a class that was not scheduled to graduate until the following year. Imagine the audacity of a student who cared so little for the sense of order that she wanted to get her diploma early and even make a public spectacle of the deed.

CHAPTER SEVEN

TEACHERS

CHEERS, TEARS, FEARS, AND JEERS

A teacher affects eternity;
he can never tell where his influence stops.

HENRY ADAMS
The Education of Henry Adams

The headquarters of the National Education Association, the organization that represents 1.8 million of the country's teachers, is just five blocks from the White House. On the last Friday in September, 1979, the morning of the 18th, the distance between the two buildings seemed to disappear. It was the day that Jimmy Carter and his friends from the NEA celebrated one of the premier accomplishments of American political lobbying: the creation of the U.S. Department of Education, a plum the size of a watermelon. The small band of NEA staff members who left the headquarters building early that Friday morning and sauntered down 16th Street toward Pennsylvania Avenue were exhilarated with their sense of triumph. A compromise bill approving the Department of Education as the thirteenth Cabinet post had won final passage in Congress the previous day. Now, all that remained before the establishment of the department was the signature of President Carter —and that was as certain as the NEA's endorsement of Carter in the 1980 election.

It was a cocky group of NEA political operatives who made their way to the White House that morning, joking and wisecracking as they strolled by the Russian Embassy, the Capital-Hilton, the Sheraton-Carlton, and other staid institutions lining 16th Street. Near Lafayette Park, within sight of the north portico of the White House, they passed the offices of the AFL-CIO, the bastion of organized labor, where one of the group made an obscene gesture as if to say, "We won and you lost." The American Federation of Labor–Congress of Industrial Organizations and its teachers' union, the American Federation of Teachers, had not supported the establishment of the Education Department. The AFT was not about to endorse a pet project of its arch rival, particularly when that project was intended by the NEA to demonstrate how much power it could wield.

When they reached the White House, the NEA staff members joined more than 100 members of the group's board of directors and other NEA officials in the East Room, where they were to be addressed by President Carter. It was a gathering predestined from the moment in 1976 when the NEA broke its nonpartisan tradition of more than a century to make its first endorsement in a presidential election, stamping its imprimatur on the Democratic standard-bearer from Georgia, who promised in return to work for the creation of a Cabinet post for education. It was a quid pro quo of the sort to bring smiles to the ghosts of Tammany.

The battle was arduous, particularly in the House of Representatives, where dubious Congressmen wondered why the needs of schools and colleges could not continue to be met through the Office of Education, a longstanding division of the Department of Health, Education, and Welfare. The margin of passage in the House was 210 to 206 on the original bill, and 215 to 201 on the compromise. But Jimmy Carter was able to deliver his payoff to the organization that had sent thousands of campaign workers into the field on behalf of his bid for the presidency.

While the rank and file milled about the East Room that autumn morning, the upper echelon of the NEA leadership waited eagerly in the lobby outside the State Dining Room, beneath watchful portraits of Presidents past, for Mr. Carter to arrive from the west wing so that they could accompany him into the East Room in triumphant procession. Someone was clutching a copy of the *Washington Star,* whose headline proclaimed, "Carter Wins Education Dept." As soon as the President stepped from the elevator that had brought him from the Oval Office, the celebrants gathered around him and Rosalynn, displaying the newspaper and posing for a quick round of photographs—Mr. and Mrs. Carter, NEA President Willard H. McGuire, NEA Vice President Bernard Freitag, and NEA Executive Director Terry Herndon. Then, all smiles, they strode together through the Cross Hall, past the Red Room, the Blue Room and the Green Room, and into the East Room, where Jimmy Carter and the NEA representatives basked in their shared glory. Shortly after leaving the White House that day, the NEA board of directors endorsed the President's unannounced candidacy for renomination.

IN UNION THERE IS STRENGTH

The love-in between the White House and the NEA symbolized the increased political influence of teachers in the United States. Politicians from the president on down assiduously court the endorsements of the NEA and the only other major teachers' organization, the AFT. And top officials of both groups dispense their recognition in the manner of ward bosses conferring indulgences. Few candidates for public office dare get on the wrong side of groups they believe can marshal large blocs of voters, as the two teacher unions claim to be able to do. The NEA, for instance, boasts that it has members in every congressional district in the country, an omnipotence shared by few other membership organizations. The strength of the smaller AFT is concentrated in the large cities, but the ability to turn out voters in places like New York, Philadelphia, Chicago, New Orleans, St. Louis, and Cleveland is not taken lightly by office seekers in those locales.

The goal of organized teachers, like organized workers of any sort, is power—the ability to win concessions that are in the interests of the members. Those who enact and administer the laws are in the best position to help teachers, and so the

NEA's entry into presidential-level politics was the natural culmination of its enlarging involvement in elections for Congress and the state legislatures. Such U.S. senators as Claiborne Pell of Rhode Island, Howard Baker of Tennessee, and Max Baucus of Montana have made no secret of their appreciation of the NEA's role in helping them attain election victories in their home states. When Jimmy Carter journeyed to the NEA's national convention in the summer of 1976 seeking support in his quest to reach the White House, the NEA was ready to go all the way and back a presidential candidate who sympathized with its ambitions, particularly the desire for a Department of Education. It did not harm Carter to have as his running mate Walter Mondale, who had a long history of cooperation with the NEA and whose brother, William, known as Mort, was president of the NEA in Minnesota. Mort Mondale was later transferred to NEA headquarters in Washington, just up the street from where his brother, the Vice President, was working.

By 1980, the NEA was so deeply immersed in politics that its members were able to gain about ten percent of the 3,331 delegate positions at the Democratic National Convention, providing a crucial bloc of votes for Jimmy Carter's renomination fight with Edward M. Kennedy. No other single group was better represented at Madison Square Garden, and it was in recognition of this newly won clout that the NEA's Terry Herndon was chosen to introduce Vice President Mondale to the convention for his acceptance speech. NEA volunteers were in the vanguard of the Carter-Mondale campaign throughout the primaries and into the fall of 1980. The NEA's political action committee during 1979 and 1980 was also pumping money into the campaigns of friends running for Congress, including such recipients as Michigan's Howard Wolpe ($8,000), Pennsylvania's Robert Edgar ($4,500), and Texas's Jack Brooks, and Vermont's Patrick Leahy ($3,000).[1] The AFT, which had backed Senator Kennedy before the convention, shifted to President Carter after he won renomination and, along with the NEA, threw its support into the unsuccessful reelection struggle.

The NEA and the AFT are the Hertz and Avis of education, competitors difficult to tell apart. They vie for the right to represent teachers in contract negotiations, but both want essentially the same benefits for their members. Yet, they must appear somewhat different if there is to be a rationale for their separate existence. Thus, when the NEA promoted the idea of a separate Cabinet-level Department of Education, the AFT opposed it. When the NEA linked its fortunes to Jimmy Carter in the 1980 Democratic primary elections, the AFT endorsed Kennedy. This is not to say necessarily that if the NEA had taken different positions the AFT would have backed the Department of Education and favored President Carter in the primaries. But the NEA's role certainly made the AFT predisposed to go in the opposite direction. Edward B. Fiske has observed that "if the NEA came out in favor of lunch pails, the AFT would oppose them."[2]

As it happens, the AFT was probably right about the Department of Education, as unneeded a Cabinet agency as ever there has been. Ronald Reagan's instinct was correct in feeling that the agency was unneeded. It is as if the NEA decided to seek a Department of Education simply to show that it had enough influence to get what it wanted. The Office of Education within the former Department of Health, Education, and Welfare served the nation's educational needs at the federal level quite adequately. Most of the new Department's expenditures are decided not by the policies of its Secretary, but by automatic funding formulas that could be overseen by a battalion of clerks. When the Department of Education began with a budget of some $14 billion, more than one-third of the money was accounted for by two programs, the $3 billion Title I of the Elementary and Secondary Education Act and the $2.4 billion Basic Educational Opportunity Grants. Both programs were bookkeeping exercises to distribute funds to which the recipients were entitled automatically by virtue of financial need.

Joseph A. Califano, Jr., the former Secretary of HEW, was not sympathetic to the idea of yanking the "E" out of his agency and making it a separate department. His attitude helped cost him his job when President Carter decided to dismiss several Cabinet officers midway through his term, a bit of window-dressing that did nothing to improve the merchandise in the store. Califano was convinced that the creation of the Department of Education was just one more instance of office holders bowing to pressure. Reflecting on the situation after he had left government, Califano commented: "We have a government plagued by special interests and the problem will be aggravated here because the special interest isn't even the group to be served, the children, but the NEA."[3]

History has shaped the NEA and the AFT differently. Like brothers raised in separate households, they bear a resemblance, but have acquired attributes that set them apart. The American Federation of Teachers is a product of trade unionism, incubated in the womb of the American Federation of Labor. Its heritage is the cacophony of the streets, where its members learned early to join their brothers and sisters in strident expressions of solidarity. The NEA was fashioned from different cloth, a mantle to the educational establishment from the time of its founding in 1857 under the guidance of respected members of the profession. Its way was that of polite conversation over tea, partaken of by men and women with proper manners. The NEA was late in adopting a forceful stance because for most of its existence it viewed itself as a professional organization, more like the American Medical Association than like the United Auto Workers. Members of the NEA would no sooner have walked a picket line than have made a pilgrimage to Red Square. The NEA even accepted principals and superintendents into its ranks.

The AFT was seen as an upstart bunch of unruly radicals who tarnished the reputation of teachers. The NEA collaborated with the movers and shakers, sponsoring momentous studies, issuing somber statements. The NEA was the palatable alternative to trade unionism for those who could not imagine themselves part of a movement that included steelworkers, truck drivers, and day laborers. The AFT provided the initial militancy that propelled teachers into collective bargaining. The AFT was firmly ensconced in the labor movement while the NEA was still suspiciously eying unionism as a peril to the classroom teacher. And within the AFT, it was Local 2 in New York City, the United Federation of Teachers, that set the beacon by which teachers throughout the country gauged their course toward activism. The contract signed between the city and the UFT in 1963 was a historic document, the first comprehensive negotiated labor agreement on behalf of teachers anywhere in the United States.

Technically, the United Federation of Teachers is a unit of the national union, the AFT, but if ever a dog was wagged by its tail, this is surely such an animal. The UFT and its sister groups in the New York State United Teachers organization account for more than 40 percent of the AFT's entire membership, placing the center of power at the UFT's Park Avenue headquarters in New York City, not at the AFT's national office in Washington. The AFT was a national union in search of a constituency until collective bargaining spread out of New York and into other big cities, where the affiliation with the AFL-CIO gave the AFT an entree to labor-oriented urban teachers. In 1974, Albert Shanker, the dominant figure in New York City's UFT, added the presidency of the national union to his collection of titles. It was a mere formality, because Shanker by then was in all but official designation the national chief of the union.

Power is the lubricant of Albert Shanker's soul, and he exercises it with the benign despotism of all great union leaders. "Power is a good thing; it's better than powerlessness," he once said.[4] Shanker's influence has spread through a weekly column carrying his picture that runs as a paid advertisement in the *New York Times* on Sundays. It is so popular that the *Times* has listed it in the index it distributes to libraries, a distinction accorded to probably no other advertisement. A skilled debater and a deft bargainer, Shanker has been an effective advocate for all teachers. Despite his often dour visage, he has a quick wit and appreciates levity. One day, for example, he walked past a leftist demonstrator who was handing out leaflets and repeating the title: "Is There an Alternative to Shankerism?" The mischievous Shanker could not resist the opportunity. He approached the man, listened to him repeat the slogan and said, "For me, there's no alternative."[5]

Indeed there isn't. And countless teachers around the country found during the 1970s that for them there was also no alternative to militancy. The NEA was influenced by the AFT and eventually became every bit as much of a union and as thoroughly militant, though the NEA never joined the AFL-CIO. For all teachers, however, whether in the NEA or the AFT, it became clear that only by organizing would they win the basic rights to which workers are entitled. Until organizing began, each teacher had been on her own in dealing with school officials. "Her" in this case because until 1950, women comprised 78.7 percent of the teaching force in elementary and secondary schools. They were women who were expected to remain prim and preferably unmarried, devoting their lives to their pupils. If a teacher happened to marry, she certainly was supposed to know better than to show up pregnant in front of a room full of students. Not only was a teacher dropped from the payroll at the first sign of pregnancy, but she was also denied benefits accorded to other kinds of medical leaves. It took a ruling by the U.S. Supreme Court in 1974 to establish the right of teachers to maternity leave, as well as the right to begin it when they wanted.[6]

That teachers were so bullied was in keeping with the prevalent attitude that self-denial was the sine qua non of a schoolteacher's life. It was a prudish existence not far removed from that of the men of an earlier era who arrived penniless in the New World as indentured servants, obligated to teach children of the landed gentry in exchange for their eventual freedom. Josiah Royce, the philosopher, wrote in 1883 that a teacher might find "that his non-attendance in church, or the fact that he drinks beer with his lunch, or rides a bicycle is considered of more moment than his power to instruct."[7] One can almost visualize those risqué teachers, taking clandestine spins on their satanic bicycles. It was not until more than half-way through this century that teachers began to shake free of the rigid codes of conduct imposed on them by school boards and administrators. One teacher, Minnich Revonna, remembered that when she started teaching in a small Oklahoma town in the mid-1950s she was told where to live, not to use tobacco or alcohol, not to get involved in politics, and to attend church regularly. Add the bicycle restriction and it might as well have been the teacher whom Royce was describing three-quarters of a century later.

Just how much times have changed would have been evident to a visitor to Iowa in the winter of 1979–80, when thousands of elementary and secondary school teachers, NEA members from throughout the state, fanned out in canvassing the 2,500 precincts that eventually gave a majority of their delegate votes to Jimmy Carter. What was happening in Iowa was the result of a loosening of fetters during the previous two decades, when teachers came to realize that if they had wanted to live in monasteries they could have joined religious orders. Fortified in their resolve by increasing numbers of men who were entering the profession, veteran teachers joined younger ones in asserting the rights that had been trammeled for so long. Often, they turned to the courts for protection. In Illinois, a court ordered a teacher reinstated after he had been dismissed for writing a letter to a newspaper criticizing the school board.[8] In Mississippi, a court declared a regulation invalid after it had been used to block the appointment of a teacher who was the mother of an illegitimate child.[9] In Georgia, a court ordered a school board to rehire a teacher who had been fired for living in a commune.[10]

Between them, the National Education Association and the American Federation of Teachers have inalterably changed the circumstances of the nation's schoolteachers, giving them the boost they needed to win dignity, better pay, and job security. The question now, though, is whether the tables have been turned so far that there are no longer places at them for the students. The bargaining power that teachers gained during the 1960s and 1970s came at the expense of almost everyone else who had anything to do with the schools. The authority of principals, superintendents, and school boards was weakened. Exacerbating the situation was the fact that teachers asserted themselves at the same time that the courts, state legislatures, Congress, and federal agencies were undercutting school officials. The cumulative impact of these shifts in power has been to make it more difficult to run the schools effectively.

LOSS OF MANAGEMENT CONTROL

Principals, who are supposed to provide the leadership in each school building, have suffered most. Rendered impotent by a straitjacket of regulations and contractual restrictions, principals find it harder to maneuver. "The combination of judicial restraints and concessions to the teachers' union has eroded almost to the vanishing point the ability of principals to manage their personnel," William Raspberry remarked in the *Washington Post.*[11] What provoked Raspberry's comment was the loss by principals in Washington of the ability to choose their teachers, a development owing to union seniority rules and a court order that teachers at different steps on the salary schedule be dispersed in ways that equalized expenditures among schools. Leadership requires making the best of circumstances, but a principal unable to select any of his staff may be without a built-in source of support for his programs.

What is happening is that those who ostensibly set policy and administer the schools have lost many of their prerogatives. They are left holding a steering wheel unattached to the chassis. And like an automobile out of control, the schools sometimes veer aimlessly. Increasingly, one aspect of the program after another is placed beyond the purview of school officials—class size, the length of the school day, lesson plans, teacher assignments. It is no great surprise that teachers want more influence over the conditions in which they work. A school district errs if it fails to involve teachers in formulating decisions that affect the classroom. It has been amply demonstrated that teachers teach best when they believe in what they are doing. But it is quite another matter for elected and appointed policy makers to be stripped of authority over the enterprise they are supposed to be running.

The unremitting battle by organized teachers in New Jersey to expand the scope of collective bargaining illustrates the problem that school boards have in trying to stay in control. Collective bargaining came to New Jersey in 1968 with the passage of an enabling act by the legislature. By 1974, teachers had gotten the state's legislators to expand the list of negotiable items to include a wide number of areas that would seriously undercut the ability of school boards to set policy and the opportunity for superintendents and principals to administer. A landmark decision by the New Jersey Supreme Court in 1978, however, held that school boards were negotiating away many powers that the legislators had never actually authorized them to give to teachers.[12]

Apparently, New Jersey's school board members were not the only ones in the country who were so generous with teachers. A study has shown that school boards in other states have also bargained away authority in excess of what was permitted by law. One can only speculate on the reasons for such largesse, but in all likelihood, these school boards were either inept or intimidated. New Jersey's school boards were directed as a result of the court ruling to limit their bargaining to matters involving hours of work, compensation, and fringe benefits. Once again, after 1978, school boards were to remain responsible for such items as teacher assignment, class size, curriculum, decisions to reschedule snow days, the formulation of lesson plans, productivity studies, qualifications for employment and promotion, testing, and the use of teacher aides.

Yet, in each legislative session since then, lobbyists for the teachers have persuaded lawmakers to introduce bills that would rescind the court decision and reopen the way to widening the scope of issues on which teachers could legally bargain. The New Jersey School Boards Association, referring to one of the latest in a series of unsuccessful attempts by teachers to wipe out the court verdict, said in 1980: "Enactment of this bill would overturn a decision of the Supreme Court which specifically prohibited bargaining on such subjects. At that time, the Supreme Court of New Jersey declared, 'the interests of teachers do not always coincide with the interests of students.' Board members not only make the decisions based upon the needs of the students, but also seek public input and are ultimately responsible to the public."[13]

A question arising ever more frequently across the country these days is whether board members and administrators can ever regain their lost powers. The outlook is dim. After a particularly long and bitter teachers' strike in the fall of 1978 in Levittown, New York, on Long Island, the *New York Times,* in a front-page story, hailed the ostensibly tough stance of Levittown's school board as a sign of a new determination by school boards to hold the line against the demands of teacher unions. The article cited settlements by other school boards in New York State and Connecticut as further examples of this hardened position. "School boards have seen the wisdom of standing up to union pressure," the newspaper quoted Richard L. Ornauer, president of the school boards association on Long Island.[14]

The kudos was premature. Neither the terms of the settlement nor the special nature of the schools in Levittown warranted the contention that this was a model of school board resistance. To be sure, it was an important event, as would be the resolution of any strike in which 14,000 students missed 34 days of instruction. And it occurred in the quintessential suburb, a community that rose from the potato fields in the wake of World War II to give returning veterans tiny Cape Cod houses for $7,000. Quiet and free of pollution, Levittown was a pleasant spot for middle-class families to raise their children. But gradually they started paying higher and higher prices for their Shangri-la on the plains of central Long Island. There is virtually no business or industry to fatten the tax rolls in Levittown, and the burden has fallen entirely on the hapless homeowners, who have ended up with higher tax rates than those who own homes in the other 55 school districts of Nassau County. But not enough revenue has been generated to enable the Levittown school system to lift the salaries of its teachers above the county's lowest range.

The teachers felt justified in striking for better pay and many of the residents sympathized with them. Some teachers, feeling guilty over robbing the children of instruction, even offered classes in the basements of some homes during the strike. But what are the taxpayers to do when taxes have already soared to exorbitant levels? Both sides—teachers and taxpayers—were "right." To assert, though, that this was a victory for the taxpayers is to overlook the terms of the settlement. Yes, the teachers agreed to freeze their salaries during the first year and a half of the four-year contract, but for the remainder of the period they were to get raises totaling 14 percent. In addition, provisions for their job security were strengthened, and they kept health and welfare benefits that the school board had tried to get them to give up.

What the experience in Levittown and in some other school districts that recently have undergone wrenching negotiations indicates is that during the leaner years of the 1980s teachers will find it increasingly difficult to get the kinds of raises to which they became accustomed in the past two decades. But if school boards cannot produce salary increases they are going to be under tremendous new pressure to yield to teachers on other fronts. Thus, the temptation will be to give teachers, in lieu of more money, strengthened job security provisions and greater control over items pertaining to the classroom. It will be argued that such concessions can be made at little cost to the taxpayers. Just how much the cost will be to the pupils in terms of the inability of principals and other supervisors to exercise control over their education is incalculable.

Educators have yet to gain a full understanding of the consequences of union power. One of the most important studies of the impact of collective bargaining on the schools, conducted by the Rand Corporation, concluded that, "because of contractual provisions regulating teacher working conditions, principals have less latitude than before in managing their own buildings." It added, though, that "collective bargaining does not seem to have affected significantly either classroom operations or the quality of educational services that teachers provide to students."[15]

Obviously, teachers are concerned about the viability of the schools since that is where they earn their livelihood. But that need not mean that the interests of teachers and students always coincide, as the New Jersey Supreme Court noted. The Rand study found that teacher-evaluation procedures were mentioned in 65 percent of the contracts. The more control teachers have over their own evaluations, the more difficult it will be to remove those who are inept. School hours were the subject of 58 percent of the contracts. Neither teachers nor any other workers seek more hours on the job, but shorter work days and fewer weeks given to instruction cannot possibly accrue to the benefit of students. Criteria affecting the transfer of teachers from school to school and the right of teachers to refuse reassignment were covered in almost 30 percent of the contracts. Such provisions undoubtedly complicate efforts to deploy staff in ways that serve the needs of students. Language regarding class size was contained in 34 percent of the contracts. While it seems reasonable to assign fewer youngsters to each teacher, provisions of this sort frequently thwart flexibility in staffing.

Retaining the Bad Apples

The wording of contracts is not all that ties the hands of school officials. Most states have an elaborate body of law affecting the employment conditions of teachers, especially in connection with grounds for dismissal. The unreasonable intrusions into the lives of teachers show that they need protection from arbitrary dismissals, but attempts to remedy the old problem have created a new one. It is called "tenure." What it means is that after a stated length of time on the job, usually about three to five years, the teacher is locked into his position by laws so secure that not even a Houdini could extricate him.

Dismissing a tenured teacher is so difficult that many school districts do not bother trying. Frustrated school officials have seen too many situations like the one in Norwalk, Ohio, where the school system found itself spending thousands of dollars on legal fees, generating testimony that ran almost 1,000 pages, in a failed effort to fire a high school mathematics teacher who allegedly could not maintain discipline in her classroom. A court-appointed referee declared that the school system had not shown that the teacher's performance had been "grossly inefficient" and therefore recommended that her contract not be terminated.[16]

Teachers should have safeguards. Their continued employment should be based on their ability to run a classroom and teach, not on their personal beliefs or their styles of life. As it is, ten states still have no tenure laws, and teachers in those states tread a precarious path between discharging their duties responsibly and pleasing community members whose concerns may be peripheral to education. But tenure laws all too often do not operate in the public interest. "Only when teachers are guilty of the most bizarre indiscretions can you get them out quickly," said Richard T. Olcott, former acting superintendent in New Rochelle, a Westchester County suburb. "Otherwise, the best you can do is try to counsel them out of the system or, if that fails, move them to the least harmful position."[17]

Almost every parent knows of an incompetent teacher. But defining incompetence is like trying to pick up a glob of Jell-o. Teaching is more art than science; much of what takes place in the relationship between teacher and student does not lend itself to objective evaluation. There is not even agreement on the connection between what teachers teach and what pupils learn. Yet, the issue of incompetence persists. A poll of the nation's school superintendents ranked the "dismissal of incompetent staff" as a problem exceeded in importance only by those involving finance, curriculum planning, and public confidence.[18]

Esther P. Rothman, a veteran New York City teacher and principal, believes that tenure has kept thousands of teachers in the classroom who should not be teaching. "I have seen teachers defended by their unions who should not be defended—a teacher who for years regularly came to school drunk, a teacher who was absent forty Mondays of each school year, a teacher who was excessively late almost every day of the term, a teacher who frequently lost control in his classes and became violent, a teacher who actively hallucinated," she said.[19] During his first two years as chancellor of the New York City schools, from 1978 to 1980, Frank J. Macchiarola said that the system, which has more than 50,000 teachers, was able to dismiss only two for incompetence.[20] Being told of this statement, Albert Shanker responded that Macchiarola ought to hire better lawyers.[21] But what is a school system to do, even with the best legal counsel, if tenure laws make it more complicated to get rid of a teacher than it is to bring about a corporate merger. Immorality is mentioned more often in state laws than any other cause as a bonafide reason for dismissal. Terrific. That means it would not be terribly difficult to remove a teacher who raped a student in the main corridor while classes were changing. What about plain old ineptitude? What about men and women who are paradigms of rectitude but utter failures as teachers?

A study of a single state, Pennsylvania, between 1971 and 1976, gives some indication of how few teachers are removed for outright incompetence. During the five-year period in Pennsylvania, only eleven cases of dismissal for incompetence at the school district level were appealed for adjudication to the state's Secretary of Education. Presumably, these were virtually all of the formal dismissals in the state, because if there had been others they almost certainly would have been appealed, according to Henry J. Finlayson, the Pennsylvania school administrator who conducted the study.[22] Six of the eleven cases contained such additional charges as cruelty, violation of school laws, persistent negligence, and immorality, leaving only five cases strictly involving incompetence. Three of the five incompetence dismissals were upheld, but one of the three should probably have been brought as insubordination, since it concerned a teacher who had refused to obey a school board order to shave off his beard. Thus, there were apparently only two teachers removed through formal procedures purely for the reason of incompetence in the entire state of Pennsylvania during a period of five years. The record in most other states is similar.

Unions cannot be faulted for protecting their members and making it difficult to fire them. That is a function of organized labor. If it is hard to get rid of incompetent teachers, much of the blame must rest with those who enacted unreasonable laws, namely, state legislators, and those who appointed the teachers, namely, school board members. Legislators have bowed to the pressure of teachers in adopting impractical regulations. And board members have failed to take advantage of the probationary period that precedes tenure to assess novices and get rid of unpromising ones. School boards have not made certain that the supervisors they employ are given adequate time for this important responsibility. "The typical high school principal with 70 to 75 teachers doesn't have time to supervise them," Shanker said.[23]

If tenure is to be awarded only to the deserving, it is

essential that principals evaluate their new teachers and report the findings to the superintendent and his staff. A school board that confers tenure on a teacher whose performance has not been subjected to rigorous scrutiny is not fulfilling its obligation to the public. "Most districts make virtually no investment in the evaluation of teacher performance," said the NEA's Mr. Herndon,[24] who maintains that the procedures on the books are adequate for dealing with incompetence if school districts would take more care in their initial appointments. Shanker adds that the statistics showing that few teachers are dismissed for incompetence are misleading, asserting that many cases are resolved when inept teachers are confronted with the facts and resign rather than submit to formal charges. "If you have a principal who wants to remove a teacher, he can make life very difficult for that teacher,"[25] Shanker insisted, though many principals might suggest that the union leader was giving them credit for more power than they possess.

During these days when confidence in the public schools is lower than the Chrysler Corporation's profit curve, the image of public education is not bolstered by the failure of schools to act more decisively on the problem of teacher incompetence. Parents know that private and parochial schools —where teachers are not covered by most state regulations affecting teachers in the public schools—will not tolerate some of the abuses common in the public schools. The onus is on officials of public school districts to find ways to work more effectively with the existing statutes, as it is unlikely that legislatures will relax the laws and make it easier to remove incompetent teachers. But efforts to keep closer tabs on teachers should not be directed solely toward their dismissal. Preferably, school districts that find teachers with problems will help them cope and improve their performance to acceptable levels. Having made such an attempt, the districts will also have a better case against a teacher if he does not improve. "As the law stands, principals in any state who wish to recommend the discharge of incompetent or unfit teachers should keep substantial written files,"[26] said Suzanne H. McDaniel and Thomas R. McDaniel, educators in South Carolina who have studied the problem. They maintain that a school district that hopes to win its case should be able to document its efforts to help the teacher.

Teacher Burnout

Let it not be forgotten in any discussion of teacher incompetence that few teachers set out deliberately to be incompetent. It is easy to lapse into cynicism about the quality of teaching, but this overlooks the fact that some inept teachers were once doing an adequate job. Teaching is solitary work, in which a man or woman is the lone sentry in an outpost called a classroom. A teacher on the job is without immediate support and counsel, bereft of professional colleagues to whom he or she may immediately turn. For hours at a time, there is only the world within four walls, and it is populated by a single adult. The only break of consequence may come at lunch, a hurried respite in the company of battle-scarred colleagues. Is it any wonder that in such a setting skilled and dedicated people sometimes stumble?

This is the age of teacher "burnout," a word widely used to explain a multitude of problems facing teachers. NEA President McGuire describes burnout as "a condition that results from stress, tension, and anxiety."[27] Teachers throughout New York State reported in a survey that dealing with disruptive children in the classroom was the single greatest cause of their stress.[28] That stress was heightened by fear of personal attack. A study sponsored by the federal government in 1977 found that 17 percent of the nation's teachers lived in constant fear of being assaulted, a situation obviously not conducive to a sense of well-being that leads to good teaching. The National Education Association said that for 60,900 teachers the fear became reality during the 1977–78 school year.

Were there sufficient rewards to compensate for the headaches, teacher morale might be higher. But some teachers say that they find too few students who are interested in learning. Pamela Bardo left teaching in Los Angeles to become a stockbroker because she could no longer tolerate the refusal of students to do their homework.[29] When Ellen Glanz gave up teaching for a semester to pose as a student in the Massachusetts high school in which she had taught for six years, she was struck repeatedly by the unwillingness of students to take responsibility for their own learning.[30] The failure of students to carry out assignments and to turn in homework makes many teachers feel that they are wasting their time trying to educate them.

Muriel Juster, a veteran social studies teacher at Scarsdale High School, serving one of the most prestigious of New York City's suburbs, spoke of how a teacher's burden gradually becomes almost unbearable even in so affluent a setting:

> We are eager to share all of our wisdom with those we teach, but over a period of time this enthusiasm fades, to be replaced instead by a sense of boredom and frustration. In probably no other occupation does professional development correlate so poorly with success and status as in teaching. By professional development, I mean spending years to gain insight and expertise in certain subject areas—knowledge which we hope to pass on to our students and with which we can inspire them. But our success and status do not seem to depend upon our scholarship; they depend upon our ability to entertain, to be popular. We are at times like actors on a stage, except we perform more frequently—up to five classes a day—and our script must change daily. Our popularity, of course, depends not on how well we know our lines, but on how high we grade. Beyond this we also act as disciplinarians and psychologists.[31]

A lack of support from the parents of students causes some teachers to despair over the possibility of being able to change the situation. Teachers responding to a survey by the NEA listed the apathy of parents as the greatest problem affecting instruction, asserting that it contributed to the lack of discipline among students. Confronted by such overwhelming odds, some teachers do little more than go through the motions of instruction, skipping the task whenever possible. Clearly, it is in the interests of schools and students to have regular teachers on the job, but absenteeism among teachers is a problem of growing proportions. Figures from the Cincinnati schools, for example, show that the rate of absenteeism for teachers and administrators rose by 20 percent between 1976 and 1979. Throughout the country, demoralized educators are deciding it may no longer be worth their efforts to extend themselves for their students. Not only does absenteeism add to expenses because of the need to hire substitute teachers, but it also undermines educational programs. Substitutes are frequently high-priced babysitters, handed the impossible job of pulling together the threads in someone else's pattern making.

Paraprofessional Help
What could provide some relief for teachers would be more extensive use of paraprofessionals, aides who work side by side with teachers in the classroom, absorbing some of the more onerous chores and assisting instruction under the teacher's supervision. Research has shown that skillful teachers can make better use of their time when paraprofessional help is available to them. The pupil is the winner because the teacher is able to give each youngster greater attention and there are more opportunities for breaking the class into smaller teaching groups.

　　Lee County, in the rural environs of Tupelo, Mississippi, a place best known as the birthplace of Elvis Presley, is an unlikely spot for trying to prove this theory, but progress is possible wherever someone is willing to take a chance. In this instance, the risk taker was George McLean, a septuagenarian newspaper publisher who was brash enough in 1934 to give up his job as a college English instructor and buy a struggling little newspaper for $10,500. He turned the *Daily Journal* into the third-largest newspaper in the Mississippi and made enough money along the way to allow himself to take other chances, namely the gamble of investing in the public schools. Through his newspaper, Mr. McLean agreed to donate more than $1 million to the Lee County Public Schools over a period of ten years, starting in 1977. Virtually all of the money, amounting to some $110,000 annually, is being spent on the salaries of paraprofessional aides to help the school system's 25 first-grade teachers teach reading. The amazing part is that people simply do not contribute money to public schools. To churches, private schools, and hospitals, maybe, but who ever heard of someone giving $1 million to a public school system? Convention made no difference to George McLean, whose twinkling blue eyes hint at the gentle soul lurking beneath his firm exterior with its tightly set jaw. "If a child does not learn to read and compute at the beginning of his education, he is handicapped forever,"[32] said the grandfatherly Mr. McLean.

By 1979, the second full year of the program, there were already signs of improvement. The Saltillo School in the northern end of the county could not find a single second-grader reading below the national average of the California Achievement Test when the group was tested in the fall to see which children needed remedial attention. The benefit of the additional work the children got in the first-grade classrooms staffed by teachers and paraprofessionals led to unprecedented levels of achievement. A fuller appreciation of this attainment is possible when one realizes that the Lee County Schools operate no kindergartens. Youngsters enter school at the first grade, not having had the advantage of the kinds of learning-readiness training that kindergartens can use to give them a stronger start. "Every child here has a home life problem," said Ginger Seals, a first-grade teacher in the Plantersville School, which drew many of its students from a nearby trailer camp. "We have to teach them their letters, their colors, and even their names."[33] But with paraprofessionals to assist them, Ms. Seals and Carolyn Weeks, the school's other first-grade teacher, were able for the first time to give every child three hours of reading instruction a day, much of it individually or in small groups. It was a pattern similar to that adopted in the district's other five schools.

On a typical day in the Saltillo School, for example, Emily Henry was sitting on a chair facing a semicircle of nine of her first-graders. Each child, in turn, read aloud to the teacher. Across the room, Patricia Peach, the paraprofessional, was huddled with three youngsters whose workbooks were open to a page of pictures. Ms. Peach led them through the page, sounding the initial letter of each pictured object and asking them to identify those starting with an "L" sound. "This is a lamp," she said, emphasizing the first letter of the word. "You have to use your ears," she prodded the children, who were in the smallest group because they needed the most attention.

Meanwhile, seated at their desks in the areas between Ms. Peach and Ms. Henry, the other ten children in the class were working quietly at their desks, waiting their turn to sit with one of the two women.

"I see my job as supplementing the teacher, and I do whatever she asks me," Ms. Peach explained during a break. "It feels good to see a child make it who might not have made it without me here to help the teacher."[34] Like the rest of the paraprofessionals, most of whom were in their thirties and forties, Ms. Peach was a high school graduate, the only requirement for the job. She was paid $4,396 for the school year. The average annual salary of the teachers in the district—the 131st lowest of the 150 in the state—was $9,722.

Paraprofessionals have made a difference in the Lee County schools. What has occurred is not a miracle, but a case of adding one more competent adult to the classroom so that more time could be devoted to the needs of each pupil. The same improvement may be possible in other schools. It is a matter of ensuring that each child will spend more time in the pursuit of learning and that it will be twice as likely that a capable adult will be present to help him if he needs it. More teachers should have the benefit of paraprofessional assistance, an innovation that should be easier to implement in this decade of declining enrollments.

In-Service Training

Teachers also need more chance to keep up with advancing knowledge and to improve their techniques. The best way for them to do this is through continuing in-service education, courses and programs offered to teachers both in the schools in which they work and on college campuses. This need has long been recognized and is encouraged by collective bargaining agreements that award teachers pay increases in exchange for taking courses and earning academic credits. In theory, the concept is sound; in practice it is often a mockery, a perfunctory charade of meaningless credit accumulation.

What sometimes passes as in-service education may be exemplified by the New York City teacher who completed 30 credit hours of courses and submitted a transcript from Azusa

Pacific College qualifying him for $1,850 in extra pay above his regular salary for the rest of his career, plus an increment in his pension. The man, not a physical education teacher, had taken ten sports instruction courses by mail—five in the summer and five in the fall—while he continued, of course, in his regular teaching duties. The first of the courses was entitled, "The Analysis and Evaluation of Modern Trends in Coaching Baseball," and the remainder of the courses carried almost identical titles, except that they were concerned with cross country, golf, tennis, medical aspects of sport, swimming, basketball, volleyball, soccer, and track.[35]

Such abuses of in-service education would not be possible, however, unless there were institutions of higher education ready and willing to abet them. These colleges and universities, greedy for tuition regardless of questions of quality, are as guilty of duplicity as are the students. They are like the college in Boston that offered New York City teachers two academic credits for a weekend tour of Boston, credits that if earned in the classroom would have required two classes a week for three months. Perhaps it was unreasonable to expect the New York City Board of Education to have been scrutinizing such bargain-basement offerings when the school system itself was officially sponsoring after-school, in-service credits of its own for such demanding courses as International Folk Dance, Bicycle Safety Education, Chinese Cooking, and Intermediate Calligraphy.

All of this is not to say that worthwhile activities do not take place under the aegis of in-service education. It is just that school districts and teachers' organizations ought to start working together to end the free lunch and assure the public that teachers really are spending time improving their craft if that is what they are being paid to do. For the rest of this century, most school systems are going to be served largely by teachers who are already on the payrolls. It only makes sense to work assiduously at making them better teachers.

Teacher Recruitment, Licensing, and Evaluation

If jobs in elementary and secondary education were attracting the best and the brightest of the college graduates there might be more reason for confidence in the future. Formerly, there was at least the virtual built-in guarantee of lifetime employment to lure people into teaching, but the layoffs triggered by enrollment declines have ended that attraction. Now, a young person who majors in education in college does so at some risk, not knowing if there will be a job after graduation. The paradox is that the nation's school systems are suffering shortages in certain teaching areas at the same time there is a general oversupply of teachers. The insufficient number of mathematics and science teachers is just one more reflection of the profession's lost luster. Detroit schools had to reassign junior high teachers of other subjects, who had not majored in mathematics in college, to high school mathematics classes. Dallas brought back retired math teachers to fill openings. Shortages are developing because people who could teach math and science are opting for the higher salaries and better working conditions in business and industry. "We can pay them only $12,110 to start with, a bachelor's degree and no teaching experience, but they can get industrial research positions that pay $18,000 to $20,000 to begin," said Edward Cowens, deputy associate superintendent for personnel in Dallas.[36]

Increasingly, the teaching profession must stake its future on young people of lower academic caliber. The scores on college entrance tests of students planning careers in teaching are invariably lower than those of their classmates who want to go into other fields. A survey of 455,170 high school seniors planning on 19 separate occupations revealed that those expecting to be teachers averaged 17th lowest on college entrance tests.[37]

The problem of drawing top-flight talent to teaching has been exacerbated by the expansion of opportunities for women in other fields, giving them alternatives to what was formerly one of the few careers they considered. In 1969, for example, 7.2 percent of the students entering law school and 9.1 percent of those entering medical school were women. By 1979, these figures had swelled to 32.9 percent in the law schools and 27.8 percent in the medical schools.[38] Similar changes occurred during the 1970s in schools of engineering, accounting, dentistry, and business—once bastions of male chauvinism. Their doors were thrown open to women in response to both affirmative action pressures and new aspirations of women themselves, who think today in terms of options that were unimaginable to their mothers. If society had not changed, many of these young women might still be majoring in education.

The abundance of so many talented women was important to teaching because the profession has seldom been selective. Women with no place else to go provided at least some assurance of a cadre of first-rate teachers. "It is obvious that current admissions policies allow just about everyone who applies to enter teacher preparatory programs," said Doyle Watts, director of teacher education at Northwestern Oklahoma State University. He continued: "The lack of selective admissions is an extremely serious deficiency that must be corrected if high-quality applicants are to be chosen. There is no reason to believe that less ability is required to become a competent, successful schoolteacher than is necessary in other professional fields."[39] One of the few states moving in the direction indicated by Mr. Watts is Florida, where a regulation became effective in 1980 requiring that students entering teacher education programs at colleges and universities in the state have a minimum score of 835 on the SAT or 17 on the ACT. Such cutoff points are minimal, but could lead to something more significant if state officials intend something more than a public relations gesture.

Tightening requirements for entry into teacher education programs is a start toward making the profession more selective. In most states, however, once a student gets accepted into such a program all he or she has to do to be certified and licensed is complete the curriculum. Passing courses is regarded as sufficient evidence of ability to teach, though it may be that passing courses proves nothing more than the ability to pass courses. Prospective physicians, dentists, lawyers, and accountants must do more. They must pass state licensing examinations even after they have passed their courses and obtained college degrees. Some education officials and legislators are beginning to think that perhaps teachers, too, ought to submit to licensing examinations after completing college. Steps toward this goal have been initiated in several states, including Alabama, Florida, Georgia, New York, and South Carolina. The State Education Department in New York has proposed a test that would examine an applicant's communications and computational skills, pedagogical knowledge, and familiarity with the proposed special area of teaching the person wants to enter.

The Florida Teacher Certification Examination is supposed to show if the candidate has the ability to write in a logical and proper style, to comprehend and interpret written material, to work with fundamental mathematical concepts, and understand patterns of physical, social, and academic development in students. There is reason to suspect, however, that with this test, as with minimum competency tests for high school students, the state may be giving the public a false sense of security. Here is a sample question from the mathematical portion of the test, a test designed to determine if a college graduate is qualified to be a teacher:

Find the sum of 3,905,666, and 821.

    a) 3,792

    b) 4,792

    c) 11,992

    d) None of the above

The Council for Basic education lamented: "It has been, and remains, our view that the minimum competency testing of teachers can serve only to single out the most egregiously incompetent, and we are sorry that Florida apparently can do no more."[40] Florida's approach to deciding who will be permitted to be a teacher resembles the tests that are used to determine who will be allowed to drive an automobile. The high number of traffic accidents gives some idea of how ineffective such tests are in screening out poor risks. The same may be predicted for Florida's attempt to keep the lowliest graduates out of the teaching profession.

Maybe it would make little difference if the test were

difficult—which it is not—since a written examination is unlikely to reveal whether a person has the rapport, compassion, perseverance, and ability to improvise that are intrinsic to good teaching.

What is needed desperately is some systematic method of evaluating the performance of teachers once they get on the job so that they may be held accountable for the quality of their interaction in the classroom. In the early 1970s, it appeared that such a device was at hand. It was called teacher accountability, and it had wide appeal. Liberals thought it could be a vehicle for helping low-achieving children, and conservatives believed it could be a basis for justifying tighter budgets. Much of the talk until then had been about inputs— the number of dollars poured into the schools, the number of teachers employed, the number of school buildings constructed. Suddenly, there was growing interest in outputs—the number of students reading at grade level, the number of students improving their scores on mathematics tests, the number of students completing high school. All of this emphasis on determining what the schools were getting for their money pointed toward the obvious step of rating teachers according to the performance of their students.

Teacher organizations did not take warmly to the idea. "Educators stress that there are too many factors affecting what students do in school, and how well they do it, to make the present simplistic measures of accountability acceptable,"[41] Mr. Herndon of the NEA stated in helping to lead the opposition to teacher accountability. The nation's teachers were able to abort the accountability movement, which was never allowed to realize its potential. Before the 1970s ended, the notion of holding students accountable to minimum competency standards was to replace the accountability movement that had been aimed at teachers.

CHAPTER EIGHT

SCHOOL FINANCE

AN UNBALANCED SCALE

Affluent districts can have their cake and eat
it too: they can provide a high quality
education for their children while paying
lower taxes. Poor districts, by contrast, have
no cake at all.

Serrano v. Priest
The California Supreme
Court

Folks were not too brotherly and love was in short supply
during September of 1980, when 11,200 teachers went on
strike against the public schools in Philadelphia. The strike
dragged on for more than two weeks, effectively preventing
the start of the school year for the system's 220,500 students
even though some of the buildings were kept open by super-
visory personnel. Only about 2 percent of the teachers went
to work. It was the fourth work stoppage in ten years in a
school district in which only 25 percent of the eleventh-graders were reading at or above the national average. How much
good did the strike do such students? It is easier to determine
how much good the strike did the Philadelphia Federation of
Teachers, which was demanding that the district rehire more
than 2,000 teachers and other union-covered employees who
had been dismissed in response to enrollment declines and
fiscal constraints in the system's $750 million budget. All of

181

those laid off were rehired as part of the settlement, which did not even assure labor peace. The schools were shut down again five months later, when maintenance workers struck.

What happened in Philadelphia in the fall of 1980 was taken in stride because strikes by schoolteachers are no longer extraordinary. The strike is an economic weapon that has come to be used more often by teachers than by members of most other kinds of unions. Strikes by teachers are so common, in fact, that there were 242 of them during the 1979–80 school year, according to the National Education Association. Most troublesome is the growing number of strikes in which teachers, like those in Philadelphia, try to prevent school districts from implementing layoffs, which administrative officials say are essential to deal with enrollment declines and inflationary pressures. In San Francisco, for example, 3,600 teachers struck at the opening of school in September, 1979, and stayed out for a month in protest over the firing of 1,200 of their colleagues. The question of layoffs is likely to recur as a major issue during the 1980s, when fewer teachers will be needed because of falling enrollments. San Francisco's settlement, probably a harbinger, involved hiring back more than half of the teachers who had been dismissed. Moreover, everyone got a 15.5 percent raise, the irony being that much of the money to make this all possible resulted from the savings of not having to pay the absent teachers during the strike.

More than anything else, teacher strikes are about one thing: the well-being of teachers. Students do not gain when their teachers are absent and the educational process is disrupted. Furthermore, the level of a settlement with a teaching staff is crucial to the financial interests of public education because their salaries and fringe benefits account for the bulk of school budgets. As the earnings of teachers have grown more respectable, the cost of providing education has risen astronomically. In other words, the low budgets of 15 or 20 years ago were, in effect, subsidized by an underpaid teaching force. There is no way in the 1980s that both teachers and taxpayers are going to be satisfied.

Between the school years of 1969–70 and 1979–80, the average maximum salary of a teacher with a master's degree rose from $10,717 to $18,834 in districts with 6,000 or more pupils.[1] Individually, even an increase of this size does not make teachers well paid, but collectively the salaries paid to teachers help make education big business. The magnitude of the nation's investment in schooling can be seen in the $166.2 billion expenditures of elementary, secondary, and higher education, a figure that is 7 percent of the gross national product.[2]

THE BIG BUSINESS OF EDUCATION

School districts do not sell shares of ownership on the New York Stock Exchange, though they dwarf many private businesses in the enormity of their operations. New York City's school system, for instance, proposed a budget of $3.1 billion for 1981–82, an amount equal to the entire federal budget when Herbert Hoover assumed the presidency. Education is the second-largest category of government spending, exceeded only by defense, which not long ago stood second to education. Four out of every ten dollars spent by local and state governments is for education. For years, however, the fiscal side of the average big city school system was run like a mom and pop grocery store. It was not until the late 1970s that the New York City system got around to adopting computers in place of the paper-and-pencil calculations of some of its clerks. At least they were no longer wearing green eyeshades.

It took a financial disaster in Chicago during the winter of 1979–80 to show just how inept an urban school system can become in administering its finances. Carl Sandburg's City of the Big Shoulders turned out to be the City of the Empty Purse. The first inkling of the crisis came on a cold Wednesday morning in mid-November, when no bids were submitted for $124.6 million in general obligation notes that the school system was trying to sell routinely to borrow money. It was like sending out invitations to a party and having no one show up. Both Mooney's Investment Service and Standard & Poor's Corporation had downgraded the board of education's credit rating, and prospective investors considered the notes risky.

The credit raters had learned that money that the school system was supposed to be putting aside to pay off notes that had already been sold was instead being used to cover operating expenses. Desperate for immediate help to meet its payroll, the board of education turned to the state, which speeded up by one month its general aid to the school system and made it possible for the teachers and other employees to be paid.

Ultimately, though, there was no averting a disaster that had been years in the making. Within two weeks, Joseph P. Hannon, the nation's highest-paid school superintendent, had resigned his $82,500 post. Rumors as strong as a windstorm off Lake Michigan circulated through the Loop. The president of the school board and the system's two highest-ranking financial officers added their resignations before the end of November. For the first time, Chicagoans were getting a glimpse of the fiscal calamity that had been hidden from them. They also got some idea of the price they were going to pay for the popularity that Mayor Richard Daley had bought during the 1970s by refusing to raise property taxes, a policy that neither of his successors saw fit to renounce.

It gradually grew evident that some Chicago school officials, trying to eke by without enough money to pay the bills, had been deluding the public. Funds intended for one purpose were being spent for another, and Peter was not only paying Paul, but Frank and John, as well. The solvency that Chicagoans assumed existed in their school system had been achieved by elaborate legerdemain. Mayor Jane M. Byrne, gifted with hindsight, charged that the mess was the result of a "ten-year coverup by school and business officials."[3] The tangle of misallocation was so intricate that even as the scandal was unfolding the school system said that it was unable to turn over to the federal government the money that was supposed to have been deducted from the salaries of employees to meet payroll taxes. Apparently, the funds had already been diverted to some other purpose. In December, the Internal Revenue Service demanded the payment of $16 million that was a month overdue.

Three times during the bitter Chicago winter of 1979–80, the school system's employees were not paid, beginning with a payroll that was skipped just four days before Christmas. The Chicago Teachers' Union, feeling like it was playing Bob Cratchitt to the school system's Scrooge, spurned the idea of teacher layoffs and went on strike. It was not until the creation of a new superbody, the School Finance Authority, that a mechanism finally existed for cleaning up the books and restoring a semblance of fiscal order to the school system. The reorganization included the dismissal of the entire school board and the appointment of a financial officer to oversee the schools at a salary of $100,000. The record of irresponsibility left Chicago's new board of education in a position from which it could not determine its own fiscal destiny, much like a child who lost his privileges because he had abused his independence. Ruth B. Love, the school superintendent in Oakland, California, was tapped in early 1981 to fill the vacancy left by Hannon at a salary at least 50 percent higher than he had received, but she would have nowhere near the financial autonomy he had had.

Fiscal mismanagement to the degree seen in Chicago has fortunately not been widespread, or so it would appear. But other big city school systems share enough characteristics with Chicago to raise concern about the competence of their business operations. If a $1.3 billion enterprise outside the educational sphere had had such shoddy stewardship as that provided for the Chicago public schools, its stockholders would have raised an outcry. But the stockholders of a public school system are the taxpayers who seldom have any notion of what is going on in their local school business office, much less care. A joint bipartisan committee of the Illinois legislature that spent a year investigating the fiscal collapse of Chicago's schools was told repeatedly by employees of the school business office that they had been illegally transferring funds back and forth because that was the way it had always been done and no one thought to challenge it.

Joseph M. Cronin, the former state school superintendent in Illinois, thinks that what happened in Chicago should alert the public to the need for early warning systems to sound fiscal alarms if similar dangers loom in other big city school systems. Mr. Cronin, now president of the Massachusetts Higher Education Assistance Corporation, would give state authorities the power to conduct periodic audits of local school expenditures. As it turns out, the prestigious auditing firm that was retained by the school system apparently knew about the excesses, but refused to tell outside authorities because that would have allegedly been unethical and a violation of confidence. Mr. Cronin also recommends that state approval should be required for local school budgets when systems want to borrow beyond a certain percentage. In addition, he would forbid the use of capital funds for operating expenses or require that such practices be publicly noted.[4]

The board of education in Chicago was fairly typical in placing total confidence in the administrators it had picked to run the system. During a period of more than a year preceding the crisis, the board's own finance committee did not meet even once, giving an impression of fiscal health at the very time the patient was comatose. Such uninterested behavior on the part of the school board helped prop up a façade of financial respectability that was indeed outdated.

THE UNEVEN PROPERTY TAX BASE

In many ways, much that surrounds the financing of the nation's public schools is anachronistic, the product of a simpler, less complex society. The very foundation on which school finance rests in much of the country, the local property tax, is ill-suited to today's needs. The varieties of school finance throughout the country form a crazy quilt of 50 patches basted together by the flimsy thread of common purpose. The Constitution carries no mention of "education." Each of the states has been free to develop its own method of paying for public schools. No two states do it the same way.

Anyone who has ever owned a home knows about real estate taxes, the largest portion of which in most locales goes to support the public schools. It has been only during the last ten years that some attempt has been made to correct the inequities of the system. In most states, property owners still suffer the burden of unfair tax rates. Not only are the rates different in neighboring towns for seemingly identical homes, but even when the rates are the same, they usually do not produce equal revenues because one community may have vastly more taxable-property wealth per pupil than another. Thus, students, as the chief beneficiaries of local taxes, do not share equally. An accident of geography—living in a town with a huge utility plant or a large shopping center, for instance— assures one child of having much more money available to be spent on his education than is available for a youngster in a neighboring town.

Such inequities were not recognized by the courts until the 1970s. For most of America's history, the fact that public education from one place to another was subject to differences in property taxes was accepted as being as natural as some people being born with brown eyes and others with blue eyes. An inferior level of support for the education of some children was simply their lot in life. The importance of property as a symbol of wealth underpinned this approach. After all, there was a time in this country when only landholders were permitted to vote. To a growing extent, though, the tax on real estate is being seen as an inequitable and impractical method of financing schools.

It took a law suit in California to alter this historic attitude toward school finance. It was a case that forever linked the name Serrano with school finance reform. Eight-year-old John Serrano, Jr., of Mexican American ancestry was listed first among 27 Los Angeles County youngsters in whose behalf the legal complaint was filed. On August 30, 1971, the California Supreme Court upheld their suit and found the state's method of school finance illegal because it tied the quality of education to the wealth of the school district in which a family happened to reside. "By our holding today," the court declared, "we further the cherished idea of American education that in a democratic society free public schools shall make available to all children equally the abundant gifts of learning. This was the credo of Horace Mann, which has been the heritage and inspiration of this country."[5]

After *Serrano,* it could no longer be taken for granted that taxpayers and students were doomed to be penalized by the inequities of the property tax. It was a development of major proportions, overturning a foundation stone of the system of taxation. State by state, the problem of school finance rapidly gained attention through the 1970s. In some states there were court challenges modeled on *Serrano*—suits were filed in 29 other states before the end of the decade—and state legislatures elsewhere acted in anticipation of such suits. Whatever the impetus, the effect was to start the arduous task of evening out the peaks and valleys that distinguish affluent, high-spending school districts from poor, low-spending school districts. But in most states the change is still inchoate and the old systems continue to prevail. A study of the impact of school finance reforms in five states—California, Florida, Kansas, Michigan, and New Mexico—found that "in relation to the major goals that the proponents of reform have championed, the scattered victories appear somewhat hollow."[6] The Rand Corporation of Santa Monica, California, conducting the study for the National Institute of Education, concluded that the process of trying to reconcile conflicting interests has ended up perpetuating some of the inequities.

Michigan, for example, has assured a guaranteed minimum tax base for property-poor districts, but many of the inequities persist nonetheless. The situation seems to come into sharp focus in comparing Lake City and Oak Park, two school districts in Michigan. What one sees is the difference between sitting at a banquet table and foraging for the scraps. Almost three times as much money is spent on each pupil in Oak Park, usually the first- or second-highest spending district in the state, as in Lake City, the perennially lowest spending district. Part of the difference reflects the willingness of an education-oriented public in Oak Park to tax itself more heavily, but the key factor is the discrepancy in property wealth between the two communities.

Students in Lake City subsist on a diet as austere as the quiet forests of the sparsely populated northern reaches of Michigan's lower peninsula, where the school district is situated. Missaukee County is a place of the poor and the retired, where jobs are scarce and welfare checks are a staple of the economy. The school system's 1,200 students are housed in a single sprawling structure, so overcrowded that seven portable buildings, looking like the shacks used by deer hunters in the nearby woods, have been erected on the playground to accommodate the overflow of students. The sheet metal sides keep out the winter winds and the roofs are fine so long as it does not rain. The temporary buildings have been in place almost fifteen years, symbols of destitution in a school district in which new construction is out of the question because of the cost, a school system in which only one millage increase was approved in seven years.

The course offerings in Lake City are as lean as the budget. There is no metal shop or auto shop for vocational students and no Advanced Placement courses for the college-bound. Music is taught only two days a week and youngsters count on their participation in church choirs for the bulk of their musical training. The high school tries to find the money and the space to offer a class at each level of Spanish every year, but there are not always enough funds or classrooms. Teachers in the high school get used to having 35 students per class and, aware that their region's economy is geared to the summer tourist industry, feel grateful for jobs to carry them through the long, bleak months of winter even if the average teacher is paid only $13,275 a year (compared with $22,041 in Oak Park). Money is so tight in the schools of Lake City that a teacher who had been relieved of one hour of class a day to coordinate the system's bus schedule had to be sent back to the classroom full-time in 1980. The school district could no longer afford the extra $1,000 it was paying him. The bus scheduling job was added to the workload of one of the principals, who could be assigned the task without extra pay because he was "management."

Oak Park's position as the highest-spending school district in Michigan is built on a tax base that has as its bedrock Northland, one of the nation's first massive suburban shopping centers. In addition, there are other businesses and small manufacturers scattered throughout the community. Together with the thousands of tidy, one-story ranch houses constructed in Oak Park during the migration from Detroit after World War II, there is enough local property wealth—50 percent more per student than in Lake City—to make school a bountiful educational experience for the young. It means the increased attention that is possible in classes that are only two-thirds the size of those in Lake City.

The capital budget for the system of 3,900 students has been large enough to construct a physical plant of 49 separate buildings, worth more than $35 million. Every school has its own gymnasium and library and the high school is equipped with a planetarium, a theater separate from the auditorium, and a Career Resource Room with computer terminals to help students explore occupational choices. The olympic-sized swimming pool in the high school is unlike anything in Lake City, where students have to wait until summer to do their swimming in the lake from which the town draws its name. The lavish range of programs in Oak Park runs from four separate projects for pre-kindergarten-aged children to a full array of Advanced Placement courses for those who want to work toward college credit while still in high school. In contrast to the two counselors in Lake City, Oak Park has a full staff of social workers, psychologists, and academic counselors. A program for the gifted and talented reaches from the elementary schools through high school. Music and art are available to all students; four art teachers and seven music teachers serve the six elementary schools.

Even though Michigan has not been compelled by the courts to make further alterations in its school finance system, there is no assurance that if and when that happens it will bring rapid change. The road to more equitable school finance is long and winding, dotted with hazards and slowed by complicated turns that are reminders of the difficulty of the journey. In Maryland, for example, a suit challenging the state's school finance system was filed in February, 1979, and did not go to trial until September, 1980.[7] The trial dragged on until May 1981, when the fiscal formula was found illegal. An appeal will probably push the case at least into 1982.

It is a circuitous route not unlike that followed in such other states as New York, where a school finance case that had its first hearing in front of a judge in April, 1976, was still not close to resolution in 1981.[8] A verdict in June, 1978, finding New York's method of paying for its schools illegal was being weighed by an appellate court early in 1981, and the process promised to drag on for perhaps another year if the case ended up being appealed to the state's highest court. What was eminently clear in New York was that the job of building a more equitable system of school finance would be a lengthy undertaking even after the judicial procedures have been exhausted and the final ruling has been rendered.

A special task force preparing for such an eventuality in New York State pointed out in 1980, even as the case was being argued, that readjusting the school finance system would involve a great deal beyond a court ruling. It would require a series of complicated decisions by the legislature in order to comply with the court directives. There would have to be judgments as to which of the state's 744 school districts were most entitled to extra amounts of money and in what sums. According to the special task force, inequities in property wealth alone are probably not a sufficient measure of need because they tell nothing about differences from one district to another in household income, the varying costs of teachers' contracts, or the expense of educating disproportionate numbers of pupils with special needs. In addition, large municipalities have the burden of providing public services that are not a concern of smaller communities that can divert a larger portion of their tax base toward public schools.

Any decision about implementing a new finance decision would also have to answer the question of whether or not to put expenditure limits on high-spending districts while allowing low-spending districts to catch up.[9] This is an important issue in New York, where per pupil spending in the highest district is six times larger than in the lowest district. Finally, there is the issue of where to find the money to pay for these changes, which the special task force estimated would cost the taxpayers of the state an extra $1 billion. This would come on top of the $10 billion that New York is already spending on elementary and secondary education—$4 billion from the state and $6 billion from the localities—giving New York per pupil expenditures that are already 45 percent above the national average.

The uncertainty of school finance reform is exacerbated by developments such as those in Ohio, where a trial court in Cincinnati found the state's method of paying for its schools unconstitutional, a verdict upheld by an appellate court, only to be overturned in the Ohio Supreme Court. "Local control provides a rational basis supporting the disparity in per pupil expenditures," the Ohio Supreme Court ruled, 6-to-1, in 1979, deciding that the equal-yield formula for generating state aid to the schools was legal.[10] In Ohio, with its fanatic aversion to new taxes, it was a decision magnified by a tradition of fiscal austerity that forced the 616 school districts into circumstances that were not only inequitable, but churlish as well. State and local taxes are kept so low in Ohio that after paying them, people have more of their personal income remaining than the citizens of all but five other states.[11] During the decade of the 1970s, Ohio's eight largest cities put school finance issues on the ballot 31 times and only 2 of the items passed.[12]

Ohio law traditionally required that school districts live within the income generated each calendar year. End-of-the-year deficits were forbidden, and until the law was changed in 1980, schools in many parts of the state would close in November and December because their budgets were not sufficient to carry them through the entire year. It happened in Ohio cities large and small—the experience in Toledo in the late 1970s was typical. The voters in Toledo simply would not agree to assess themselves the additional taxes that could have kept the schools open. Instead, educators were forced to stagger from one tax levy defeat to another, leading to repeated school closings. Toledo's 50,000 schoolchildren learned to live like Mother Hubbard's dog. Bare cupboards were the rule.

THE HOSTILE PUBLIC

The necessity of winning election approval for each tax rate hike means, in effect, seeking a vote of confidence every time a school system wants to boost revenues. Votes of confidence are not easily won in an era in which faith in public education is at a low point. The difficulties of properly financing the schools are inextricably tied to many of the day's most pressing concerns. The mine field of public opinion through which school officials must tiptoe as they wend their way to budget increases is peppered with explosive issues. People are bitter over racial desegregation, the closing of neighborhood schools because of declining enrollments, and federal mandates that siphon off funds for the disabled and the disadvantaged. Worries over discipline and faltering test scores have added to the public's wariness over investing more of its money in schools. Doug Sites encountered some of these feelings when he was a senior at Rogers High School in Toledo in the fall of 1977, when he and other students were helping campaign in the community for a school tax increase. "People told us they wouldn't go for it because there was too much drinking and too many drugs in the schools. That was a pretty poor excuse. They were talking about no more than 4 percent of the students."[13]

Many white residents of Toledo were inclined to believe the worst about the schools because they felt alienated from a system with a growing proportion of black students. It was a situation that in some other Ohio cities was exacerbated by the specter of busing for desegregation. Federal judges who issue desegregation orders cannot be voted out of office, but irate citizens can refuse to cast their ballots in favor of more money for school systems that are affected by those judicial rulings. Legislative mandates also determine what is possible in the schools. "I used to balance the budget by putting a few extra children in a classroom, but I'm not permitted to do that anymore," said Frank Dick,[14] who spent 13 years as superintendent in Toledo before being forced to resign as a scapegoat during the budget crisis. The legislative mandates form a chain that constrains the flexibility of school administrators. In Ohio, the legislature, not the local school board, sets minimum staffing requirements for teachers, nurses, truant officers, librarians, and guidance counselors. It is probably best that the state uphold such standards, especially in a place as parsimonious as Ohio, but the result leaves little maneuverability in the budget.

In Toledo, the effort to stretch meager resources left the school system without enough administrators to provide the basic leadership essential to any staff. In-service education for teachers was abandoned. When new programs in reading and mathematics were introduced, there was no money to train teachers in how to use the unfamiliar material, which was like giving someone an expensive computer without an instruction manual. It was obvious that Toledo's school system was being allowed to slip into an abyss of neglect for want of adequate funding. The city's movers and shakers, accustomed to running Toledo like a modern-day, overgrown version of a company town, conceded that a tax boost was necessary, but they did not want it to be too high, because their industrial properties would have to carry much of the burden. A 6.1-mill increase was set as the highest amount acceptable to business, and it mattered not that those most knowledgeable about the schools argued that the sum was too small. Tomorrow's calamity was buying today's burnished image. Even the muckamucks from the city's newspaper monopoly shamelessly played the game, predicating editorial support for the increase on an agreement that the amount be limited to 6.1 mills.

At least one parent, Virginia Fortino, saw through the dirty gossamer of civic leadership that the power brokers had draped over themselves. She castigated them at a public meeting at which the school board was to set the official amount of the millage increase to be put on the ballot. Said Fortino: "A revitalized downtown Toledo is very nice. However, who will be working in those buildings in the future when the children of today have been shortchanged on their education?"[15] Despite such criticism, the 6.1-mill figure was accepted by the school board. Toledo's educators geared up for their fifth levy campaign in two years. After four straight losses, they were experienced, albeit cynical, in coining slogans and taking to the hustings. There was even a war chest of $75,000 from the business establishment to hire a professional media manipulator of the sort who normally plied his talent in behalf of political candidates.

It worked. The schools had closed for lack of money a week before the election, and a sympathetic public approved the operating tax increase. It was a victory worthy of King Pyrrhus. But then Ohio is also the state whose highest court subsequently declared that "local control provides a rational basis supporting the disparity in per pupil expenditures."[16] Toledo was not alone in its resistance to higher school taxes; the 1970s marked the end of an era of automatic support for the schools. In the 1960s the nation's voters were still approving more than 70 percent of the school tax issues submitted to them, but by the middle of the 1970s the rate of acceptance had dropped to less than 50 percent.[17]

It would be a mistake, though, to view the erosion of support for budgetary items on the ballot as representing a dissatisfaction limited to education. In what other area of public expenditure is the citizenry permitted the luxury of an election? Tax revenues are spent on welfare, public safety, health and hospitals, higher education, and defense without the public right of disapproval. The public schools just happen to have the misfortune of having their funding subject to election. People think their taxes are high—all their taxes—and they have no other way of venting their frustration. Imagine what would happen if they could vote on welfare payments.

The 1980s will be a harsh decade for public education. Disenchantment with the public schools is rife. A symptom of the problem is the growing popularity of nonpublic schools, which now enroll almost 11 percent of the nation's elementary and secondary students. Greater acceptance of nonpublic education by families that traditionally supported the public schools raises the possibility of further defections if parents are suddenly given the financial wherewithal to exercise free choice. There are signs of this happening under a Reagan administration and a conservatively leaning Congress. There is strong backing in both the House and the Senate for a bill that would allow families tax credits for money spent for elementary and secondary school tuitions. Such a device would undoubtedly boost enrollments in private and parochial schools and it would cost the U.S. treasury billions of dollars in taxes. Tuition tax credits are a threat to the future of public education, but many people do not care because they view private and parochial schools as offering a kind of education that they think public schools are incapable of providing. Families are turning away from the public schools in search of better discipline, more dedicated teaching, and a stronger orientation toward traditional values.

Increasingly, the public schools are being abandoned to the poor, many of whom are minority members as well. It is a situation not likely to help the schools when they turn to the taxpayers for more money, as was discovered in Toledo. Furthermore, whether they are poor or wealthy, white or black, a growing proportion of those taxpayers are middle-aged and elderly people without any children in school, almost guaranteeing an expanding source of resistance to increased expenditures for public education. Add to this the economic woes with which the nation began the decade and it is clear why the outlook for adequate financing of public education is so depressing. Buffeted on one side by inflation and on the other by recession, the bemused citizen does not want to hear about the needs of schools. He has his own needs and cannot afford the interest payments on his credit cards, much less consider taxing himself more heavily for the public schools.

Citizens discovered a new outlet for these frustrations in the late 1970s. It is called tax limitation and, like so many fads, was conceived in California, where a couple of members of the state legislature, Paul Gann and Howard Jarvis, introduced a proposal to limit property taxes to 1 percent of market value. It was approved by the state's voters in 1978 under the title of Proposition 13, denoting its position on the ballot. Passage of the issue sent tremors up and down a state that thought it was accustomed to earthquakes. Proposition 13 was a disaster of a new variety, one that could destroy without leaving outward evidence of damage. Property tax rates had to be slashed by as much as 50 percent in some communities. While school buildings and other public facilities would remain standing, the services inside would eventually have to be reduced drastically. The full impact of Proposition 13 on the public schools will not be known until at least 1982 or 1983 because surpluses in the state budget were distributed to local governments in the years immediately after passage of the measure to minimize the effect of the lost property tax revenues. Soon, though, Californians will have a taste of the brew they have concocted.

Elected officials bear a good deal of the blame for the allure that gimmicks like Proposition 13 have for the voters. Those charged with overseeing public expenditures have not inspired the confidence of the taxpayers. Even the public schools, which probably have less waste proportionately than most other areas of government, are not run in ways that assure taxpayers that their money is being spent responsibly. Exasperated by the abuses, the people take the only course open to them: voting to limit the amount of money that will be placed in the hands of elected and appointed officials. Public unrest is of such dimension that in California, two years after the passage of Proposition 13, voters almost approved Proposition 9 as well. That measure would have cut the state income tax in half, reducing revenues by an estimated $4 to $5 billion.

The progeny of Proposition 13, as fecund a sire as ever appeared, showed up on the ballots of almost a dozen states in 1980. Though most of the initiatives were defeated, the voters of Massachusetts could not resist the seductive siren. Liberal Massachusetts, the only state to give its electoral votes to George McGovern in 1972, the only state since Reconstruction to send a black to the U.S. Senate, adopted by a wide margin in 1980 an issue to limit property taxes to 2.5 percent of market value, making it likely that up to $1 billion—much of it earmarked for education—would be withheld from tax collections throughout the state. It was no accident that Massachusetts was one of the first states to join the tax revolt. Taxachusetts is the sardonic nickname by which residents of the Bay State define their plight of trying to squeeze by in the second most heavily taxed state in the country, exceeded only by Alaska.

As justified as their anger may be, however, taxpayers cannot expect effective schools to operate on a pittance. Teachers cannot have their salaries frozen when everyone around them has a rising income—even if inflation does consume most of it. If, indeed, the tax limitation measures do remain in force and spread to more states, there will be no way in which schools can be financed in anything like the fashion of the past. California is already shifting more and more of the burden of financing the public schools to the state treasury, the only practical step under the circumstances.

The silver lining in this dark cloud is of unintended origin, but forcing state governments to take over more of the responsibility for paying for local schools may expedite school finance reform. If the state is dispersing most of the money on which school districts are dependent, it can more easily overcome the disparities of local property wealth. The state can make certain that the amount of money available per pupil is more nearly the same in every school district. This is a major goal of school finance reform, and its realization could be hastened by limitations on local property taxes.

Hawaii

The ultimate attempt to remove local disparities in school funding is found in Hawaii, where the entire state comprises a single school district. The state has assumed all of the cost of local education, spending approximately the same amount of money on each pupil whether he attends an urban school in bustling Honolulu or a rural school on the most remote island in the archipelago. The income from all of the state's taxable wealth flows into a general fund and then is doled out, school by school, to equalize spending. All of the teachers in the state are paid on a single salary scale, and no town, however affluent, may levy additional local taxes to enrich its schools beyond those in the rest of the state. Hawaii is the nation's showplace of tax equalization in education, a place where the amount of money spent on a child's education is not a function of local property wealth. The state's general fund, drawing revenues from sources as diverse as personal income taxes, excise taxes, and traffic fines, pays all the bills for all of Hawaii's 170,761 students.

One of the arguments favoring this sort of equalization in school finance—aside from the equity it provides property owners—is that it will narrow the advantages that one student may have over another. What Hawaii has found, though, is that despite its system of school finance, students do not achieve equally. Invariably, those from families of higher socioeconomic background outperform those of more modest background. Scores on standardized achievement tests are strikingly different even though students are ostensibly supported equally in the classroom. All of which may indicate that equal opportunity for children who are handicapped by family disadvantages may depend not on spending the same amount on them as is spent on other youngsters, but on spending more.

This, of course, is the theory behind such compensatory aid programs as Title I of the federal government's Elementary and Secondary Education Act. In fact, the availability of this kind of assistance for students of impoverished background means that more money is spent on their education in Hawaii than on the education of most other students, who do not get any additional support beyond the basic state allocation. So, even in a place like Hawaii, there is not the same absolute funding level for every student. Per pupil spending also varies somewhat throughout the state because the salary schedule awards higher pay to more experienced, older teachers. This means that unless teachers are assigned around the state with an equal proportion of older and young teachers in every school, there is no way of ensuring equal expenditures in each school. Schools on Oahu, the state's principal island, spend more per pupil simply because seniority rules give veteran teachers a choice of schools and many of them would rather be in urban areas. What Hawaii's effort at equalization demonstrates is the difficulty, perhaps the impossibility, of designing a finance system that delivers equal educational opportunity. But Hawaii has at least given it more of a try than any other state.

FAMILY CHOICE OR VOUCHERS

Regardless of how closely other states model their systems of school finance after Hawaii's, there remains the issue in all states of building more freedom of choice into the reforms. Imagine a situation in which a family had no choice about where to shop. Living at a certain address, in other words, would mean that a family would be required to use a specified supermarket and a specified department store, as well as a specified movie theater (even when the film is not desirable) and a specified physician. There would be no leeway for alternatives—the only way to buy groceries elsewhere would be to change residences and live on a street with a different designated supermarket. This far-fetched vision of compulsory consumerism is exactly what most Americans face when it comes to selecting public schools for their children. Public schools are monopolies of the worst sort. A family moves into a house or apartment and is told that if it wants to use the public schools, only the school designated for that neighborhood is acceptable. Furthermore, in most cases, families cannot even choose among the several teachers who may be teaching at a particular grade level. A student is assigned to a class and that is that.

This problem could be addressed as part of school finance reform if schools were made more responsive to family choice. A mechanism for such a change might be the education voucher, a kind of IOU issued by local governments for each child that would give parents some leverage in selecting schools. The school the student decides to attend gets the voucher from the family and then redeems it, receiving a cash payment from the local government on behalf of the youngster. Vouchers would have equal redemption value except for those issued for disabled and needy children, which would be worth more because such pupils are presumably more expensive to educate. While vouchers could lay the public open to the hucksterism of those who would advertise for and solicit students, taking advantage of the naiveté of some parents, this is not an insurmountable problem. Colleges and universities have adopted the most overt forms of promotion in recent years as they have widened their quest for students, and these practices, however odious, have not destroyed higher education.

The education voucher has been a concept in search of an advocate since the late 1960s. Mention of the idea can be traced to Adam Smith, who thought it might be a good method by which government could give parents the money to hire teachers for their children. In 1969, the U.S. Office of Economic Opportunity contracted with the Center for the Study of Public Policy, a Harvard-related group in Cambridge, Massachusetts, to develop a voucher plan that could be given a trial run.[18] The attraction of vouchers is the same now as it was a decade ago. If parents have the power to determine which school their children attend, then it has some ability to hold the school accountable for the youngster's performance. Under such circumstances, there would be more incentive for schools to produce favorable results because ineffective schools would have a difficult time attracting and holding students.

All of this implies greater responsibility for parents, some of whom undoubtedly would not fulfill their obligations. But the system could provide for the placement of students whose parents do not handle the task themselves. There are also ways that have been suggested by experts of preventing schools from discriminating against minority youngsters in the admissions procedures. The federal government's interest in vouchers was tied to the wish that poor people have something like the kinds of choices open to affluent families who can afford nonpublic school tuitions.

Several school districts in scattered parts of the country turned down the federal government's offer to operate an experimental voucher system. The one school system to run a voucher experiment was Alum Rock, an impoverished, predominantly Mexican American kindergarten-to-eighth-grade district serving part of San Jose, California. Alum Rock was probably enticed more by the prospect of an infusion of federal funds than by the concept itself. The five-year trial, which began in 1972, was artificial from the start because it was limited to the public school system. Vouchers helped extend the range of offerings in the public system and many families availed themselves of the opportunity for choice, but the experiment in Alum Rock was considerably less than a success.

This one poor experience is hardly reason enough to abandon the idea of vouchers. Under more favorable circumstances, in a test that would include private and parochial schools, vouchers might satisfy the needs of many families. The problem of such a system is not that it is unworkable, but that it could undermine the public school system. Many families would use vouchers as passports to cross the border into non-public elementary and secondary education. Public schools would be decimated by the emigration of their students. Public education as a unifying force of nationhood would be immeasurably weakened. Though the public schools have abused their monopoly by settling into complacency, the introduction of vouchers—as appealing as they may be—would be a lethal antidote. The apparent remedy of vouchers ought to be kept on the shelf for now.

The alternative is for public schools to give people the advantages of vouchers without students having to desert public education, making public schools so attractive that families prefer them. More should be done to make the public schools responsive to the needs of students and to let families choose educational programs, the schools, and the teachers for their children. A student should be able to attend any appropriate public school that serves his needs, regardless of its locale, and a variety of educational choices should be available to facilitate a proper match between pupil and program.

There is already a model for this approach in the magnet schools that have been established in some school districts to promote voluntary racial integration. Schools like the Mario Umana Harbor School of Science and Technology in Boston are examples. In New York City, there is Mark Twain Junior High in the seedy Coney Island section of Brooklyn, a neighborhood school with an entirely minority enrollment until a federal judge ordered it desegregated. Mark Twain has been converted into a junior high for the gifted and now draws talented white, black, and Hispanic youngsters from throughout southern Brooklyn. Entrance is voluntary, based on performance in elementary school and on potential in one of the areas in which the school offers enrichment—athletics, creative writing, music, mathematics, science, and industrial arts.

In San Diego, the Valencia Park School was able to raise its proportion of white students from 1 to 30 percent in a single year by accepting volunteers for what has become a laboratory school for the teacher education program at San Diego State

University. A new staff of master teachers was recruited from throughout the system to serve as teacher-trainers; a paraprofessional aide and at least one student-teacher were assigned to work with the veteran teacher in each classroom.

Such innovations and the chance for students to be a part of them should not have to depend on desegregation. There is no reason why the same concepts cannot be used in districts that are virtually all white or all black. Desegregation does not have to be the only excuse for giving students choices. Everyone connected with public education has a stake in bringing about these changes. Both California and Michigan have seriously entertained the idea of instituting voucher systems. If proponents of public education do not take steps to adopt the best features of vouchers and apply them to public schools, then people are going to demand that government help them switch to private and parochial schools, where they think they can get what they want for their children. The public schools cannot compete for students whose parents want a religiously based education for their youngsters. Parents have a right to seek that in parochial schools, though it is not incumbent on the public to pay for it. But most other families simply want an educational system that is more responsive. This can be offered through the public schools and, if it is not, then as sure as Ronald Reagan was elected President, the public schools are going to lose their monopoly.

CHAPTER NINE

PARENTS

MORE THAN COFFEE
AND CAKE

> Growing up is a serious business.
> He, Cal, would not be young again,
> not for anything. And not without
> sponsors: a mother and father,
> good fortune, God.
>
> JUDITH GUEST
> *Ordinary People*

Bay St. Louis, at the southern tip of Mississippi, where the sparkling waters of the Gulf of Mexico kiss the white sandy beaches with the gentleness of an affectionate lover, is a paradigm of the changing South. Fifty miles east of New Orleans, the town has been a favored weekend and summer retreat of city dwellers who enjoy the slower pace of Bay St. Louis, with its courtly turn-of-the-century homes that they have helped renovate. Gradually, though, Bay St. Louis has entered latter-20th-century America. The drilling platforms perched out of sight like parasitic centipedes sucking sustenance from the bed of the sea are symbols of the town's pivotal geographic locale, which make it a base for companies servicing the oil rigs. The recession-resistant economy of the Bay St. Louis region has been bolstered by an influx of government installations, including a technology laboratory operated by the National Aeronautics and Space Administration. One of the area's largest plants is a DuPont facility for the processing of titanium dioxide, a whitening agent that lends an appearance of purity to products ranging from toothpaste to stationery.

Not that every vestige of the old life has been cleaned away from Bay St. Louis. The fishing boats still make their daily journeys into the gulf, foraging for their succulent harvest of shrimp and oysters. And the few old-line families that have dominated the town of 7,000 for generations continue to wield their silent influence, keeping out such interlopers as the jazz clarinetist from New Orleans who wanted to build a Dixieland nightclub. Perhaps the most pronounced sign of the entrenched paternalism has been in the attitudes of those who run the school system, an entity that the superintendent, who has been in office more than twenty years, and the board of trustees seem to have regarded as a fiefdom.

Lana Noonan, for one, had no idea of this plantation mentality until she got involved as a member of the Parent-Teacher Organization at North Bay Elementary School, one of the four schools that serve the almost 2,000 pupils of the Bay St. Louis Municipal School District. The parents went out on their own and raised $6,000 that they wanted to use to buy air conditioners for the school so that their children would no longer have to swelter in the classrooms every fall and spring. It did not take long for the concerned parents to learn that if there were to be air conditioners or any other changes in the schools of Bay St. Louis, the superintendent and the trustees would make that decision without anyone else having much to say about it. The PTO found it difficult even to get a spot on the agenda to address a meeting of the trustees. Access to the agenda was restricted by a labyrinth of regulations intended ultimately to make certain that only groups of which the trustees approved would get the floor. Discussions by anyone other than the trustees of "wages, hours, or working conditions" of teachers was forbidden by a provision clearly meant to thwart union activities in behalf of the district's teachers. Unionism was viewed on a par with bolshevism. The policy was applied with such zeal that even someone purporting to speak for a parents' group might be denied the lectern.

Rebuffed in repeated attempts to get the superintendent and the trustees to consider their proposal for air conditioners, the parents from North Bay Elementary began to discover the extent to which citizen participation was discouraged in their school system. "What an education it was for me, an ordinary housewife who met with intimidation when I tried to do something nice for my youngsters' school,"[1] said Ms. Noonan, the mother of three, and president of the school's PTO. Ms. Noonan and other parents found that meetings of the school district's trustees were more like the gatherings of a private club whose members got together to sip mint juleps in private on the veranda. The trustees did not even bother posting notices of all their meetings, occasionally conducting unannounced meetings in violation of the state's law. When the public sliced through the veil of secrecy to attend meetings, the five trustees and the superintendent would sit huddled around a table in a charade of legality, whispering to each other as they conducted public business in tones so faint that they were barely audible.

Efforts by parents to obtain board minutes were resisted, as the superintendent announced that he would decide who was entitled to have copies of minutes and other official documents pertaining to the operations of the school district. The frustrated parents felt as though they had been trying to get minutes of meetings of the Central Intelligence Agency. A representative of the PTO who sought copies of journal entries reflecting expenditures by the district said that she was denied access to the material. Some of the women in the PTO complained of being confronted by school officials who asked them about their husbands' places of employment. The message they inferred was that if they pressed further, their husbands' jobs might be in jeopardy. Finally, numbed by a nightmare of frustration, the PTO—joined by some of the teachers—turned to the federal district court, charging that their constitutional rights to free speech, free assembly, due process, and equal protection were being violated by the superintendent and the trustees through intimidation, censorship, unreasonable delays, screening requirements, and secret meetings.[2] The suit, filed in 1979, provoked the biggest storm in Bay St. Louis since Hurricane Camille, which roared through the town a decade earlier.

An out-of-court settlement was reached as the school year was closing in the spring of 1980, an agreement by a begrudging board of trustees to revise its policies and pay $3,500 of the parents' attorney fees. The door to enlightenment has been opened a crack in Bay St. Louis, and the embittered school officials have been forced to acknowledge that parents do indeed have some rights in the schools their tax dollars support. Bay St. Louis is an extreme example of official indifference to public opinion, but it is a rude reminder of the lengths to which some school people will go to prevent parents from participating in the schools.

The idea of parent involvement is anathema to some of those in control of the schools. Never mind that parents and other taxpayers are the ones who finance the schools or that their most precious possessions, their children, are entrusted to the schools. Never mind that what happens in the schools probably has the next greatest impact after the home itself in shaping the lives of those children. Many teachers and administrators believe, nonetheless, that parents have no right to exert influence of any sort on the schools. "Public schoolpeople in America generally take a jaundiced view of parents' motives, concerns with the school, and interest in their own children," said Dwight Roper of Contemporary Research, Inc., in Palo Alto, California.[3]

Some of the procedures in schools seem designed to exclude parents and to keep them uninformed. Parents usually are not consulted on the choice of teachers for their youngsters. Most schools make no effort to involve parents in curriculum development or in the selection of textbooks. Principals are assigned to schools by central offices without regard for the wishes of parents. Codes regulating dress and behavior may be mandated unilaterally by the schools. Report cards may be so complex that they are unintelligible or so simple that they reveal almost nothing about a child's progress. Daytime meetings at the schools are scheduled with little regard for the needs of working mothers and fathers.

Marilyn Gittell, in an extensive study of citizen organizations in Boston, Atlanta, and Los Angeles, found that even where groups had been formed to give the community some

voice in the operation of its schools, their influence was frequently minimal.[4] This was especially true, according to Gittell, when organizations were comprised of low-income people. Apparently, the schools listen mostly to those who have
the power to force some attention. Congress, for example,
backed by the strength of the federal judiciary, has been able
to compel the schools to do its bidding. The individual citizen
is granted the authority to pay his taxes and keep his mouth
shut.

"The school is still perceived as a fortress in too many
places," said Carl L. Marburger, senior associate of the National Committee for Citizens in Education. "Our mission is to
convince people that the schools are theirs. Many school districts are scared to death of parents and parents are scared to
death of them. If people are invited to participate in anything
at all, it is in deciding the color of the bunting for the senior
prom. And then they are perceived as apathetic because they
don't want to do that. My dream as an advocate is the creation
of a coalition of parent-citizen groups in each state, each
served by a staff that can raise issues from their point of view."[5]

Marburger's dream is just about that: a dream. His
group is one of the few lonely outposts of an advance guard
dissatisfied with the secrecy that, like a moat around a castle,
guards schools from prying parents. The fortress Marburger
mentions is cold and forbidding, its drawbridge seldom low-
ered long enough to permit parents to gain access. Before that
happens, there will have to be wider support for the goals of
organizations like the National Committee for Citizens in Education. Operating on an annual budget of less than $400,000,
the group exerts efforts on three fronts, trying (1) to get more
information into people's hands about the way schools operate,
(2) to aid parents and others, like those they helped in Bay St.
Louis, Mississippi, gain an entree to the schools, and (3) to
monitor compliance by the schools with federal directives that
are intended to give parents input in the education of their
children.

A question that must occur to observers of the various
attempts to get citizens more active in the schools, however,
is whether citizens really want to play such a role. Often par-

ents do not bother taking advantage of the avenues that are opened for them. "Too many parents pay their school taxes, then sit back as though they had fulfilled their responsibility," the Association of American Publishers observed.[6] One provision in the minimum competency requirement taking effect for high school graduation in California in 1981 calls for the schools to hold conferences with parents of students who have failed the test so that the parents can have input in the remedial programs set up for their children. A survey of the preparations that local school districts were making for the implementation of the minimum competency requirement disclosed, though, that fewer than half of the parents of failing students were attending the conferences in 25 percent of the school districts surveyed. In one school system that sent invitations to conferences to parents three separate times, parents of only 15 to 20 percent of the students took the time to go to school in their youngsters' behalf.[7]

"We have to do a better job of opening the schools to parents and the broader community," John Yates, principal of Lumpkin County High School in Dahlonega, Georgia, said in the spring of 1981, upon taking over the presidency of the National Association of Secondary School Principals. "We are losing credibility, and much of our public no longer wants to become involved in schools."[8] Yates cited the example of his own 600-student high school, eighty miles north of Atlanta, where the parents of no more than a dozen youngsters showed up for an open house.

People take the schools for granted. Buyers of suburban homes will usually want to know something about the school system's reputation before closing a deal. But once they take up residence, they show more interest in the frequency of rubbish collections than in the dates of the school board meetings. The fact is that the reputations of school districts in the United States have absurdly little to do with the content of the curriculum or the quality of the teaching. What are generally considered desirable school systems and locales in which to purchase homes are those with many families clustered at the higher end of the socioeconomic scale. The poor have fewer options, and send their children to the trouble-plagued urban schools or impoverished rural schools that serve the only districts in which they can afford to live.

Higher-income parents are more easily able to put pressure on schools, but actually most of them do not bother. Families at all income levels seem content to remain uninvolved. A lack of time and interest may have more to do with this apathy than anything else. Even if a school allows participation in decision making by parents, few people are willing or able to miss work on a regular basis to attend a series of meetings, for example, in the implementation of a new secondary mathematics curriculum. Moreover, there is a widespread feeling that paying taxes relieves citizens of further responsibility and that they should not have to give up their precious time to do what they are hiring professionals to do for them. These attitudes, combined with the failure of most schools to reach out to solicit parent involvement, assure that citizens in most places will not be part of any meaningful process of educational decision making.

Administrators and teachers exacerbate the problem of noninvolvement when they fail to recognize the changes that are occurring in the American family. Relations with parents often are approached as though this were still a nation of Ozzies and Harriets. But the new reality is that the father who used to return from a hard day's work faithfully each evening to his homemaking wife and their two well-adjusted children is probably now living alone in a bleak apartment somewhere trying to figure out how to pay for his TV dinners after writing the weekly alimony check. The mother, who remained behind with the children in the prototypical split-level house, has joined a consciousness-raising group and works three days a week performing menial tasks in an office, struggling to reactivate and augment job skills that she has not used since she was twenty years old. And the children—yes, the children—are facing the awesome task of building their educational future on a support system of splinters. This approach may work, but, on the other hand, it may not.

Fewer children are living with both biological parents; more children are sharing a home with an adult partner of their mother who is not their father; and more children are being born into homes in which no father resides or ever will reside. By 1990, only half the households in the country are expected to contain a married couple: The remaining households will contain only one adult or an unmarried couple living together, and schoolchildren will live in many of these homes. By 1978, more than half of the nation's mothers—whether living with another adult or not—were in the paid labor force, and the proportion will continue to grow. Apparently, the family portrait of the immediate post-World War II era, the never-divorced couple of working father, homebound mother, and their children, is becoming so rare that it may soon be an artifact appropriate for the Smithsonian. Such families are expected to comprise 14 percent of all households in 1990.[9]

For the sake of the children, however, schools cannot ignore the implications of these changes. A report in 1980 said that students from one-parent families were less likely to be high achievers and more likely to be low achievers, more likely to be tardy, truant, and subject to disciplinary action, more likely to transfer from school to school, and twice as likely to drop out of school.[10] Others who have examined the plight of students from one-parent families have found the situation less dire, but still worthy of special concern. "Schools have an important role to play in the lives of single parents and, more particularly, their children," stated the National Association of Elementary School Principals, which cosponsored the aforementioned study with the Charles F. Kettering Foundation. It concluded that: "An important beginning is the mere recognition that they exist as a valid family unit." The National PTA has added its official voice, noting that schools sometimes make single parents feel like outcasts. This view was echoed by the National Committee for Citizens in Education, which in its own survey of 1,200 single parents in 47 states in 1980 found that in fewer than 5 percent of the cases did the parent without custody receive information about school activities from the school and that in fewer than 7 percent of the cases did that same person get a copy of the youngster's report card from the school.

Among the numerous proposals for better serving such

students and their parents are some worthy of immediate implementation. Schools should erase from their lexicon the phrase "broken home" and the assorted perjoratives so often applied to single-parent situations. Furthermore, teachers and administrators ought to abandon the self-fulfilling prophecies that children from such a background will automatically have problems. Schools should maintain records that include the addresses of both parents when they do not live together so that both mother and father may maintain a connection with the school. Identical reports should be sent to each parent, and the noncustody parent should have an equal opportunity to confer with teachers and staff.

This is not to say that single parents, any more than married ones, are entirely innocent and that schools are always guilty when it comes to parental noninvolvement. Parents of all kinds tend to sit back and let their school board members get involved for them. Judged by the low level of participation in the public schools by parents and other citizens, grassroots democracy is withering away. It is not for lack of fertilizer, which is abundant at school board meetings. Taxpayers are simply too willing to delegate all responsibility for the schools to the few people who are willing to assume the heartache of school board service. Those fulfilling this role, whether appointed or elected, are better educated and wealthier than their fellow citizens. Typically, they are from families with incomes of more than $40,000. Sixty-three percent of them have completed four or more years of college. Ninety percent of them are white, and more than seven of every ten are men. Usually, few outsiders attend their meetings and neither side— school board, nor public—tries very hard to communicate with the other. An informal survey of 759 school board members from around the country showed that more than one-third had contact with parents in their districts on school business fewer than three times a month.[11] Systematic contacts are frequently nonexistent. The result is that few taxpayers have any notion of what is happening in the schools.

If school board members were always diligently striving to represent the interests of their fellow citizens, they might compensate somewhat for these omissions. But sometimes board members seem to be spokesmen for the superintendent instead of for the public. "Most board members do not view their role as representing, or speaking for, 'the public'; rather, they view it as speaking *for* the administration *to* 'the public'," [12] commented one group of experts on the subject of school governance. School board members sometimes allow themselves to become rubber stamps for the superintendents they hire.

This is fine with some superintendents who are glad not to have school board members poking into the affairs of the district. Some superintendents sweep enough problems under the rug to choke a Hoover, and would rather leave those problems out of sight. One of a superintendent's most effective devices for deflecting inquiry is obfuscation, needlessly complicating matters so that the laymen on the board feel inadequate. Board members seldom have time to learn the nuances of the job. Few districts allot board members their own staffs. Consequently, board members are often dependent on the superintendent for the very information they would need to challenge him. Perhaps that is why so many school boards spend so little time on matters of substance, instead devoting disproportionate attention to the seating plan for commencement or the brand of typewriter to purchase for the school office.

Some of the worst hoarding of power has occurred in districts like Bay St. Louis, whose superintendents have been in office so long that they begin to think they, not the taxpayers, own the school system. It is a proprietary attitude not necessarily limited to school superintendents, but somehow it is a bit more understandable in the domain of a Henry Ford or a David Rockefeller. One district that has endured such a mentality is DeKalb County, Georgia, a comfortable bedroom community abutting Atlanta. During a period of more than thirty years, beginning in the late 1940s and ending in 1980, only two superintendents reigned in DeKalb. For all purposes the district was run to their specifications.

For the citizens, this meant not knowing what was going on in the schools. The system dispensed information to the public with the eagerness of a miser donating to charity. People even had trouble finding out the schedule for school board meetings. The situation was abetted by the local parents' organization, handmaiden to the administration. The parents' groups of the various schools in the 78,600-student system were discouraged from forming a unified organization that might exert influence at the district level. Virtually the only gatherings of the parents at the district level were social affairs, carefully watched over in paternalistic fashion by the school system's administrators. School board members did not fare much better, relying on financial figures supplied by the administration while an embarrassing surplus of $40 million accumulated by 1980, a result of maintaining taxes at a higher level than was needed to operate the system.

Change may finally be in the air in DeKalb, however. A new superintendent was hired in 1980, and there was promise of some fresh air blowing through the hidden corridors of administrative power. One lesson emphasized by those long years during which the people of the county meekly acceded to the authority of the superintendent is that the public is reluctant to get involved in the schools so long as there is the appearance of a smooth-running operation. Chicagoans played the same apathetic role. In DeKalb's case, this apparently meant that nothing counted quite so much as having an orderly, virtually all-white school system. Many of the families had fled Atlanta with the express desire of escaping the increasingly black schools. Sometimes, though, white is not enough.

In the future, it will be less common to find school districts anywhere in which an administration has the kind of free-wheeling authority that was once exercised in DeKalb. The reason for this change will have little to do with citizens asserting themselves. Instead, the boundaries of local jurisdiction will grow fuzzier as incursions by unions, legislatures, courts, and federal agencies wrest away great chunks of educational terrain on which outsiders never dared trespass in former years. Is it any wonder, then, when school boards and administrators will be losing strength that the outlook is not encouraging for ordinary parents? One symbol of the shift away from local control is the statistic showing that in 1975, for the first time in American history, the amount of revenues supplied to the schools by state and federal sources exceeded local sources.[13] All the money, of course, originates in the same place—the taxpayer's pocket—but when it is redistributed by the state and federal governments, the legislatures and Congress can set the terms.

This need not mean that parents must abandon all hope of having input in the education of their children, doing nothing but signing an occasional report card. If they choose, parents can fight to be partners in the schools. But they will have to find new and more effective methods for participation. The National PTA, for instance, was supposed to facilitate such a partnership. Too often, though, during those years when the PTA was the only outlet for parents, it played sycophant to teachers and administrators. Only recently has the organization become more consistently assertive. Virginia Sparling, the president of the National PTA, does not like to be reminded of the obsequious reputation of her group. "We have become more activist," she said in an 1980 interview.[14] And indeed the PTA has shown signs of change. The PTA was instrumental in keeping conservatives from ousting progressives on the school board in Newport News, Virginia. The PTA monitored the collective bargaining process in Louisville, Kentucky. The PTA mobilized parents to keep kindergartens from being eliminated in New Smyrna Beach, Florida. Now, the PTA has launched an Urban Education Project to help raise the quality of schooling in the big cities.

It remains to be seen if the PTA can be successful in its new efforts to portray itself as an effective force for parents' rights in an era when some parents are no longer satisfied with melting into the background at their children's schools. Dissatisfaction with the PTA is reflected in the steady loss of membership, which fell from 11,791,431 in 1965 to 6,069,438 in 1980.[15] Clearly, the PTA is trying to speak with a stronger voice, less willing to be a demure partner to the school establishment. But the tune has changed and the PTA may already be out of step. New forms of parent involvement could make the PTA an anachronism.

The near absence of the PTA in the life of inner-city schools was one of the reasons for federal legislation mandating the formation of parent councils in schools to advise on policies involving government-supported programs. The most extensive of these efforts is in behalf of Title I of the Elementary and Secondary Education Act, which provides remedial funds. Every school with at least 75 students in a Title I program is supposed to have an advisory council of parents and other community members. Similar requirements have been adopted for other federal education programs for the disadvantaged, including Follow Through, Head Start, bilingual education, and the Emergency School Aid Act, which sponsors projects connected to desegregation.

There are about 60,000 Title I advisory councils in the country with a total of some 900,000 members. In addition, an estimated 150,000 people serve on the councils formed for the other federal education programs. This is the most extensive parental involvement ever mandated for the schools. Little is known, though, about how it is working. Apparently, the results are uneven; some school principals have played show-and-tell with the councils, while others have truly let parents get involved in substantial ways. The first comprehensive examination of the federally sponsored councils is to be completed in 1981 by the Department of Education.

Don Davies, president of the Institute for Responsive Education, based in Boston, and one of the nation's authorities on parental participation in the schools, had this to say about the councils: "Regulations or guidelines for participation are often ambiguous, frequently different or contradictory from one program to another and inevitably confusing for those charged with implementation. No attention is given to problems of multiplicity of groups or duplication of efforts, especially at the school level."[16] A separate council is required for each federal program and, as Davies implied, a principal may carry the burden of having to recruit and work with three or four councils in the same school, ending up with almost the same individuals serving on each. Congress has sidestepped the issue of consolidation, preferring to create the impression that several viable councils can operate simultaneously in the same school, hardly a possibility in a suburban school, let alone in the ghetto.

Where an advisory council for a Title I program is effective, parents are kept informed of the educational progress of their children, brought into the classrooms as volunteers, and taken along to assist on field trips. The successes and frustrations are shared with the parents, who sometimes help the school find needed resources in the community. The idea of creating the councils was to ensure a forum through which parents could feel they had a stake in the education of their youngsters. It was hoped that the parents would transmit their concerns to their children, who would benefit from knowing that their mothers and fathers thought school was important enough to get involved. Probably the most important function of the federal mandate, even if it has not fulfilled its promise, has been to introduce some semblance of parent involvement in schools where parents might otherwise be excluded from participation. Congress improved the concept in 1978 by providing that the councils use part of their money to train members in the intricacies of the Title I legislation so that they would be more likely to offer sound advice.

As a result of the federal government's interest in parent advisory councils, some states have been stimulated to promote the establishment of such councils in all schools, whether or not they have extensive federal programs. California, Florida, and South Carolina were among the first states to take this initiative, and their experiences seem certain to influence what other states do about advisory councils in the 1980s. The mandate for advisory committees in Florida was part of a legislative package aimed at equalizing financial support for education throughout the state.

A look at the advisory committee at Cypress Elementary School in Pompano Beach, along Florida's Atlantic coast, gives some idea of what has happened in one of the better situations. It also demonstrates the vital role of the principal in determining whether or not such a venture will succeed. The principal in this case was Al Capuano, a transplanted New Yorker, who was an open and responsive administrator. When he arrived at the school in 1977, there was no advisory committee even though the law had been in effect for four years. Mr. Capuano quickly found out which parents were most interested in the school and invited them to form the nucleus of an advisory committee, which grew to ten members by accepting anyone who wanted to join. The law says membership may include teachers, parents, and community members, as well as students, for committees at secondary schools. Cypress Elementary offered a fertile cross-section of families—two-thirds white and one-third black—from which to draw members.

Soon, the committee was meeting monthly in the one-story, concrete-block school, consulting regularly with Capuano on a variety of decisions. Capuano used the committee as a sounding board in developing a discipline policy. On another occasion he let the committee serve as an appeal board, though he was not obligated to accord it that role. A mother who had waited until after the deadline to request a change in her child's class assignment had complained about the inflexibility of the policy. Capuano left it up to the committee to decide whether an exception should be made for the youngster. The committee upheld him, refusing to allow the student's transfer. Capuano also turned to the committee when the school had a choice of using a portion of its discretionary budget either to rent a copying machine or hire an additional teacher's aide. The committee opted for the copier and Capuano followed that advice.

The Florida legislature tried to give the advisory committees more latitude in 1978 by adopting the Educational Improvement Projects Act, a $500,000 program of mini-grants for which advisory committees throughout the state compete. Individual grants of $500 to $5,000 are used for such purposes as hiring directors of school volunteer programs or running programs to train parents to help their children with homework, or carrying out community relations projects. There is also a requirement in the law that all advisory committees assist in the preparation of annual reports for their schools, providing the parents with information about such items as the building budget and achievement scores on tests. The legal language has the proper sound for those who favor greater participation by parents, but in most cases it is really the principals who compile the reports, relegating the parents to a minor role.

The brief history of advisory committees in Florida indicates that involving parents in the schools can be a slow and cumbersome process. Few of Florida's school boards embraced the legislation enthusiastically and the turtle's pace at which implementation has proceeded says something about their continuing attitudes. Similarly, many of the building principals did not strain themselves ferreting out volunteers to serve on committees when prospective members failed to bang down the schoolhouse doors. A survey in 1977 showed that only about 10 percent of the potential committees had been formed.[17] More recently, during the 1979–80 school year, Mary Fedler, a doctoral candidate at the University of Florida, conducted a survey of committees throughout the state as her dissertation project. Her findings reinforced the earlier examinations by the Institute for Responsive Education, disclosing that much remains to be done before schools in Florida conform with the spirit of the law. The enabling legislation made it possible for the school PTA to be designated as the building's advisory committee, and some school boards have followed this practice as the least threatening solution to what they deem an unfortunate intrusion into their bailiwick.

The experience with parent advisory groups in Florida and elsewhere reaffirms the suspicion that inserting any type of new entity into an existing hierarchy, including the organizational structure of a school, is not easy. Strong and specific support is needed from the legislature. The more vague the mandate, the more likely that local school officials will find ways of resisting the law and manipulating it to their advantage. The Institute for Responsive Education noted the "apparent paradox that strong action by central governments is necessary for the promotion and nurturing of grassroots democracy."[18] It also seems necessary to do more to stimulate and train the volunteers who serve on committees, as well as to allay the trepidations of principals and teachers so that they do not feel threatened by the involvement of parents.

It would be a mistake, though, to conclude on the basis of the weak and ineffectual start of advisory committees in most of Florida's school districts that citizens do not want committees or that the public is unable to carry out the functions.

Perhaps there is an analogy between the advisory committees and some of the emerging nations in underdeveloped parts of the world. People who have not had the chance to influence their own affairs—as most people have not had when it comes to the schools—cannot immediately behave as if they have had such experience. If parents do not seek out the chance to sit on advisory committees it could be that, after a lifetime of being told that their advice was not welcome, it is difficult for them to take seriously an invitation to participate.

Marshall Harris, who helped frame the Florida legislation when he was on the staff of Governor Reubin Askew, is now the liaison with the advisory committees as head of the Florida Education Council, an arm of the State Education Department. Harris concedes that the accomplishments of the law have fallen short of what was envisioned, but he remains convinced that setting up the committees was one of the most important moves the state has made in education. "I think the advisory committees are a key ingredient for improving the quality of schooling," Mr. Harris said. "It is shortsighted for the people in the schools not to take advantage of the desire by parents to play a greater role. The research is clear that where there is a consensus among teachers, administrators, and parents about what they want to do, the likelihood of achieving it is extremely high. Furthermore, in our state, with the large proportion of older people, schools are having an increasingly difficult time vying for resources. This way the schools can team up with the taxpayers."[19]

On a local level, Chicago has its own school advisory councils, groups with their roots planted firmly in the 1960s, when urban unrest set the stage for change—or at least the illusion of change. In 1970, the city's board of education mandated the creation of an advisory council in each of Chicago's decentralized school districts, which now total 20. The councils, composed of parents, community members, teachers, and even some high school students, meet monthly during the academic year. Virtually any topic relating to the schools may be discussed with the district superintendent, though the bodies can make no decisions in their own right. They exercise power only to the extent that they can influence the district

superintendent. Some of the district superintendents appreciate the guidance of the councils and others ignore them.

Surprise followed surprise in Chicago: Two years after
creating the district advisory councils, the board of education
authorized similar groups at each of the city's 650 school buildings. The school advisory councils, like those at the district
level, have no independent decision-making powers, acting
only as sounding boards for the principals. The school advisory
councils were, however, given a role in the selection of principals, an extraordinary authority that delighted parent advocates. Few school districts in the country have permitted
parents to participate in the choosing of principals. In Chicago,
the school advisory councils appointed committees to screen
and nominate candidates for the principalships. The board of
education reserved to the city's general school superintendent
the final appointment, but in the beginning he concurred with
most nominations.

This venture in participatory democracy did not win
favor with the Principals' Association in Chicago, which went
to court several times during the 1970s to challenge the propriety of public involvement in the selection of principals.
Respect for the process was further weakened by Superintendent Hannon, who decided increasingly to make appointments without regard to the role of the advisory councils. The
councils struggled to preserve their role, even making certain
to include both blacks and whites in their lists of nominees
after the federal government directed Chicago to step up staff
integration, but by 1980 the short experiment was moribund,
the life squeezed out of it by the various pressures against the
councils. The closing of schools because of enrollment declines
was putting principals out of their jobs and contributing to a
pool of people who had to be reappointed before any new
principals could be considered.

Sometimes the promise of citizen participation is little
more than an attempt to lull a quiescent public into thinking
it has something to say about the schools. Occasionally, though,
genuine involvement appears where it is least expected. Salt
Lake City, for example, is not exactly a den of radicals. The
Mormonism that permeates the area has helped shape a citi-

zenry accustomed to hierarchical lines of authority, and boat-rockers have a good chance of ending up in the drink, swimming against a powerful tide of conformity. Yet, the community councils that have been formed at each of the schools in Salt Lake City allow for greater public input than is found in many other of the nation's schools, including those in districts that are supposedly more liberal.

Most of the credit for this innovation belongs to M. Donald Thomas, a superintendent with self-confidence enough not to consider parents a threat to the school system. Mr. Thomas assumed the superintendency in 1973, stepping into a vise in which he was squeezed on one side by a public that had lost trust in the schools and on the other side by a school board that did not know how to communicate with parents. Salt Lake City was a troubled school district in which enrollment had dropped by more than 25 percent and funding problems were undercutting whatever stability remained. Mr. Thomas immediately began exploring a concept he called "shared governance" as a way of renewing the faith of the people in their schools.

As a result of Mr. Thomas's plan, every building in the school system now has a council composed of nine persons— the principal, the president and vice president of the school's PTA, and six other individuals from the neighborhood, usually including a student if the building is a high school. Councils serve in both advisory and decision-making capacities. The decisions are anything but monumental, but do affect the life of the school. In Salt Lake City, for instance, each council has the power to determine how the particular school will meet the state requirement of 27½ class hours a week. If the council desires, for example, the school can have longer schooldays from Monday through Thursday so that classes on Friday may meet for only a half-day. The council also decides how to allot the budget each school gets for the payment of athletic coaches and teachers of extracurricular activities, determining the priorities for the kinds of teams and clubs the school will sponsor. The council, as well, sets the format for regularly scheduled conferences between teachers and parents.

In addition, the council designates representatives who

sit on the committees that make a range of decisions for the school from selecting textbooks to choosing a new principal. When issues have districtwide significance or the legal authority of the board of education is involved, a school community council can not do more than advise. Thus, if a council decides that one of the teachers in the school is not performing to standard, the most it can do is bring the matter to the attention of the school board. The central administration will respond by setting in motion the specific machinery that Thomas has designed for dealing with questions of teacher competence. There is the possibility of a formal review of the teacher's work, as well as a procedure that Salt Lake City calls an "audit," in which the standardized test scores of the teacher's classes are studied to measure the progress that the youngsters have achieved under that teacher.

A look at the council at Highland High School and its recent accomplishments points to the sorts of action that can be taken by such groups. Concern with automobile traffic might seem a mundane interest by contrast with the educational issues in a school, but at Highland the congestion in the streets around the school was so bad that a student was killed in an accident. The traffic pattern in the immediate neighborhood, dangerous in the best of times, was almost beyond control during the hours before and after the school day, when the streets filled with the cars of the many students who drove to schools. Affluence, after all, is the mother of traffic jams—what better place to find the symbols of that affluence than in the parking lot of an upper-middle-class high school. The council could not make the cars disappear, but it could induce the city's road department to formulate a plan for relieving congestion and making the streets safer.

Two of the other contributions of the council at Highland involved its efforts to get an addition built for the gymnasium and to develop a program for improving the study habits of the school's students. The gym addition required the authorization of the board of education, and the council organized a lobbying campaign that ultimately won that approval. In addressing study habits, the council was responding to the concerns of many parents who were dismayed by how little their youngsters seemed to be getting out of school. A professor from the University of Utah was hired by the council to give a voluntary eight-week course on study habits. So many students signed up for the class during the 1980–81 school year that it might become a regular feature at the school.

The council's greatest impact on the educational program may come from its request that the school system reexamine its graduation requirements. During the four years from the ninth through the twelfth grade, students have to take a total of only twelve mainline courses, known as "solids" in Salt Lake City. An average of three solids a year in a schedule fleshed out with make-work electives allows students to glide through high school with a minimum of effort. A committee under the council's sponsorship started delving into the question of requirements during the 1980–81 school year. Eventually, the result of its deliberations may be a series of proposals for strengthening the curriculum.

Assuring parents of input into the schools through councils and committees is desirable, but it does not relieve parents of the responsibility for reinforcing education in the home. They owe it to their children to support education out of the classroom as well as in it. Help of this kind can take many forms, ranging from disciplining youngsters and inculcating good attitudes toward teachers to listening to children read aloud and drilling them in multiplication tables. This is not something that comes naturally to all mothers and fathers, parenthood being one of the jobs for which neither training nor credentials are required. In his *Republic,* Plato envisioned an ideal state in which the only people eligible to be rulers would be those who by virtue of age, education, and experience had established their qualifications. Since parenthood requires no such test, it would be well if more agencies began assisting schools in guiding parents in ways to help in the schooling of their children.

One of the few organizations that exists for this purpose is the Home and School Institute (HSI), which Dorothy Rich started on a shoestring in 1965. HSI is based on the idea that the schools, no matter how good they may be, cannot do an optimum job of educating children without reinforcement from parents. The nonprofit organization, not an arm of any school system, operates independently, sponsoring workshops and publishing materials to help parents, teachers, and administrators do more to promote relationships between home and classroom.

A typical HSI workshop runs from 8:30 to 5 on four successive Saturdays, teaching parents to help their children to develop skills in mathematics and reading through activities that they can carry out in the home. An affiliation with Trinity College in Washington, D.C., enables HSI to award academic credits for its workshops. Another of the group's projects has involved the preparation of "Home Learning Recipes," practical suggestions for using objects and chores around the house to teach basic skills. One difficulty Ms. Rich has found, however, is that many parents do not want to bother attending workshops or inconvenience themselves in any way for something they consider peripheral to their lives. So, HSI is exploring other ways of getting information to parents, including the possibility of reaching them at their places of employment.

While the schools pay obeisance to the idea that parents should reinforce classroom learning, few schools do much to equip parents for the task. At best, many of them offer no more than an open school night during which the parents troop from classroom to classroom and emerge with nothing more than tired feet. Houston has at least tried to improve this approach with its Operation Fail/Safe. The program began in 1978, when the school system designated two days in the fall and two more in the spring for parents of elementary pupils to visit their children's schools. The public was blitzed with a media campaign befitting a political election. The message was proclaimed on television and radio, from newspapers and billboards. Parents throughout Houston were urged to show up at their children's schools on appointed nights. Upon arrival, they were greeted by teachers and told of school policies relating to attendance and promotion. The teachers reviewed test scores and marks with the parents. Finally came the pièce de résistance, a personalized computer printout of each child's reading level and reading interests on a sheet to take home. Libraries across the city had already made preparations to supply lists of books that corresponded to the levels and interests of the youngsters as indicated on the printouts. In addition, as a pilot project in 50 of the schools, the computer also generated for the parents lists of vocabulary words and drills in word-attack skills programmed to meet the individual needs of their children.

An innovation of a different sort was tried in Fowler, California, where John Taylor, the superintendent, wondered why the children of some low-income minority families were successful in school, while other children from similar families failed. In 1977, the school district identified a group of successful students and sent teams of teachers and principals into their homes to discover what accounted for the higher achievement of these children. At least three common themes ran through almost all the homes: (1) the parents knew a lot about what was happening in school and kept in touch with teachers so that they would know what was expected of their children; (2) the parents saw school as a key to upward mobility and encouraged good attendance; and (3) there was in each child's life, even though these were usually one-parent families, another adult besides the parent—grandparent, neighbor, or aunt—who was a source of additional emotional and psychological support. The combination of these factors led to a strong emphasis on doing homework, though in some instances the home was so crowded that it meant reserving study time in the bathroom. These were children whose television-viewing was regulated and who had assigned chores around the house. There was organization and structure in their lives, and it apparently carried over into the classroom.

Each year since the study, the Fowler district has run a program for 15 to 20 parents, trying to make them familiar with what was learned about children in families of socioeconomic background similar to theirs. In some cases, the parents attending the program have been paid with funds from the Comprehensive Employment Training Act (CETA). Superintendent Taylor claims no miracles, but there have been improvements in achievement scores that he thinks can be traced to the program.

Clearly, as has been found in Fowler and in other places,

parents can have an effect on what happens in the classroom. It is important that at the very minimum they lend encouragement to their youngsters. Studies of home-based reinforcement of school behavior have shown conclusively that when parents consistently show approval for good work in school it encourages their children to try harder. Regular notes back and forth between parents and teacher, for example, can prod a youngster to do better.

A recognition of the importance of home attitudes in school success underlies the campaign that the Rev. Jesse L. Jackson has conducted to raise the achievement of blacks in inner-city schools. Using his theatrical flair, Jackson has gone into school auditoriums across the land to exhort young people to forsake drugs and other temptations so that they can do their best in school and aspire to responsible jobs. Chanting slogans and swearing oaths, the youngsters promise to try harder. Jackson's Push for Excellence has also enlisted parents, asking them to be sure that their youngsters follow through on their pledges to do homework. Push for Excellence has yet to advance very far beyond theatrics, but the notion of getting parents to support homework is worth pursuing in any event.

Three of every five 17-year-olds in all kinds of high schools—inner-city, suburban, rural—say they spend less than five hours a week on homework. This is happening in their senior year of high school, the point in their education when they should be hitting their stride and honing study habits for college. But too many students find that school is not demanding. Fifty-three percent of the teen-agers surveyed by the Gallup Poll asserted that they did not have to work hard in school.[20] Apparently, many teachers do not even assign homework because they assume their students will not do it. Other teachers do not give homework because they do not want the nuisance of having to mark it.

Parents know better than anyone else whether their children are doing homework. There is no reason why parents cannot confer with teachers to be certain that homework is assigned and to discuss ways that they—the parents—can collaborate to be certain that the assignments are completed.

Ellen Glanz, the Massachusetts high school teacher who posed as a student to see how the other half lived, offered a good rationale for homework. She said that homework helps pinpoint learning problems, extends the breadth of the lesson without taking away classtime, prepares students for the next day's discussion, and cultivates independent problem solving.[21]

Some parents are so dissatisfied, not only with the failure of schools to assign homework, but with what happens in the classroom itself, that they have taken the education of their children into their own hands. Literally. These parents keep their children out of school and educate them at home, assuming the teaching themselves. They are people like Joe and Susan Bruno, who stopped sending their son, Max, to school when he was halfway through the first grade in early 1980. The dining room of their home on the top floor of a four-story brownstone in the Park Slope section of Brooklyn became Max's classroom. He was joined by his brother, Damon, who would have entered kindergarten in the fall of 1980, but remained home to be educated with Max.

Joe Bruno, who has been a butcher and a real estate salesman, and who never completed college, stayed home each day to teach his children, while Susan Bruno went off to her job as a secretary in Manhattan. The Brunos obtained a copy of the minimum curriculum requirements from the New York State Education Department and built a teaching program around it. The antique oak dining table became Max's school desk each morning as the breakfast dishes were cleared and his father handed him a lined notebook into which the day's assignment had been written.

On one particular morning, Max, a brown-haired, brown-eyed child with a resemblance to his father, opened the notebook to read the following words: "The other day we were talking about division. I showed you the symbol for division. It is $\div$ or $\overline{)}$. If you see $6 \div 3 = ?$ you read it as "6 divided by 3 equals ." And in a mixture of script and printing the explanation of division continued, ending in a long list of exercises that Max was to answer. It was a neat assignment, lasting from nine to ten o'clock, in which Joe Bruno had cleverly combined reading, writing, and arithmetic to give his 7-year-old son a rigorous taste of the basics. Joe Bruno confessed that he was weaning Max from printing and moving him into script as quickly as possible because it was easier for Joe to write the lessons in script. Joe Bruno would puff on a cigarette and sip coffee as Max attacked the division problems. Occasionally, Mr. Bruno would look over Max's shoulder, tap a finger on the page and say: "Hmm, check that one out." Damon, curled up on a chair next to Max, watched his brother for a while and then asked his father to work with him on his alphabet. As he felt the urge, Mr. Bruno would make a phone call or go into some other part of the house to attend to a task. The boys might spar or distract each other briefly, but always returned to the work at hand. Every now and then, Mr. Bruno would ask Max a question about the lesson to be certain he understood what he was doing. Sometimes he would have Max read aloud to him. Max, a strong, sure reader, moved confidently through his work, apparently enjoying himself and giving the impression that life without classmates could be normal.

But it was not normal, and even though Joe Bruno maintained the regimen for five hours a day—giving his son science lessons from materials purchased from the National Geographic Society and improvising geography lessons on a large map of Europe that had been hung in the kitchen—Max Bruno was not in a schoolhouse and the Bruno family was skirting the edges of the law. Despite state regulations in New York that permit children to be educated at home if certain requirements are met, the Family Court was suing to get Max back in school and Mr. Bruno had hired a lawyer to fight back. "He would probably pick up as much information in school," said Mr. Bruno, "but his attitude toward himself and toward what he learns wouldn't be as good. All of the tests and grading in schools are built on comparative performance and it's an unhealthy way of seeing oneself."[22]

John Holt, the author, who has promoted the idea of home education through his Boston-based organization, Growing Without Schooling, estimated that about 10,000 families around the country are teaching their youngsters at home. "The courts have been swinging pretty heavily to the side of the parents where they have done sufficient homework and can come in with a strong statement of what they are doing and back it with a good legal case," Holt said.[23] The question, though, is whether home education is in the best interests of the children. It is an extreme response to the very real inadequacies of public education. Perhaps before resorting to such a measure parents might first do more to become actively involved in trying to improve the system, rather than simply abandoning it.

One way to encourage families to remain allied with public schools is to reduce the frustrations of those who find the system intractable. Layer upon layer of bureaucracy, buttressed by tomes of rules and regulations, sometimes make parents seeking information feel like Dorothy in the Land of Oz. Even where accessibility is encouraged, parents may remain intimidated by authority, hesitant and unsure in their approach to administrators and teachers. While the schools have no responsibility to give assertiveness training to parents, steps could be taken to make it easier for parents to have an impact. The Swedish parliament did it for their countrymen in the early 19th century by giving them an ombudsman to help lone individuals gain redress from government. It is an idea that every school system in this country ought to consider. Ombudsmen have been used by various governmental bodies in the United States and even by some universities, beginning in the 1960s. But probably no more than a couple dozen school systems have ombudsmen.

One of those districts is Ann Arbor, Michigan, where Robert L. Potts has been ombudsman since 1970, making him one of the nation's first public school ombudsmen and probably the person who has held such a position longest. Mr. Potts believes that communications problems are inherent in bureaucracies and that the views of parents and students are likely to get chewed up in the machinery of a school system unless there is someone like an ombudsman. His job was established by the school board, and he reports directly to the superintendent without any intermediaries to blunt his role. While the superintendent could recommend the dismissal of the ombudsman, only the school board could actually take such action.

Student discipline is involved in the largest number of cases brought to Potts's attention and so one of his main tasks is to ascertain if students were penalized justly. He finds that the ombudsman is pivotal in helping minority members win assurance of equitable treatment. One case not long ago involved a black student on the football team whose parent complained to Potts that the lad was not getting all of the playing time he deserved because the coach was allegedly discriminating against him. Potts brought together the principal, the coach, the parent, and the student. The outcome of the conversation was that the coach decided to give the youngster more playtime. This is the stuff of which successful schools are made, and any school system could benefit from a process that resolves differences and alleviates misunderstandings. Almost every family with a child in school has at one time or another felt the need for an intermediary—someone to step in when problems between teachers and students cannot be reconciled, when rules are administered unfairly, when parents cannot get a sympathetic ear.

There is some disagreement over whether an ombudsman should be an impartial mediator or an advocate. Either role has merit, though advocacy is probably what parents need most. Above all, the ombudsman must be independent, free from the pressure of those who would weaken his effectiveness and threaten to take away his job. This means that an ombudsman probably ought to serve under a contract that cannot be abrogated except under special circumstances. He should be accountable only to the school board, the body directly representing the public. He should have direct access to the superintendent and all other personnel in the system. It is best if the ombudsman has the respect of both educators and the public, as well as a familiarity with the schools.

In the end, whatever helps students and makes schools more successful serves the larger purpose of strengthening public education for the next generation. Parents are the key to this process. While ombudsmen can pave the way for them, parents should have the opportunity to participate in their own right. But defining the extent of their role is not as easy as it may appear to some advocates. The school district in Rochester, New York, for instance, has gone so far as to let a parent serve as an observer to the Board of Education's collective bargaining negotiations with the Rochester Teachers' Association. Leaders of parent organizations jointly compiled a list of a half-dozen acceptable representatives and the school board selected one.

Gayle Dixon, the mother of two, represented the parents in the 1978 negotiations and found the task arduous and time consuming, a chore that perhaps few parents would relish or for which they could find time. Her son was already in the first grade, and she took her preschool daughter with her to most of the meetings, making the child probably the best-known three-year-old in Rochester, Ms. Dixon now jests. But it was no joking matter at the time and Ms. Dixon reflects that "maybe it is unreasonable for other parents in the school district to expect one parent to devote that kind of time."[24] An alternative might be to assign a revolving team of parents as observers to the negotiations, but then there would be the difficulty of someone being unable to participate in a full and knowledgeable manner because he or she would get only a fragmentary view.

The problem is by no means insurmountable and Rochester is obviously on the right track in making parents privy to collective bargaining negotiations. Ms. Dixon's experience, though, demonstrates once again that parental participation requires thoughtful planning and may take a degree of refining before it works well—as Florida has discovered with the school councils. All this to say that the role of parents in the schools is simply one arm of a partnership with teachers, administrators, and school board members. There is a careful balance to maintain; what is important is that parents be included on the scale.

EPILOGUE

But I have promises to keep,
and miles to go before I sleep,
and miles to go before I sleep.

ROBERT FROST
"Stopping by Woods on a
    Snowy Evening"

What I hope I have made clear is that the quality of schools depends on adults, not kids. Young people are powerless in this drama, bit players on a stage on which their elders have all the best parts. Most youngsters want desperately to succeed. No child ever entered first grade intending to join education's casualty list. If the schools are in trouble then it is the fault of the adults. The plea for greater parental involvement is not meant to add a special interest group where there is already too much self-interest, but to strengthen the one body of adults who have the greatest stake in seeing to it that pupils prosper.

Classrooms in the lower grades of elementary schools are full of children who are eager and willing to learn. What happens, though, to extinguish the passion in so many of them as they advance to the upper grades and into secondary school? Events in those classrooms during the early years of schooling are crucial in determining what will occur just a few years later. The loss of innocence is to be expected, but when students also lose the joy of learning, then the schools themselves should be examined. The horror of events in some of the worst high schools can be best appreciated in terms of what failed to happen during those first years of schooling. One cannot overemphasize the need of every youngster for a good start. The fact that kindergarten is still not a universal experience for five-year-olds is testimony to the lack of understanding of the importance of this period.

The imperative for a strong beginning is most obvious

235

in the inner city, where models of success should be studied carefully for replication. The few schools that overcome the odds must be scrutinized, rare specimens that they are, so that their traits can be emulated in the cloning of a whole generation of similarly successful schools. Only then will public education fulfill its mandate for all the people.

A great danger at this juncture is the likelihood of a new rationale for failure, one more excuse for the schools not being able to serve their pupils properly during the 1980s. Education has been left terribly vulnerable by the economic crunch. It is a flimsy, tattered banner buffeted by a ferocious storm. School boards claim they do not have enough money to keep up with inflationary demands and they have started cutting programs. Statewide elections, such as those in California and Massachusetts for limiting taxes, are pushing the knife deeper. Finally, the Reagan administration slashing the federal budget to the quick is bound to cripple the school systems that have developed the greatest dependence on Washington, namely the big-city districts. If schools do not have sufficient funds to hire enough teachers, mount adequate programs, and maintain ample hours of instruction, then there is going to be one more very good reason why children are not learning.

An inevitable result of the new policies in Washington is that the states and cities are going to have to assume more of the burden for programs that have been financed primarily by Congress. The continuance of many health and welfare enterprises is going to take a larger share of the state and local tax dollar. Education's claim on these monies will become even shakier than it is; there is the specter of an odious competition, indeed a form of triage, as the needs of the elderly and the indigent might be weighed against those of schoolchildren.

Furthermore, the public schools must now fight a rear guard action against critics who maintain that private and parochial schools are a better educational bargain. James S. Coleman's study for the National Center for Education Statistics, released in the spring of 1981, indicated that students in nonpublic schools learn more than students of comparable background in public schools. Coleman insisted that the importance of the study was that it drew attention to the attributes of successful schools and that all kinds of schools, public and private, could improve by emulating the best schools. This may be true, but the point was obscured by the haste in which observers seized on the findings as evidence of the inferiority of public education.

Were such travail not enough, education in the 1980s will have the awesome responsibility of upholding standards in a society in which the schools may be among a shrinking number of institutions concerned with quality. Young people cannot be faulted if they question values at a time when the best-selling novels tend to be the worst written, the highest-paid Americans are entertainers and athletes, and the most popular leisure-time activity of adults is watching situation comedies on television. Don't blame the kids if they wonder why education is worth the bother.

REFERENCES

CHAPTER ONE

1. *On Further Examination: Report of the Advisory Panel on the Scholastic Aptitude Test Score Decline* (New York: College Entrance Examination Board, 1977).
2. Daniel Calhoun, *The Intelligence of a People* (Princeton, N.J.: Princeton University Press, 1973), pp. 70–73.
3. Personal Interview.

CHAPTER TWO

1. Public Law 64–347.
2. Personal interview with Office of Food Services, New York City Board of Education.
3. Elaine Yaffe, "Public Education: Society's Band-Aid," *Phi Delta Kappan,* March 1980, p. 452.
4. "A Plan for a Pilot Project in School Health Service in the Public Schools of New York City," New York State Board of Regents, Albany, November 1979.
5. Arthur Bestor, *Educational Wastelands: The Retreat from Learning in Our Public Schools* (Urbana: The University of Illinois Press, 1953), p. 75.
6. *Engel v. Vitale.* (All court cases will be cited only by name.)
7. Chapter 692 of the Acts of 1979, Massachusetts Legislature, November 1979.
8. *Kent v. Commissioner of Education*
9. *Armstrong v. Kline.*
10. Personal Interview.
11. *Rowley v. Hendrick Hudson Central School District.*
12. *Tatro v. State of Texas.*
13. *Southeastern Community College v. Davis.*
14. Jerome C. Winegar and Geraldine Kozberg, "An Open Letter to Friends of South Boston High School," June 1978.
15. Statistics provided by the Council of the Greater City Schools, Washington, D.C., based on 1979 reports.
16. Gary Orfield, "The St. Louis Desegregation Plan: A Report to the Federal District Court," May 1980.
17. Median prices as of January 1981 from National Association of Home Builders for new house and from National Association of Realtors for existing house.
18. Letter to Jack P. Taylor, Superintendent of the School District of the City

of Saginaw, from Kenneth A. Mines, Director, Office for Civil Rights, Region V, Chicago, Ill. Sept. 30, 1975.

19. Ibid.

20. T.H. Bell, Official statement released by the U.S. Department of Education in Washington D.C., Feb. 2, 1981.

21. Noel Epstein, *Language, Ethnicity and the Schools: Policy Alternatives for Bilingual-Bicultural Education* (Washington: Institute for Educational Leadership, 1977), p. 18.

22. Alan Pifer, "Bilingual Education and the Hispanic Challenge," Annual report of the Carnegie Corporation, June 1980.

23. John Sawhill, "The Collapse of Public Schools," *Saturday Review*, Aug. 4, 1979, p. 17.

24. Personal Interview

25. "Teacher Workload Study," San Diego City Schools, November 1979.

26. *Digest of Education Statistics 1980,* National Center for Education Statistics, U.S. Department of Education, Washington D.C. p. 71.

27. Neil Postman, *Teaching as a Conserving Activity* (New York: Delacorte Press, 1979), p. 49.

28. Marie Winn, *The Plug-In Drug* (New York: The Viking Press, 1977).

29. From a class assignment.

30. "Excerpts from the National Survey on Drug Abuse: 1979," issued by the National Institute on Drug Abuse, U.S. Department of Health and Human Services, Rockville, Md., June 1980.

31. *On Further Examination: Report of the Advisory Panel on the Scholastic Aptitude Test Score Decline.*

CHAPTER THREE

1. Personal Interview.

2. *Debra P. v. Turlington.*

3. "Adult Functional Competency: A Summary," University of Texas, Austin, March 1975.

4. "New Jersey College Basic Skills Placement Testing, April 24, 1980–September 18, 1980, Aggregated by New Jersey Sending High Schools," New Jersey Basic Skills Council, Department of Higher Education, Trenton, Feb. 20, 1981.

5. "Report of the National Academy of Education, Committee on Testing and Basic Skills to the Assistant Secretary for Education," Washington, D.C., Feb. 23, 1978.

6. Personal Interview.

7. Roger T. Lennon in a speech at the 19th Annual Michigan School Testing Conference, Ann Arbor, Mich., Mar. 7, 1979.

8. "Minimum Standards: Three Points of View," International Reading Association, Newark, Del., Undated.

9. Personal Interview.

10. "Proficiency Assessment in California: 1980 Status Report of Implementation of the Requirements of AB 3008/76 and AB 65/77," California State Department of Education, Sacramento, 1980.
11. Personal Interview.
12. Ibid.
13. Harold Howe II in keynote address to National Conference on Achievement Testing and Basic Skills, Washington, D.C., March 1978.
14. Fred M. and Grace Hechinger, *Growing Up in America* (New York: McGraw-Hill, 1975), p. 104.
15. Ibid., p. 105.
16. *Digest of Education Statistics 1980,* p. 63.
17. Ibid.
18. "UNESCO Statistical Yearbook," United Nations, New York, 1977.
19. *Griggs v. Duke Power.*
20. *Debra P. v. Turlington.*
21. Personal Interview.
22. "The Practitioner, A Newsletter for the On-Line Administrator," National Association of Secondary School Principals, Reston, Va., May 1980.
23. Personal Interview.
24. Ibid.
25. Ibid.
26. Personal Interview.
27. Personal Interview.
28. Official explanation of a resolution adopted by Community School Board 8, New York City, December 1979.
29. Personal Interview.
30. *The New York Times,* Week in Review, Dec. 9, 1979, p. 6 IV.
31. "Minimum Competency Testing: A Report of Four Regional Conferences," CEMREL, Inc., St. Louis, Mo., 1978, p. 30.
32. *Doe v. San Francisco.*
33. *Donohue v. Copiague.*
34. *Hoffman v. Board of Education.*

CHAPTER FOUR

1. "City Wide Tests: April 30–May 25," Board of Education, Newark, 1978.
2. Compiled from various reports of the National Assessment of Educational Progress, Education Commission of the States, Denver.
3. "Dropouts in the Cleveland Public High Schools, 1976–1978," Office on School Monitoring and Community Relations, Cleveland, Undated.
4. Ibid.
5. *Giving Youth a Better Chance: Options for Education, Work, and Service,* Carnegie Council on Policy Studies in Higher Education (San Francisco: Jossey-Bass, Inc., 1979), p. 4.
6. Ibid.

7. Jacob Abramson, "The Effect of Continuity of School Environment on Reading Achievement of Fifth Grade Pupils," Presented at Northeastern Educational Research Association Annual Convention, Ellenville, N.Y., Oct. 30 to Nov. 1, 1974.
8. "Eleventh Annual Ranking of Schools by Reading Achievement," Board of Education, New York, December 1980.
9. James S. Coleman, *Equality of Educational Opportunity* (Washington, D.C.: U.S. Department of Health, Education, and Welfare, 1966), p. 325.
10. Christopher Jencks, *Inequality: A Reassessment of the Effect of Family and Schooling in America* (New York: Basic Books, 1972), p. 255 and p. 8.
11. Christopher Jencks, *Who Gets Ahead: The Economic Determinants of Success in America* (New York: Basic Books, 1979).
12. "Central City Schooling: Money Can Make a Difference," Potomac Institute, Washington, D.C., pp. 5–6.
13. Personal Interview.
14. Personal Interview.
15. Personal Interview.
16. "A Foundation Goes to School: The Ford Foundation Comprehensive School Improvement Program 1960–1970," Ford Foundation, New York, 1972, p. 33.
17. Ann Kurzius, "The School Principal: A Closer Look," *American Education*, November 1979, p. 43.
18. *Basic Education*, Council for Basic Education, Washington, D.C., February 1980, p. 5.
19. Personal Interview.
20. Personal Interview.

CHAPTER FIVE

1. Personal Interview.
2. *A Decade of Gallup Polls of Attitudes Toward Education* (Bloomington, Ind.: Phi Delta Kappa, Inc., 1978).
3. "Organizations for the Essentials of Education," a joint statement by twelve education groups including the International Reading Association, Newark, Del., 1978.
4. "Math, Science and Social Studies Curriculum: Retrospect and Prospects," National School Boards Association, Washington, D.C., 1979.
5. Editorial in *The National Elementary Principal,* January 1980.
6. "Three National Assessments of Science: Changes in Achievement, 1969–77," National Assessment of Educational Progress, Denver, June 1978.
7. Personal Interview.
8. Jane M. Armstrong, "Achievement and Participation of Women in Mathematics: An Overview," Education Commission of the States, Denver, March 1980, p. 13. For more information see "Anxiety and Mathematics:

An Update," by Sheila Tobias and Carol Weissbrod in *Harvard Education-al Review*, February 1980, pp. 63–68.

9. "National Council of Supervisors of Mathematics Position Paper on Basic Mathematical Skills," January 1977.

10. Vincent J. Glennon, "In Mathematics Education: Our Greatest Need," *Phi Delta Kappan*, May 1980, p. 593.

11. Personal Interview.

12. Marjorie Kirrie, "Teaching Writing in the World that Writing Built," *College Board Review*, Spring 1978, p. 14.

13. Thomas C. Wheeler, *The Great American Writing Block* (New York: The Viking Press, 1979).

14. Timothy Shanahan, "The Writing Crisis: A Survey and a Solution," *Phi Delta Kappan*, November 1979, p. 216.

15. Diana Buell-Hiatt, "Time Allocation in the Classroom: Is Instruction Being Shortchanged?" *Phi Delta Kappan*, December 1979, pp. 289–290.

16. John B. Carroll, "A Model of School Learning," *Teachers College Record*, May 1963, pp. 723–733.

17. See the various publications during 1979 and 1980 of the Beginning Teacher Evaluation Study of the Commission for Teacher Preparation and Licensing, Sacramento, Calif.

18. Barbara Heyns, *Summer Learning and the Effects of Schooling* (New York: Academic Press, 1978), p. xii.

19. "Special Report on the NIE Compensatory Education Study," National Advisory Council on the Education of Disadvantaged Children, Washington, D.C., 1979.

20. Roger Reger, "Learning Disabilities: Futile Attempts at a Simplistic Definition," *Journal of Learning Disabilities*, October 1979, p. 34.

21. Benjamin S. Bloom in a news release issued by the University of Chicago, Office of Public Information, Oct. 6, 1976.

22. Personal Interview.

23. Burton L. White, *The First Three Years of Life* (Englewood Cliffs, N.J.: Prentice-Hall, Inc., 1975).

24. Alice Klein, "Saturday School's Impact on Students, Parents and Teach-ers: A Summary of Six Years of Research Findings," Parent-Child Early Education Project, Ferguson-Florrisant School District, Ferguson, Mo. Un-dated.

25. Janis E. Woods, "Attitudes of Elementary Principals and Kindergarten Teachers Toward Mandatory Kindergarten and Optional Pre-Kindergar-ten Programs in Iowa," unpublished graduate thesis, University of North-ern Iowa, April 1979.

CHAPTER SIX

1. Dennis Gray in testimony to U.S. House Subcommittee on Elementary, Secondary and Vocational Education, Washington, D.C., Feb. 5, 1980.

2. Fred Hargadon in letter to secondary schools prepared by Stanford Committee on Undergraduate Admissions and Financial Aid, Palo Alto, Calif., Oct. 24, 1978.
3. Personal Interview.
4. Personal Interview.
5. Informal survey by the National Association of State Universities and Land Grant Colleges, Washington, D.C., 1973.
6. "Strength Through Wisdom: A Critique of U.S. Capability, A Report to the President's Commission on Foreign Languages and International Studies," U.S. Government Printing Office, Washington, D.C., November 1979, p. 5.
7. S. Frederick Starr, "Foreign Languages in the American School," a background paper prepared for the President's Commission on Foreign Languages and International Studies, Washington, D.C., November 1979.
8. James Q. Wilson in a speech to the Scarsdale Conference on the College-Preparatory High School, Scarsdale, N.Y., Oct. 2, 1980.
9. Personal Interview.
10. Robert Kirkwood, "The Annual Report of the Executive Director of the Commission on Higher Education," Middle States Association of Schools and Colleges, Philadelphia, Aug. 1, 1980, p. 6.
11. Michael W. Kirst in background paper prepared for the California State Board of Education, Jan. 10, 1980.
12. Statistics from the central headquarters of the City University of New York, Spring 1981.
13. Jill Conway in news release issued by Smith College, Northampton, Mass., April 15, 1980.
14. Harold L. Enarson, "Reading', Righting and Mathematicks," Speech to the educators' luncheon of the Ohio Congress of Parents and Teachers Annual Convention, Columbus, Ohio, Oct. 24, 1977.
15. Personal Interview.
16. "High School Graduates: Projections for the 50 States," Western Interstate Commission for Higher Education, Boulder, Colo., November 1979.
17. William Ehlanfeldt in speech at the Wingspread Conference on Marketing in College Admissions, Racine, Wis., Nov. 7–9, 1979.
18. "Joint Statement on Principles of Good Practice in College Admissions and Recruitment," National Association of Secondary School Principals, Reston, Va., September 1980.
19. Personal Interview.
20. Personal Interview.
21. Personal Interview.
22. Personal Interview.
23. "The Prospectus Issue of Simon's Rock of Bard College Prospectus," Great Barrington, Mass., Winter 1980, p. 2.
24. Personal Interview.
25. Statistics provided by College Entrance Examination Board, New York.
26. Personal Interview.

27. Personal Interview.
28. Personal Interview.
29. Personal Interview.

CHAPTER SEVEN

1. *NEA Reporter,* December 1980, p. 2.
2. Edward B. Fiske, *The New York Times,* Week in Review, Jan. 22, 1978, p. 9 IV.
3. Personal Interview.
4. Personal Interview.
5. Personal Interview.
6. *Cleveland Board of Education v. LaFleur.*
7. Josiah Royce, "The Freedom of Teaching," *Overland Monthly,* 1883.
8. *Pickering v. Board of Education.*
9. *Andrews v. Drew Municipal Separate School District.*
10. *Doherty v. Wilson.*
11. William Raspberry, *Washington Post,* July 16, 1976, p. A27.
12. *Ridgefield Park Education Association v. Ridgefield Park Board of Education.*
13. New Jersey School Boards Association in news release, May 13, 1980.
14. "Education Boards See Levittown as a Model for Resisting Strikes," *The New York Times,* Nov. 20, 1978, p. 1.
15. Lorraine McDonnell and Anthony Pascal, "Organized Teachers in American Schools," Rand Corporation, Santa Monica, Calif., February 1979, p. IX.
16. *Barbara Hart Couture v. Board of Education of Norwalk City School District.*
17. Personal Interview.
18. "Annual Status and Opinion Survey," American Association of School Administrators, Arlington, Va., 1979–80.
19. Esther P. Rothman, *Troubled Teachers* (New York: David McKay Company, 1977), p. 251.
20. Personal Interview.
21. Personal Interview.
22. Harry J. Finlayson, "Incompetence and Teacher Dismissal," *Phi Delta Kappan,* September 1979, p. 69.
23. Personal Interview.
24. Personal Interview.
25. Personal Interview.
26. Suzanne H. McDaniel and Thomas R. McDaniel, "How to Weed Out Incompetent Teachers Without Getting Hauled into Court," *The National Elementary Principal,* March 1980, p. 35.
27. Willard H. McGuire, "Teacher Burnout," *Today's Education,* November –December 1979, p. 5.

28. From a survey by the New York State United Teachers, Albany, November 1979.

29. Pamela Bardo, "The Pain of Teacher Burnout: A Case History," *Phi Delta Kappan,* December 1979, p. 252.

30. Ellen Glanz, "What Are You Doing Here? or Schooldays for the Teacher," Occasional Paper 26 by the Council for Basic Education, Washington, D.C., May 1979, pp. 16–17.

31. Muriel Juster in speech to the Scarsdale Conference on the College-Preparatory High School, Scarsdale, N.Y., Oct. 2, 1980.

32. Personal Interview.

33. Personal Interview.

34. Personal Interview.

35. From an official college transcript (dated May 8, 1978) in the files of the Office of Personnel, New York City Board of Education.

36. Personal Interview.

37. "College Student Profiles: Norms for the ACT Assessment," 1980–81 Edition, American College Testing Program, Iowa City, Iowa.

38. Statistics provided by the American Association of Medical Colleges and the Law School Admissions Council.

39. Doyle Watts, "Admissions Standards for Teacher Preparatory Programs: Time for a Change," *Phi Delta Kappan,* October 1980, p. 120.

40. "More About Testing Teachers," *Basic Education,* Council for Basic Education, Washington, D.C., December 1980, p. 14.

41. Terry E. Herndon, "Why Teachers Get Mad About 'Accountability,'" *Compact,* January–February 1974, p. 26.

CHAPTER EIGHT

1. "Salary Schedules, 1978–80," Research Memo, National Education Association, Washington, D.C., 1980.

2. *Digest of Education Statistics 1980,* p. 23.

3. Nathaniel Sheppard, Jr., "Chicago Mayor Accuses Schools of Hiding Fiscal Woes," *The New York Times,* Dec. 6, 1979, p. 26.

4. Joseph M. Cronin, "Big City School Bankruptcy," Policy Paper 80–03 of the Institute for Research on Educational Finance and Government, Stanford University, Palo Alto, Calif., October 1980.

5. *Serrano v. Priest.*

6. Stephen J. Carroll, "The Search for Equity in School Finance: Summary and Conclusions," Rand Corporation, Santa Monica, Calif., March 1979, p. v.

7. *Somerset County Board of Education v. Hornbeck.*

8. *Levittown v. Nyquist.*

9. "Research Findings and Policy Alternatives: A Second Interim Report," The New York State Special Task Force on Equity and Excellence in Education, New York, September 1980.

10. *Cincinnati Board of Education v. Walter.*
11. "A Special Report on Taxes," Table 4, Citizens Public Expenditure Survey, Inc., Albany, N.Y., March 1981.
12. Information provided by the Ohio Department of Education.
13. Personal Interview.
14. Personal Interview.
15. Testimony at an open hearing of the Board of Education, Toledo, Oct. 5, 1977.
16. *Cincinnati Board of Education v. Walter.*
17. *Digest of Education Statistics 1980*, p. 72.
18. "Education Vouchers: A Preliminary Report on Financing Education by Payments to Parents," Center for the Study of Education Policy, Cambridge, Mass., March 1970.

CHAPTER NINE

1. Personal Interview.
2. *North Bay Elementary Parent-Teacher Organization et al. v. J. D. McCulloch et al.*
3. Dwight Roper, "Parents as the Natural Enemy of the School System," *Phi Delta Kappan*, December 1977, p. 239.
4. Marilyn Gittell et al., "Citizen Organizations: Citizen Participation in Educational Decisionmaking," Institute for Responsive Education through a subgrant with the Graduate School and University Center of the City University of New York, July 1979.
5. Personal Interview.
6. "Parents Guide to More Effective Schools," Association of American Publishers, New York, Undated.
7. "1980 Back-to-School Package," California State Department of Education, Sacramento, Aug. 9, 1980.
8. "New NASSP President: Let's Open Doors," National Association of Secondary School Principals, Reston, Va., Mar. 9, 1981.
9. George Masnick and Mary Jo Bane, "The Nation's Families: 1960–1990," Joint Center for Urban Studies of MIT and Harvard University, Cambridge, Mass., 1980.
10. "The Most Significant Minority: One-Parent Children in the Schools," National Association of Elementary School Principals and the Institute for Development of Educational Activities of the Charles F. Kettering Foundation, Arlington, Va., July 28, 1980.
11. "School-Community Communication: School Board Members and their Constituents," National School Boards Association, Washington, D.C., 1980, p. 7.
12. L. Harmon Zeigler, Harvey J. Tucker, and L. A. Wilson, "How School Control Was Wrested from the People," *Phi Delta Kappan*, March 1977, p. 536.

13. *Digest of Education Statistics 1980,* p. 71.
14. Personal Interview.
15. Statistics provided by the National Congress of Parents and Teachers, Chicago.
16. Personal Interview.
17. Luvern L. Cunningham et al., "Improving Education in Florida: A Reassessment," Prepared for the Select Joint Committee on Public Schools of the Florida State Legislature, February 1978, pp. 268–269.
18. Ross Zerchykov and Don Davies with Janet Chrispeels, "Leading the Way: State Mandates for School Advisory Councils in California, Florida and South Carolina," Institute for Responsive Education, Boston, August 1980, p. 135.
19. Personal Interview.
20. "A Study of Attitudes Toward the Public Schools Among American Teenagers," Charles F. Kettering Foundation, Dayton, Ohio, 1980.
21. Ellen Glanz, "What Are You Doing Here? or Schooldays for the Teacher," pp. 19–20.
22. Personal Interview.
23. Personal Interview.
24. Personal Interview.

INDEX

ABOUT THE AUTHOR

GENE I. MAEROFF, an education writer for the *New York Times*, spent the entire decade of the nineteen-seventies reporting on issues and trends at schools and colleges across the United States for the newspaper. His work has won first-place awards in competitions sponsored by the Education Writers Association, the American Association of University Professors, and the International Reading Association. Mr. Maeroff, the author of *The Guide to Suburban Public Schools*, has contributed to other books and to numerous magazines including *The New York Times Magazine, Saturday Review, New York Magazine, Parents Magazine, Parade, Seventeen*, and *Phi Delta Kappan*. Born and bred in Ohio, Mr. Maeroff now lives in Manhattan and is the father of three teen-agers—Janine, Adam, and Rachel.